Priase for *Engineering Resilient Systems on AWS*

The authors have taken the AWS Shared Responsibility Model for resilience and brilliantly expanded it in this book. When we introduced the AWS Shared Responsibility Model for resilience in 2021, our aim was to create a simple framework for understanding resilience in the cloud. The authors, all experienced resilience experts, build on that foundation. They dive deep into the principles and practices that empower teams to design resilient and scalable workloads on AWS, continuing our mission of enabling users.

—*Seth Eliot, former Global Reliability Lead,*
AWS Well-Architected

An indispensable guide for any IT professional, this book masterfully underscores the critical importance of AWS resilience and seamless integration. With its clear, step-by-step instructions, it not only demystifies complex concepts but also empowers readers to build robust, scalable, and future-proof cloud solutions.

—*Patricia A. Thompson, Lockheed Martin, Systems Engineer*

This book does an excellent job of applying theoretical concepts to real-world techniques for building resilient cloud applications. I wish this resource had been available when I first began exploring resilience in distributed systems.

—*Michael Haken, Senior Principal SA, AWS*

As a computer science undergraduate new to modern cloud application development, this book gave me a solid foundation in building resilient architectures with AWS CDK.

—*Ben Schwarz, Clemson University student*

Engineering
Resilient Systems on AWS
Design, Build, and Test for Resilience

Kevin Schwarz, Jennifer Moran, and Nate Bachmeier

Engineering Resilient Systems on AWS

by Kevin Schwarz, Jennifer Moran, and Nate Bachmeier

Copyright © 2025 Kevin Schwarz, Moran Services LLC, and Nate Bachmeier. All rights reserved.

Published by O'Reilly Media, Inc., 1005 Gravenstein Highway North, Sebastopol, CA 95472.

O'Reilly books may be purchased for educational, business, or sales promotional use. Online editions are also available for most titles (*http://oreilly.com*). For more information, contact our corporate/institutional sales department: 800-998-9938 or *corporate@oreilly.com*.

Acquisitions Editor: John Devins
Development Editor: Corbin Collins
Production Editor: Katherine Tozer
Copyeditor: Sonia Saruba
Proofreader: Vanessa Moore

Indexer: nSight, Inc.
Interior Designer: David Futato
Cover Designer: Karen Montgomery
Illustrator: Kate Dullea

October 2024:   First Edition

Revision History for the First Edition
2024-10-11:   First Release

See *http://oreilly.com/catalog/errata.csp?isbn=9781098162429* for release details.

978-1-098-16242-9

[LSI]

Table of Contents

Part II.   Reliable Trading Portal

Part III. Discovering Trading Opportunities

Preface

The need for resilient systems has reached unprecedented levels. This book explores the nuances of designing and implementing durable systems on Amazon Web Services (AWS). As technology becomes integral to enhancing customer experiences across industries, creating high-performing and resilient systems has become a top priority. Users now expect applications to be continuously available, raising the bar for system reliability.

Two key trends drive this book's purpose: the increasing complexity of modern infrastructures and the growing importance of system reliability. As systems become more intricate, potential failure points multiply. Simultaneously, the costs associated with downtime or data loss have increased significantly. In this landscape, traditional approaches to system resilience fall short.

Many assume that cloud-based workloads are inherently resilient. While cloud infrastructure provides tools for building more robust systems, it doesn't guarantee resilience. Effectively using the cloud demands a thorough understanding of both the platform and resilient architecture principles. This book aims to bridge this knowledge gap by examining best practices, architectural patterns, and a real-world example workload. It serves as a comprehensive guide for engineers, architects, and IT professionals.

Resilience encompasses more than just technology; it involves people and processes as well. While the book primarily focuses on hands-on technology, Part I reviews people and process aspects, covering best practices for change management, failure handling, and incident response. We recognize that even with solid technology, inadequate people and processes can hinder achieving true resilience.

The book begins by exploring fundamental resilience principles and their relevance in today's IT landscape. It then examines how AWS can help customers build more resilient workloads by leveraging its services and orchestrating them to create systems that withstand impairments. Each chapter builds upon the previous one, offering step-by-step guidance and insights from extensive field experience. Whether you're an experienced AWS practitioner or new to the platform, this book aims to equip you with the knowledge and tools needed to build enduring systems.

By emphasizing practical implementation and providing a holistic understanding of resilient system design, this book serves as a valuable resource for professionals working with AWS. The inclusion of a fictitious financial consumer application offers a real-world context for the discussed principles and strategies. Our goal is to contribute to a future where building resilience into systems becomes instinctive and central to exceptional system design. The skills and strategies you gain from this book will empower you to build more resilient systems from the outset.

Conventions Used in This Book

The following typographical conventions are used in this book:

Italic
> Indicates new terms, URLs, email addresses, filenames, and file extensions.

`Constant width`
> Used for program listings, as well as within paragraphs to refer to program elements such as variable or function names, databases, data types, environment variables, statements, and keywords.

`Constant width bold`
> Shows commands or other text that should be typed literally by the user.

`Constant width italic`
> Shows text that should be replaced with user-supplied values or by values determined by context.

 This element signifies a tip or suggestion.

 This element signifies a general note.

 This element indicates a warning or caution.

Using Code Examples

Supplemental material (code examples, exercises, etc.) is available for download at *https://github.com/engineering-resilient-systems-on-aws/AvailableTrade*.

If you have a technical question or a problem using the code examples, please send email to *support@oreilly.com*.

This book is here to help you get your job done. In general, if example code is offered with this book, you may use it in your programs and documentation. You do not need to contact us for permission unless you're reproducing a significant portion of the code. For example, writing a program that uses several chunks of code from this book does not require permission. Selling or distributing examples from O'Reilly books does require permission. Answering a question by citing this book and quoting example code does not require permission. Incorporating a significant amount of example code from this book into your product's documentation does require permission.

We appreciate, but generally do not require, attribution. An attribution usually includes the title, author, publisher, and ISBN. For example: *"Engineering Resilient Systems on AWS* by Kevin Schwarz, Jennifer Moran, and Nate Bachmeier (O'Reilly). Copyright 2025 Kevin Schwarz, Moran Services LLC, and Nate Bachmeier, 978-1-098-16242-9."*

If you feel your use of code examples falls outside fair use or the permission given above, feel free to contact us at *permissions@oreilly.com*.

O'Reilly Online Learning

 For more than 40 years, *O'Reilly Media* has provided technology and business training, knowledge, and insight to help companies succeed.

Our unique network of experts and innovators share their knowledge and expertise through books, articles, and our online learning platform. O'Reilly's online learning platform gives you on-demand access to live training courses, in-depth learning paths, interactive coding environments, and a vast collection of text and video from O'Reilly and 200+ other publishers. For more information, visit *https://oreilly.com*.

How to Contact Us

Please address comments and questions concerning this book to the publisher:

O'Reilly Media, Inc.
1005 Gravenstein Highway North
Sebastopol, CA 95472
800-889-8969 (in the United States or Canada)
707-829-7019 (international or local)
707-829-0104 (fax)
support@oreilly.com
https://www.oreilly.com/about/contact.html

We have a web page for this book, where we list errata, examples, and any additional information. You can access this page at *https://oreil.ly/EngineeringResilientSystems*.

For news and information about our books and courses, visit *https://oreilly.com*.

Find us on LinkedIn: *https://linkedin.com/company/oreilly-media*.

Watch us on YouTube: *https://youtube.com/oreillymedia*.

Acknowledgments

This book would not have been possible without the invaluable feedback and contributions of many talented individuals. The authors would like to extend their heartfelt gratitude to Mike Haken, whose insightful feedback profoundly shaped and elevated the quality of this work. Sean Mullen, a valued member of the AWS resilience community, provided his expertise and contributions. Special thanks to Patricia Thompson, an exceptionally skilled technical writer, whose clarity and precision significantly enhanced the book's readability. Finally, we want to express our sincere appreciation to Ben Schwarz for his tireless efforts in meticulously testing and refining all the hands-on exercises, ensuring a seamless learning experience for our readers. Your collective dedication and support have been instrumental in making this book a success.

From Kevin

I owe much of my learning to the smart people I work with, both at AWS and the customers who allow me to contribute to the modernization and migration of their systems to AWS. Being involved in complex projects throughout my career has constantly inspired me to crack open books, build example applications, and come up with solutions where they did not exist. The need to make these systems performant and resilient to meet customer expectations and grow business is the part of technology that gets me up in the morning. I'm grateful to the engineers and leaders of each project I've learned from and contributed to.

I am personally grateful to my wife, Catherine, and two children, Ben and Amy. They not only supported me while I wrote this book, but rallied me to take on the opportunity. Both of my children have gone on to study computer science in college, inspiring me to keep learning and exploring the art of the possible.

From Jennifer

I am deeply grateful to my colleagues in the AWS resilience community. It is an incredible honor to be part of such a remarkable team that is truly making a difference in helping our customers build more resilient workloads on AWS. The individuals in this community are some of the most brilliant and innovative people I've had the pleasure of working with, tirelessly solving complex resilience challenges for our customers.

On a personal note, I want to extend my heartfelt gratitude to my husband, Tom, for his unwavering support throughout this writing process. And, as promised, a special shout-out to all the amazing kids in my life: Kaylee, Jack, Jordyn, Michael, Dylan, and Kamryn.

From Dr. Nate

To my wife Pei-Chi, your unwavering support and patience made this book possible. Thank you for standing by me through this journey. To Eli, Maya, and Milo—thank you for filling our home with laughter and reminding me of life beyond the keyboard. I'm deeply grateful to the AWS community for your collective wisdom and willingness to share knowledge. Your insights have been invaluable.

This project was longer and more challenging than I anticipated, but also immensely rewarding. I hope the pages that follow provide you with practical value in your quest to build reliable systems. Your success would make the long nights worthwhile.

Lastly, to all the engineers who've faced the "it worked in staging" conundrum—this book is for you. May it help us build systems that perform reliably not just in our test environments, but in the unpredictable world of production at scale.

## PART I

Foundations

Traditionally, resilient design involved a series of established practices centered on physical infrastructure, redundancy, and failover mechanisms within a company's data center. However, these practices have evolved significantly with the advent of cloud computing. This book helps you understand the differences between traditional resilient design and resilient design in the cloud.

Organizations typically invest in duplicate hardware systems, such as servers, storage devices, and network components. This redundancy ensures that if one piece of hardware fails, another can take over without significant disruption.

To safeguard against catastrophic events, like natural disasters, companies often maintain multiple data centers in different geographic locations. Data and applications are replicated across these sites to enable failover if one data center becomes inoperable. Detailed disaster recovery plans are developed and regularly tested to ensure business operations can be quickly restored following a major incident. These plans often include backup procedures, manual intervention steps, and predefined recovery time objectives (RTOs). Monitoring hardware performance and regular maintenance is crucial for preemptively addressing potential issues before they lead to system failure.

While these methods have been effective, they come with significant costs and complexities. The capital expenditure required for duplicate hardware, the operational costs of running multiple data centers, and the complexity of managing and maintaining these environments can be substantial.

In contrast, resilient design in the cloud leverages the inherent capabilities and services that cloud platforms like Amazon Web Services (AWS) provide. Cloud platforms can automatically scale resources up or down based on demand. This elasticity helps maintain performance and availability without the need, in most cases, for over-provisioning resources, which is a common practice in traditional setups. The AWS cloud has a global network of data centers. Applications and data can be distributed across multiple regions and availability zones, ensuring high availability and fault tolerance without organizations needing to manage physical infrastructure. Some AWS services include automated recovery options or self-healing mechanisms that can, for example, automatically replace failed instances and distribute traffic to healthy instances, minimizing downtime. AWS offers managed services for databases, messaging, storage, and more. These services come with built-in redundancy and failover capabilities and can abstract away some of the complexity associated with building resilient systems. AWS operates on a pay-as-you-go model, which can be more cost-effective than the significant up-front investment in physical infrastructure.

The shift from traditional resilient design to cloud-based resilient design represents a significant evolution in how organizations ensure the availability and reliability of their systems. While conventional methods focus on physical infrastructure and redundancy, cloud-based approaches leverage cloud platforms' flexibility, scalability, and automation. This book will explain that shift and how to consider resilience in your AWS cloud environment.

## CHAPTER 1

Introduction

Resilience refers to a system's ability to withstand and recover from disruptions, failures, or unexpected events. It's about preventing failures and ensuring the system can gracefully degrade, recover quickly, and provide some functionality even under stress.

So, how does an organization achieve resilience? Achieving this goal requires an ongoing pursuit on the part of organizations to invest in cloud expertise and engineering, automation tools, and a willingness to embrace a culture of continuous learning in resilience.

People, Processes, and Technology

Creating resilient systems involves more than just technology; it also requires integrating people and processes. While technology provides the tools and platforms for resilience, the people who implement and manage these tools and the processes they follow ultimately determine the success of resilient system design.

The Role of People

People are the driving force behind resilient systems. Skilled professionals, including business stakeholders, engineers, architects, operators, and other specialists, bring the necessary expertise to design, implement, and maintain these systems. Knowledge of the technical landscape and the organization's business requirements ensures that the systems are built for optimal performance and resilience as required by the business.

Continuous training and development are essential for adapting to the rapidly evolving technology landscape. Ensuring that the team has up-to-date skills and knowledge allows team members to effectively utilize new tools and methodologies for resilience.

Building resilient systems requires cross-functional collaboration. Clear communication among teams, such as product, development, operations, and security, ensures that all aspects of the system are considered and that business requirements are addressed.

The team's ability to respond quickly and adapt is required in the face of disruptions. A well-prepared and agile team can swiftly implement contingency plans, troubleshoot issues, and restore services, minimizing downtime and impact.

The Role of Processes

Processes provide the framework within which people operate, ensuring consistency, efficiency, and alignment with organizational goals. Well-defined processes standardize best practices, reduce errors, and enhance the system's resilience.

Detailed incident response plans outline the steps to be taken during various disruptions. These plans should be regularly updated and tested to ensure effectiveness when actual incidents occur.

Implementing a change management process helps mitigate the risks associated with system updates and modifications. By carefully planning, testing, and monitoring changes, you can prevent unintended consequences that compromise system resilience.

Ongoing monitoring of system performance and regular reviews of resilience strategies ensure that the system remains robust against evolving disruptions. This process includes collecting data, analyzing trends, and making informed adjustments to improve resilience.

Comprehensive documentation of systems, processes, and incident histories facilitates knowledge sharing and ensures that all team members are informed and prepared. This practice helps maintain consistency and reduce dependency on individual expertise.

Integrating People, Processes, and Technology

Creating resilient systems requires a holistic approach integrating people, processes, and technology. Technology provides the tools, but only with skilled people to implement and manage it, and well-defined processes to guide its use, can the full potential of the technology be realized.

Empowering teams with the right tools and training, and fostering a continuous learning and improvement culture ensures they can effectively leverage technology to build resilient systems. It's important to ensure that processes are designed to support and enhance the capabilities of the technology in use. This alignment helps maximize efficiency and effectiveness, leading to more resilient systems.

Encouraging a mindset focused on resilience across the organization helps proactively identify and address potential issues. This cultural shift ensures that resilience is not just an afterthought but an integral part of system design and operation.

Building resilient systems is a multifaceted endeavor that goes beyond the deployment of advanced technology. It requires the concerted efforts of skilled professionals, guided by well-defined processes, to ensure that systems can withstand and recover from disruptions. By recognizing the critical roles of people and processes, you can create a robust foundation for resilient system design, ensuring continuous and reliable service delivery in an ever-changing technological landscape.

Shared Responsibility Model

The AWS Shared Responsibility Model for resilience is a concept that every organization should understand. It is important to know where the responsibility lies between *of the cloud* and *in the cloud* to successfully build resilient workloads on AWS.

This book shows you how to take advantage of *of the cloud* while building *in the cloud*. With this knowledge, you can start engineering resilient workloads. In February 2021, AWS introduced the Shared Responsibility Model for resilience to clarify the responsibilities of AWS and its customers. This model outlines the distinct responsibilities of AWS, *of the cloud,* and its customers, *in the cloud,* regarding resilience.

Figure 1-1 shows this model, a framework to assist you in achieving cloud resilience. It clearly defines the roles and responsibilities of AWS as the cloud service provider and the customer as the custodian of their data and applications.

This model clarifies your role in ensuring the resilience of your workloads hosted on AWS. While AWS safeguards the underlying infrastructure (physical data centers, networking, and virtualization platforms) and AWS services, your responsibility lies in architecting, building, testing, and operating your workloads on AWS in a way that promotes resilience.

You understand your specific business needs, regulatory requirements, and risk tolerance levels best, so you are best positioned to tailor your resilience strategies to align with these unique factors. By taking ownership of your responsibilities within the shared model, you can customize and implement resilience measures most suitable for your specific use cases while adhering to resilient best practices.

You are responsible for data governance and security specific to your applications. Good data governance requires flexibility, allowing you to adjust resources and configurations, and implement new resilience controls to ensure scalability and adaptability in response to changing circumstances. You must ensure data availability and recover to a usable state in case of data corruption. You are also responsible for ensuring compliance with relevant regulations within your portion of the shared model, as you have the domain knowledge and insight necessary to meet these requirements for your industry.

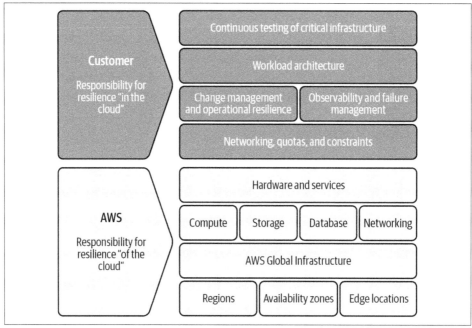

Figure 1-1. AWS Shared Responsibility Model for resilience

Ultimately, you are responsible for managing data and application resilience risks. By actively participating in the Shared Responsibility Model, you can assess risks, identify vulnerabilities, and implement mitigation strategies to minimize the impact of potential impairments. This proactive approach to risk management is essential for maintaining business continuity and protecting critical assets during disruptions.

AWS Responsibility

First and foremost, let's touch upon service-level agreements (SLAs). As a cloud provider, AWS offers SLAs to customers for its services. These agreements specify the level of service that AWS commits to delivering. Generally, SLAs define metrics relating to service reliability, availability, performance, and support. SLAs are financial contracts that establish trust and accountability between cloud service providers and their customers. They provide customers with assurance regarding the reliability and performance of cloud services and set clear expectations for the level of service they can expect to receive.

However, while AWS SLAs are a useful baseline, it's important to complement them with your tailored objectives that align closely with your business goals, performance requirements, and risk tolerance. This approach ensures that you comprehensively understand your workload's performance and reliability, and can take appropriate actions to optimize and manage it effectively.

We will discuss resilience goals in more detail in "Setting Objectives" on page 9.

In the context of systems and computing, fault isolation refers to the practice of designing and implementing systems that limit the impact of failures. Fault isolation can help ensure the reliability and availability of your applications by isolating impacts or failures within the fault isolation boundary where they occurred.

The AWS global infrastructure is an example of designing with fault isolation in mind. The infrastructure is a vast network of regions, availability zones, and data centers in key geographic areas worldwide. Each AWS Region has several *Availability Zones* (AZs), essentially isolated data centers with redundant power, cooling, and networking infrastructure. These AZs are linked by high-speed, low-latency connections, creating a highly resilient and fault-tolerant network, as shown in Figure 1-2.

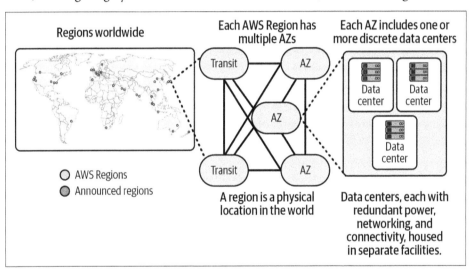

Figure 1-2. AWS global infrastructure

You can leverage the AWS global infrastructure to build and operate resilient workloads. Your architectures should span multiple Availability Zones within an AWS Region to achieve redundancy and fault tolerance. This way, you can achieve high availability and resilience, as any impairments of a zonal service or resource in one zone would not impact the availability of resources or zonal services in other Availability Zones. You can also deploy your workloads across multiple AWS Regions for an additional layer of fault isolation. Each AWS Region is isolated from the others, with its own set of Availability Zones. By replicating your data and workload across multiple AWS Regions, you can withstand regional impairments or disasters and maintain business continuity within your designed recovery objectives.

In addition to the existing AWS Regions, AWS has announced regions that have been publicly disclosed but are not yet available for general use. While these announced regions are not immediately usable, they can be factored into your long-term resilience planning, allowing you to prepare for future expansions of your global infrastructure footprint.

AWS also operates edge locations distributed worldwide. You can leverage the edge to cache and deliver content closer to end users, reducing latency and enhancing the resilience of your applications.

> An AWS *edge location* is a point of presence (PoP) within the AWS global network infrastructure. These PoPs are distributed globally, and strategically placed in major cities and regions worldwide. The primary purpose of these locations is to provide AWS services to end users with low latency and high data transfer speeds.

Additionally, you can run computing and processing data at the edge using Amazon CloudFront functions and AWS Lambda@Edge, which run closer to end users or devices.

Customer Responsibility

This section examines some of the methodologies, principles, and frameworks that you, the customer, can use when engineering and operating on AWS to meet your responsibilities as part of the Shared Responsibility Model.

When designing your system for resilience, we recommend working backward from the failure modes that can occur within it. We discuss this when we get to "Workload Architecture" on page 13. Still, if we take a simple example, we know that if a server gets terminated for any reason and there is no other server to take its place, then we see a single point of failure. So, if we were to design a resilient system, we would create this server with redundancy, preventing this failure.

Another important aspect of resilience is identifying whether a failure is happening within your system. Do you have the observability to identify the signal from that failure mode? And what happens when your observability detects that failure? Do you have alarms configured to either send notifications to a team, automatically mitigate the failure, or both?

You will want to test for these failures to validate that your processes are working as expected. The best practice is to automate and build these tests into your continuous integration and continuous delivery (CI/CD) pipeline. Most of our systems' failures are self-inflicted, and because of this, change and failure management processes are important.

Finally, you want to get to a point where you practice continuous resilience, incorporating all the lessons from your hard work into your resilience lifecycle. This section explores all of these topics in depth.

Let's start with setting your resilience objectives.

Setting Objectives

Building resilient systems requires setting clear goals to guide your efforts. These goals establish a roadmap for fortifying your system against disruptions, ensuring it can withstand failures and recover quickly.

By defining "resilient" for your specific system, you can effectively prioritize resources, measure progress, and ultimately minimize the impact of downtime on your business and its stakeholders.

Business impact analysis and risk assessment

A business impact analysis (BIA) and risk assessment are two processes that work together to understand potential threats to your system and how they can impact your business operations. The business conducts a BIA and risk assessment to help define resilience goals.

A *BIA* identifies and prioritizes critical business processes, systems, and resources. It is crucial in ensuring business continuity, going far beyond technology considerations. It delves into the heart of an organization's operations, identifying critical processes, dependencies, and the potential ripple effects of disruptions. By understanding these intricate relationships, businesses can proactively address vulnerabilities and develop strategies to maintain essential functions despite unexpected events.

A BIA acknowledges that businesses are complex ecosystems where people, processes, and technology are interconnected. It recognizes that disruptions can impact IT systems, the workforce, supply chains, customer relationships, and overall reputation. By analyzing these diverse elements, businesses can develop comprehensive continuity plans that safeguard their most valuable assets, ensuring resilience and minimizing downtime.

A *risk assessment* proactively identifies potential threats and vulnerabilities that could disrupt your system. These include natural disasters, cyberattacks, hardware failures, software bugs, and human error. The assessment then evaluates the likelihood of each threat occurring and the severity of its potential impact.

Understanding the likelihood and severity of different risks helps you develop a more targeted approach to building system resilience. You can prioritize mitigation strategies for the most probable and impactful threats or critical applications, ensuring your system is better prepared to handle real-world challenges.

Resilience goals

When defining resilience goals, two key metrics are *recovery objectives* and *availability goals*. Recovery objectives define the maximum acceptable downtime after a disruption before functionality needs to be restored. At the same time, availability goals specify the percentage of time a system must be operational.

Why are resilience goals important? They help prioritize resources toward the areas that matter most, adapting to each system's unique needs. For instance, an electronic trading platform with financial transactions might require stricter recovery objectives than a company website with mostly static content.

Furthermore, defining resilience goals establishes measurable targets to track progress and assess your system's overall resilience.

Recovery objectives

The *recovery time objective* (RTO) specifies when you aim to recover your critical systems and resume normal business operations after a disruptive event.

The *recovery point objective* (RPO) specifies the maximum acceptable age of the data that an organization is willing to lose in a disaster or disruptive event.

Both are expressed as a specific duration, typically hours, minutes, or days, and are based on the recovered systems' or processes' business requirements, operational needs, and criticality. A shorter RPO indicates a lower tolerance for data loss, requiring more frequent backups or data replication to minimize the amount of data at risk. Conversely, a longer RPO may be acceptable for less critical data or applications that can tolerate longer periods of data loss without significant impact.

Downtime, defined as when a system is unavailable, can be caused by various factors like hardware failures, software bugs, or even natural disasters. The definition of downtime itself can vary depending on the organization. Downtime is usually not binary, either up or down, but varying shades of this. You may define downtime when error rates reach a certain point or when latency exceeds a certain threshold. It is important to have this conversation and define these goals with the business stakeholders to understand their expectations of the system and then convert those into the appropriate technology measurements. Even a few seconds of downtime can have severe consequences in mission-critical fields like healthcare or finance, so any interruption might be unacceptable. On the other hand, a noncritical system like an internal company directory might tolerate a few hours of downtime as long as users can still access other resources.

Bounded Recovery Time (BRT) refers to the maximum tolerable duration within which a system, process, or organization must be restored to an operational state following a disruption. Establishing a BRT is essential for effective resilience planning, as it provides a clear target for recovery efforts and helps prioritize resources. BRT is not merely a technical metric; it aligns with the overall BIA by considering the potential consequences of prolonged downtime. By defining an acceptable BRT, you can ensure that recovery strategies are tailored to minimize financial losses, reputational damage, and operational disruptions. BRT serves as a guiding principle for resilience, driving the development of robust backup systems, redundant infrastructure, and well-rehearsed recovery procedures.

The three Ms

MTBF, MTTD, and MTTR are all metrics that can be valuable in setting resilience goals by providing insights into your system's uptime and downtime characteristics:

Mean time between failures (MTBF)
    Measures the average time between failures or incidents that cause downtime. It represents the expected time between failures in a system or component. MTBF indicates the predicted reliability of a system or component over time. A higher MTBF value indicates that the system or component is more reliable and experiences fewer failures on average, resulting in longer intervals between failures.

Mean time to detect (MTTD)
    Measures the average time to detect an incident or failure within a system or application. MTTD is an important performance indicator in incident management and response processes, as it reflects the effectiveness of your monitoring and detection capabilities in identifying issues and abnormalities. A shorter MTTD indicates that incidents are detected more quickly, allowing for faster response and resolution. This helps minimize the impact of incidents on service availability, performance, and user experience. Effective monitoring, alerting, and automated detection mechanisms contribute to reducing MTTD and improving overall incident response efficiency.

Mean time to repair/recovery (MTTR)
    Measures the average time to repair or recover from a failure or incident that causes downtime. It represents the time it takes to restore the system or application to regular operation after failure. MTTR is a key performance indicator in incident management and response processes, reflecting the efficiency and effectiveness of your incident resolution and recovery efforts. A shorter MTTR indicates that incidents are resolved quicker, minimizing downtime

and promptly restoring the system or application's regular operation. Effective incident response processes, automation, and well-defined recovery procedures contribute to reducing MTTR and improving overall system resilience and availability.

Figure 1-3 shows the three Ms on a timeline.

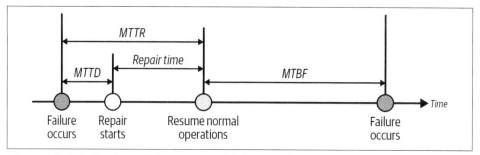

Figure 1-3. Relationship of Ms on an availability timeline

MTBF and MTTD can inform your recovery objectives. These metrics provide a historical perspective on how often your system experiences failures and how long they typically last. By understanding these averages, you can set a realistic recovery objective that reflects the time needed to recover from an outage based on past experiences. MTTR influences your BRT. A lower MTTR translates to a faster recovery, allowing you to set a tighter BRT time as your goal. Knowing your historical MTTR helps you determine an achievable target for how quickly you can restore functionality after a disruption.

First, when setting resilience goals, you want to establish your baselines. Analyze your historical data to establish MTBF, MTTD, and MTTR baseline values. Then, you can set improvement goals. As you implement resilience strategies, aim to improve your MTBF (reducing failures) and MTTR (faster recoveries). Make sure you are aligned with business needs. Consider the financial impact or user experience disruptions caused by downtime.

Use this information to set recovery objectives and BRT goals that balance technical feasibility with business needs.

You can build a more resilient system that aligns with your organization's specific needs and downtime tolerance by continuously monitoring these metrics and striving to improve them. Remember, these metrics provide historical averages, and actual failures might deviate. However, they offer valuable insights to set realistic and achievable resilience goals. By setting clear resilience goals, aligning them with recovery objectives and availability goals, and implementing strategies to achieve bounded recovery times, you can build systems that are more resistant to disruptions and minimize the impact of downtime on your operations and user experience.

These will be your resilience goals for your fictitious electronic trading application, AvailableTrade. You are responsible for the AvailableTrade application, where downtime can result in revenue loss. Your system logs reveal an average MTBF of 2 weeks (336 hours) and an MTTR of 2 hours. Based on this data, set a recovery objective of 4 hours (allowing some buffer time beyond your typical MTTR). Given your business needs and current MTTR, achieving a bounded recovery time of 1 hour might be a more strategic goal to minimize downtime and its financial impact.

Now that you have set your objectives, let's learn some best practices and patterns for achieving them.

Workload Architecture

Workload architecture is the cornerstone of customer responsibility in the AWS cloud. Architecting, engineering, testing, and operating revolve around designing a resilient workload architecture.

To guide you in this endeavor, we'll begin by exploring essential frameworks that empower you to enhance the resilience of your workload. These frameworks foster continuous learning and improvement, enabling you to adapt to evolving business needs and technological landscapes and ensuring that resilience is ingrained at every phase—design, implementation, testing, and ongoing evolution.

Following this, we'll delve into fundamental resilience concepts, including high availability and disaster recovery, shedding light on how they fortify your workload against disruptions. Finally, we'll dive deeply into each facet of the Shared Responsibility Model, clarifying the customer's responsibilities in maintaining a resilient cloud environment.

Two core frameworks, the AWS Resilience Analysis Framework and the AWS Well-Architected Framework, are invaluable pillars in pursuing resilient system design on AWS. Let's start our journey here by closely examining each of these frameworks, uncovering how they can equip you to build robust and dependable systems within the AWS ecosystem.

AWS Resilience Analysis Framework

The AWS Resilience Analysis Framework (RAF) is a comprehensive methodology designed to assess and enhance workload resilience. It provides a structured approach to identifying potential failure modes within user journeys that your applications support. At its core, the framework aims to identify vulnerabilities and weaknesses, enabling you to proactively address potential points of failure and implement resilience strategies to prevent or minimize the impact of disruptions. By conducting a thorough resilience analysis, you can gain insights into your current resilience posture, prioritize areas for improvement, and develop actionable plans to enhance resilience. RAF identifies the desired resilience properties of a workload. Desired properties are what you want to be true about the system.

Resilience is typically measured by availability, and RAF has defined five properties that are the characteristics of a highly available distributed system: redundancy, sufficient capacity, timely output, correct output, and fault isolation. When a desired resilience property is violated, it could cause a workload to be unavailable or perceived to be so. Based on these desired resilience properties, RAF identifies five common failure categories: single points of failure, excessive load, excessive latency, misconfigurations and bugs, and shared fate (SEEMS) that can cause a resilience property violation.

These failure categories provide a consistent method for categorizing potential failure modes:

Single point of failure (SPOF)
> Violates the redundancy resilience property. A failure in a single component disrupts the system due to a lack of redundancy.

Excessive load
> Violates the sufficient capacity resilience property. Overconsumption of a resource through excessive demand or traffic prevents the resource from performing its expected function. This can include reaching limits and quotas, which cause throttling and rejection of requests.

Excessive latency
> Violates the timely output property resilience property. System processing or network traffic latency exceeds the expected time, service-level objectives (SLOs), or SLAs.

Misconfiguration and bugs
> Violates the correct output resilience property. Software bugs or system misconfiguration leads to incorrect output.

Shared fate
> Violates the fault isolation resilience property. A fault caused by any of the previous failure categories crosses intended fault isolation boundaries. It cascades to other parts of the system or other customers.

While these are not exhaustive, and you may have other resilience property requirements, RAF gives you a good starting point for thinking about how failure modes affect the resilience of your workloads, and working toward corrective, preventative, or mitigation measures.

You will use RAF in this book as we work through your example application. You will create failures aligning with SEEMS, and implement preventative measures or mitigations to maintain the corresponding resilience property.

 You can find the prescriptive guidance for the AWS Resilience Analysis Framework used in this book at the AWS "Resilience Analysis Framework" documentation (*https://oreil.ly/lnKwc*).

AWS Well-Architected Framework

The AWS Well-Architected Framework is a set of principles and best practices that helps architects, developers, and engineers design, build, test, and operate secure, efficient, high-performing, and resilient workloads on Amazon Web Services (AWS). It serves as a blueprint to help you navigate the complexities of the cloud and establish a strong foundation for your cloud infrastructure.

The framework is based on six key pillars: Operational Excellence, Security, Reliability, Performance Efficiency, Cost Optimization, and Sustainability. Each pillar defines best practices for designing, building, and operating workloads on AWS. Here, we'll focus on the Reliability and Operational Excellence pillars for resilience.

The Reliability pillar of the AWS Well-Architected Framework ensures that workloads perform consistently and predictably, even under varying conditions. It focuses on building systems that can withstand disruptions and minimize downtime while maintaining availability, resilience, and fault tolerance. Key areas of emphasis under the Reliability pillar include architectural best practices, fault tolerance mechanisms, recovery strategies, and performance optimization to enhance the reliability of AWS workloads.

The Operational Excellence pillar of the AWS Well-Architected Framework is about optimizing operational processes and procedures to efficiently manage and maintain AWS workloads. It highlights the importance of automating tasks, continuously improving processes, and empowering teams to make informed decisions. Key areas of emphasis within the Operational Excellence pillar include defining operational standards, implementing automation, monitoring and logging, incident management, and resource optimization to enhance the efficiency, reliability, and security of AWS workloads.

You can find the prescriptive guidance for the AWS Well-Architected Framework used in this book at "Reliability Pillar: AWS Well-Architected Framework" (*https://oreil.ly/tND1v*) and "Operational Excellence Pillar: AWS Well-Architected Framework" (*https://oreil.ly/UVjn7*).

High availability

High availability (HA) focuses on preventing downtime or minimizing its impact during minor disruptions, ensuring your system remains operational most of the time. These disruptions are typically caused by hardware or software failures within the system itself. HA systems employ automated recovery and self-healing mechanisms to mitigate these failures.

One key concept of high availability is redundancy. These systems typically utilize redundant components such as servers, storage, applications, and data replication. If one component fails, another seamlessly takes over, minimizing service disruption and ensuring continuity.

High availability is not just about uptime; it's also about efficiency. These systems often possess self-healing capabilities like automatically restarting failed applications. This reduces the need for manual intervention and speeds up recovery times, bolstering confidence in the system's resilience and the efficiency of your investment.

Highly available systems are designed with adaptability, empowering you to handle increased traffic or workload demands. They are often horizontally scalable, meaning they can effortlessly adapt to real-time needs, ensuring high availability even under heavy load. This flexibility allows you to optimize resource utilization and cost while maintaining availability, giving you greater control over your system's performance.

Effective management is important for achieving high availability. Centralized management tools empower administrators to monitor system health, configure components, and efficiently perform maintenance activities. Advanced monitoring capabilities track system performance, resource utilization, and potential issues, enabling proactive identification and resolution of problems before they escalate into outages. Additionally, real-time alerting mechanisms notify administrators of possible issues or failures, facilitating prompt intervention and minimizing downtime.

To learn more about availability, see the AWS whitepaper "Availability and Beyond: Understanding and Improving the Resilience of Distributed Systems on AWS" (*https://oreil.ly/3ypzk*).

Disaster recovery

Disaster recovery is an essential part of business continuity. It focuses on recovering from disasters that can cause complete system outages. These plans cover both the technological aspects of recovery and the human resources and established processes needed to restore operations effectively.

Defining a disaster recovery strategy involves a systematic approach, including identifying critical business functions, prioritizing recovery objectives, establishing RTOs and RPOs, and designing a comprehensive recovery plan outlining specific steps to be taken during and after a disaster. Proactively addressing disaster recovery in this way helps you protect your operations, data, and reputation, ensuring a swift and efficient return to normalcy even after a catastrophic event.

Disaster recovery in AWS differs significantly from traditional on-premise workload recovery strategies. The AWS Global Infrastructure helps mitigate concerns related to spare hardware, natural disasters, fire risks, and power outages. Failing servers can be easily replaced, and the distribution of availability zones within a region can help minimize the impact of power interruptions, fires, and natural disasters.

When considering potential disaster scenarios in AWS, the focus shifts toward failure modes that could render primary workloads inoperable. These scenarios may include data corruption, regional service impairments, and problematic deployments. Understanding these unique challenges in the cloud environment empowers you to tailor your disaster recovery strategies accordingly, ensuring the continuity of your critical applications and services.

Disaster recovery strategies

Let's examine each disaster recovery strategy shown in Figure 1-4, with recovery objectives as the dimension.

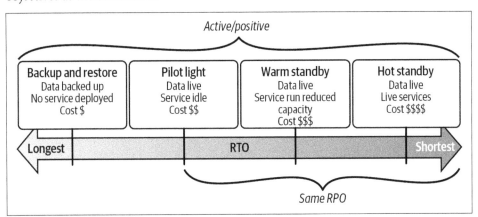

Figure 1-4. Disaster recovery strategies

The *backup and restore* strategy involves regularly creating backups of critical data and system configurations, which are stored in a secure and separate location. This strategy is fundamental and suitable for most organizations. It's cost-effective and ideal for situations where a complete system outage isn't a critical concern. However, recovery times can be longer depending on the complexity of the restore process.

A backup and restore strategy should not be confused with backing up data. While regular data backups are essential for protecting against data corruption (whether accidental or malicious), a comprehensive backup and restore strategy goes beyond mere backup creation. It encompasses the entire process of backing up data and ensuring the capability to efficiently and reliably restore all critical components of your workload, including data, configurations, networking infrastructure, and compute resources in the event of a disruption or disaster.

Data backups are a fundamental component of any workload, acting as a safety net against data loss. They are required to be part of your overall data management strategy. However, a well-defined backup and restore strategy is a holistic approach that ensures you can recover your data and restore your entire operational environment within a time frame that aligns with your recovery objectives.

The *pilot light* strategy maintains a minimal, preconfigured infrastructure in a recovery environment. This "pilot light" can be scaled up during a disaster using automation tools and scripts to provision additional resources and deploy application components. This strategy suits scenarios where recovery time objectives can support the time for scaling out resources in a disaster. It's ideal for less critical applications or limited budgets.

The *warm standby* strategy replicates the production environment infrastructure and data in a separate recovery environment. This replica is kept synchronized with the primary environment but doesn't actively process transactions. Some computing resources are running for a warm standby, which differs from a pilot light where there are none. In a disaster, the recovery environment can be more quickly scaled up than a pilot light to handle production traffic and take over operations. This strategy is a good choice when downtime is costly, but a hot standby might not be justified. It balances cost and recovery time objectives, with you deciding how warm you want your recovery environment to be.

The *hot standby* strategy maintains a fully operational and synchronized copy of the production environment in a separate recovery environment. This redundant environment is ready to take over operations in a disaster with minimal downtime. The exact number of computing resources in the production environment run for a hot standby. This strategy is ideal for mission-critical applications where even a brief outage can have significant consequences. It ensures the fastest possible failover, but comes at a higher cost due to the need to maintain a fully operational replica.

By carefully considering your business needs, resilience goals, and budget constraints, you can select the most appropriate strategy and implement a comprehensive disaster recovery plan. Remember, a well-tested and documented disaster recovery plan is critical for ensuring business continuity during disruptions.

Multi-region considerations

Developing multi-region workloads on AWS involves considerations and trade-offs that you must understand to create efficient and cost-effective AWS multi-region workloads.

If your business drivers require it, consider using multi-region architectures. These drivers may include compliance with regulatory requirements that mandate data storage within specific regions, such as data sovereignty. Global and geographically dispersed user bases may require multi-region deployments to improve performance by reducing latency. Multi-region deployments can also provide redundancy and mitigation for your system's specific failure modes, such as an AWS regional service impairment. In a disruption in one AWS Region, the workload can be failed over to another, reducing downtime.

While multi-region systems can offer significant benefits for high availability, scalability, latency, and compliance, they can also introduce additional complexity in managing and operating geographically dispersed resources, as well as additional infrastructure, resources, and data transfer costs.

Aligning your technical decisions with your business strategy is key to successful multi-region deployments. You will also have to consider the balance between data consistency and latency. Replicating data across multiple regions ensures data availability and resilience but introduces data consistency and synchronization challenges. To balance data consistency and latency, you can implement strategies such as multi-master data stores, eventual consistency, or conflict resolution mechanisms; however, depending on the complexity of your workload, this can prove challenging to achieve and operate.

You will also need to decide on a failover strategy and the granularity of your failover. Deciding the level at which to failover (entire system, application, service, user journey, or portfolio) has advantages and disadvantages. If you choose not to failover a whole system, one consideration should be how upstream and downstream services will behave with dependencies running in a different region. You should comprehensively test these failover scenarios to validate performance and latency impacts. This ensures that timeouts and retries won't cause cascading failures during an actual failover.

By understanding business drivers, considerations, and trade-offs, you can design efficient and cost-effective multi-region architectures on AWS that deliver optimal performance, resilience, and scalability while meeting your business requirements.

To learn more about multi-region considerations, see the "AWS Multi-Region Fundamentals" whitepaper (*https://oreil.ly/_EFTI*).

Networking

Networking can be nuanced within the AWS Shared Responsibility Model. While AWS owns and maintains the underlying global network infrastructure, ensuring its resilience, your responsibility lies in building your networking layer on top of it. This includes configuring virtual private clouds (VPCs), routing, and establishing connections between on-premises data centers and AWS.

A resilient network architecture is essential for uninterrupted critical business operations, particularly in sectors where even brief downtime can lead to significant financial losses or reputational damage. These networks ensure business continuity through redundant data transmission paths, failover mechanisms, optimized performance, reduced latency, and efficient data transfer among users, applications, and services.

Crucially, networks play a vital role in disaster recovery plans by providing alternative communication paths and failover mechanisms. This enables the replication and recovery of data during disaster scenarios.

When designing your AWS network, consider leveraging native AWS services and features that support data replication across regions. Services like Amazon S3 Cross-Region Replication, Amazon Aurora Global Database, and Amazon DynamoDB global tables offer built-in replication capabilities, simplifying the process compared to building your networking pathways using AWS Direct Connect or AWS VPN.

By adhering to best practices and effectively utilizing AWS services, you can create a network architecture that withstands various disruptions, including hardware and software failures, power outages, cyberattacks, network congestion, and resource limitations. Identifying these failure modes and conducting experiments allows network administrators to implement preventative measures, prepare backup plans, and respond effectively to minimize downtime and maintain network stability.

To optimize traffic routing, employ load balancers to distribute incoming traffic across multiple instances or resources. AWS load balancers automatically scale and distribute traffic to healthy instances, ensuring high availability and fault tolerance. Deploying load balancers across multiple availability zones further enhances availability and resilience. Amazon Route 53 enables you to configure various routing policies and health checks, directing traffic to healthy resources and distributing the load across multiple instances or regions. This minimizes the impact of failures within any single fault isolation boundary.

Establish private connectivity using AWS Direct Connect or AWS VPN for secure and reliable communication between on-premises resources and AWS services. This reduces reliance on the public internet for service-to-service communication.

Finally, implement network monitoring and automation tools to track network performance, detect anomalies, and trigger automated incident responses. Identifying and resolving potential issues is key to minimizing downtime and maintaining a resilient network.

Quotas

Effective management of service quotas on AWS is essential for organizations leveraging cloud services. Service quotas are predefined thresholds that restrict the maximum usage of AWS resources or operations within an account or AWS Region. These quotas help maintain the AWS environment stability, reliability, and cost-effectiveness.

Exceeding service quotas can lead to resource exhaustion, causing service degradation or outages. By staying within predefined quotas, you mitigate the risk of service disruptions and ensure the availability and performance of your applications and workloads.

Start by gaining a comprehensive understanding of the various service quotas imposed by AWS. These quotas vary across different AWS services and dictate the maximum number of resources or operations allowed within an account or AWS Region. This knowledge will empower you to make informed decisions about your resource usage.

To learn more about quotas, see "AWS Service Quotas" (*https://oreil.ly/p1ABH*).

Implement monitoring and quota management strategies. Continuously monitor resource usage metrics using tools like AWS CloudTrail and Amazon CloudWatch. Integrate alarms into your observability platform to trigger automatic quota increase requests when predefined thresholds are met.

Leverage the AWS Service Quotas API to request quota increases for specific services or resources, and automate quota checks and requests within your deployment and infrastructure management processes. This proactive approach allows you to identify and address potential quota limitations before they impact your services.

Optimize resource allocation by prioritizing critical workloads and applications. Use AWS resource tagging to categorize and track resource usage, facilitating efficient allocation based on business priorities and usage patterns. This minimizes wastage and maximizes resource utilization. Review and optimize resource usage and allocation regularly. By analyzing usage patterns, identifying optimization opportunities, and implementing measures to improve resource efficiency, you can be reassured that your AWS resources are utilized effectively, minimizing costs and maintaining service availability.

Change Management

Managing change effectively lends itself to seamless application operation and maintaining operational resilience. A structured change management process mitigates risks, maintains stability, prevents unintended consequences, ensures compliance, promotes collaboration, facilitates rollback and recovery, and encourages continuous improvement.

Establish a formal change control process that outlines how changes are requested, evaluated, approved, implemented, and documented. With its clear roles and responsibilities for all stakeholders, this process empowers each individual, safeguards against potential disruptions, mitigates risks, maintains stability, and prevents unintended consequences. Foster effective communication and collaboration among cross-functional teams involved in the change management process. Encourage open dialogue, feedback sharing, and knowledge exchange.

Prioritize the ability to roll back changes in case of unforeseen issues. Develop and regularly test a well-documented rollback plan, making it readily accessible for swift action. Alternatively, mitigation strategies like fixing forward, isolating and redirecting traffic, or degrading functionality should be established if complete rollback isn't feasible.

Conduct risk assessments for proposed changes, evaluating factors like downtime risk, data loss risk, and security implications. Thorough testing and validation before implementing changes in production environments instill confidence in the impact of these changes on workload resilience. Maintain detailed documentation for all workload changes, including rationale, implementation details, and associated risks. This documentation is a valuable reference for future change management activities and troubleshooting.

Leverage automation tools and scripts to streamline change management processes and minimize manual errors. Where automation isn't possible, implement methods to reduce errors in manual processes, such as two-person verification and well-documented procedures. Implement monitoring and reporting mechanisms to track the impact of changes on workload resilience. Monitor key performance indicators (KPIs) and metrics to identify deviations from expected behavior.

Regularly evaluate and refine change management practices based on feedback, lessons learned, and industry best practices. Update change management policies, procedures, and documentation to ensure they remain effective and aligned with business objectives.

Failure Management

Failures are inevitable in modern technological environments despite careful planning and implementation. Therefore, having a well-defined failure management process can help mitigate risks and maintain operational efficiency. This process provides a structured framework for effectively anticipating, identifying, and responding to failures, minimizing downtime, and swiftly initiating recovery measures. Timely resolution of failures is crucial for fulfilling regulatory mandates and mitigating financial losses from service interruptions.

To establish an intuitive failure management process, configure monitoring thresholds and alarms to trigger alerts based on predefined criteria, such as abnormal resource utilization, performance degradation, or service disruptions. Automated alerts can notify relevant teams promptly, enabling them to take corrective action or initiate automated remediation scripts before failures escalate.

Another key aspect of the failure management process is the development of response playbooks. These playbooks outline predefined response actions for different failures and incidents, and are best created collaboratively with cross-functional teams. This collaboration is essential for defining response procedures, escalation paths, and communication protocols for various scenarios, ensuring a comprehensive and effective incident response.

Integrate automation tools and scripts into the incident response system to automate remediation actions and response workflows. This can include automated scripts for restarting services, reallocating resources, rolling back configurations, or triggering failover mechanisms. Leverage infrastructure as code (IaC) and configuration management tools to automate resource provisioning and configuration during incident response. Additionally, consider implementing orchestration tools or workflow automation platforms to orchestrate complex incident response workflows and coordinate remediation actions across multiple systems and teams. Utilize workflow automation capabilities to define conditional logic, decision points, and dependencies within response workflows.

Continuous improvement is a cornerstone of any failure management process. Thorough post-incident and root cause analysis (RCA) for failures or incidents is essential for identifying contributing factors, lessons learned, and areas for improvement. Regularly reviewing and updating the automated incident response system, based on feedback from post-incident reviews and infrastructure or application architecture changes, is critical. Conducting periodic tabletop exercises, simulations, and drills to test the automated response system's effectiveness and identify improvement areas is also essential. The goal is to continuously optimize response playbooks, automation scripts, and workflows to enhance the efficiency, accuracy, and effectiveness of failure management processes.

Observability

Observability provides real-time insights into system performance, health, and behavior, serving as a proactive tool. It plays a pivotal role in preventing disruptions by enabling you to identify and address potential issues before they escalate into significant disruptions.

At the heart of observability are three pillars: logs, metrics, and traces. Each pillar offers a unique perspective on your system's functions, contributing to a comprehensive understanding of its overall health and performance.

Logs

Logs are a detailed journal of your system's activities, capturing specific events within your application or infrastructure. They often contain timestamps, messages, and relevant data about each event. By analyzing logs, you can gain valuable insights into the chronological order of events, troubleshoot specific issues, identify root causes of errors, and understand user behavior patterns.

Metrics

Metrics are numerical measurements that provide a quantitative view of your system's performance over time. They represent continuous data streams aggregated and summarized at regular intervals. Metrics allow you to monitor trends, identify performance bottlenecks, and gauge the overall health of your system. They are essential for scaling your infrastructure and ensuring optimal resource utilization.

Traces

Traces delve into the flow of requests within your system, mapping the complete journey of a user request as it traverses different components and services. They often include timestamps, identifiers, and detailed information about each step in handling the request. Traces are invaluable for understanding complex, distributed systems where requests involve multiple services. They help pinpoint performance issues within specific parts of the request flow and identify potential bottlenecks.

While each pillar offers valuable insights on its own, their true power lies in their synergy. Logs provide context for metrics, metrics help identify trends in logs, and traces offer a detailed view of what the logs and metrics represent within a specific request flow. Analyzing all three pillars together gives you a holistic understanding of your system's behavior. This comprehensive view lets you diagnose problems effectively, optimize performance, and ensure a seamless user experience.

Furthermore, observability empowers postmortem analyses of failure incidents. By examining logs, metrics, and traces collected during and after an incident, you can gain deep insights into the root causes and underlying issues that contributed to the failure. This data-driven approach allows you to identify patterns, vulnerabilities, and areas for improvement, fostering a culture of continuous learning and refinement, ultimately leading to more resilient systems.

In the context of resilient design, observability serves as an early warning system, alerting you to potential problems before they cause significant disruptions. By leveraging observability tools and techniques, you can proactively address issues, minimize downtime, and ensure your workloads' continuous availability and performance.

Continuous Testing and Chaos Engineering

Testing is a recurring theme throughout this book, and while we will dive into it quite a bit, the subject is vast enough to warrant its own book. The fundamental principle is this: you should be testing everything. This encompasses all your application code, IaC, change management processes, failure management processes, recovery processes, observability monitoring, and alerting mechanisms. Testing should be an ongoing practice, enabling you to learn from observations and continuously enhance your systems. We will explore this further in "Continuous Resilience" on page 28.

Traditional code testing techniques, such as unit tests, integration tests, and regression tests, are pivotal in maintaining code quality and detecting potential issues early in the development lifecycle. Integrating these automated tests into your CI/CD pipeline is a must. These tests validate individual code units, ensure the smooth interaction of different modules or components, and ensure that new code changes do not lead to functionality regressions. While traditional testing effectively catches bugs, performance issues, and integration problems, it often struggles to replicate the complexities and unpredictability of real-world scenarios. Unexpected events and failures can result in severe system disruptions and costly downtime, underscoring the need for more comprehensive testing approaches.

Chaos engineering is a disciplined approach to identifying system vulnerabilities by proactively introducing controlled disruptions. It operates on the principle that intentionally injecting failures into a system can uncover weaknesses and potential points of failure before they manifest in a real-world scenario. This allows for proactive remediation, strengthening the system's resilience and ensuring it can withstand unexpected disruptions.

Traditional testing verifies that a system functions as expected under normal operating conditions. Chaos engineering, on the other hand, goes beyond the norm, intentionally pushing systems to their limits to expose vulnerabilities that may not be apparent in traditional testing scenarios. By simulating real-world failures, chaos engineering helps you understand how your systems behave under stress and identify areas for improvement.

Best practices in chaos engineering include:

Start small and gradually increase complexity
Begin with simple experiments and progressively increase the complexity and severity of disruptions as you gain confidence in your system's ability to handle them.

Define clear hypotheses and metrics
Each experiment should have a clearly defined hypothesis and measurable metrics to determine whether the system behaved as expected.

Prioritize blast radius control
Implement safeguards to limit the impact of experiments and prevent them from affecting production environments or users.

Automate experiments
Automate the execution and analysis of chaos experiments to ensure consistency and repeatability.

Continuous learning
Analyze each experiment's results, identify improvement areas, and implement changes to enhance system resilience.

Chaos engineering shifts the approach from reactive to proactive, empowering you to anticipate and mitigate potential failures before they occur. Chaos engineering represents a paradigm shift in how you approach system resilience. By deliberately introducing controlled disruptions, you can gain invaluable insights into the behavior of your systems under stress. This knowledge empowers you to make informed decisions regarding system design, infrastructure investments, and operational procedures, ultimately enhancing your technology stack's overall reliability, robustness, and resilience.

AWS Fault Injection Service (FIS) is a powerful tool for implementing chaos engineering principles, enabling you to proactively enhance your AWS workloads' resilience. It's a fully managed service that allows you to inject controlled disruptions, simulating real-world failures like EC2 instance terminations, API throttling, Availability Zone power outages, or network latency. By observing how your applications and infrastructure respond under stress, you can identify and address vulnerabilities before they impact your customers.

Using AWS FIS, you gain several key advantages:

Simplified chaos experiments
> FIS eliminates the need to build and manage your own chaos engineering tools, saving you valuable time and resources.

Safe fault injection
> With FIS, you can conduct fault injection experiments in a safe and controlled environment. This ensures that your experiments don't impact production systems, giving you the confidence to test without fear of disrupting your operations.

Comprehensive insights
> Using FIS, you gain comprehensive insights into the results of your chaos experiments. FIS offers detailed reports and metrics, helping you pinpoint vulnerabilities and prioritize remediation efforts, thereby strengthening your infrastructure's resilience.

Automated chaos testing
> Integrate FIS with your CI/CD pipelines to seamlessly incorporate chaos experiments into your regular testing processes, fostering a culture of continuous improvement.

Scalable experiments
> FIS enables you to easily replicate experiments across multiple AWS accounts and AWS Regions, ensuring consistent testing across your entire infrastructure.

By leveraging FIS, you streamline the implementation of chaos engineering on AWS. This accelerates your journey toward building more resilient and reliable systems and strengthens your confidence in your infrastructure's ability to withstand unexpected disruptions. With FIS, you can proactively identify and address weaknesses, ultimately improving the overall customer experience and minimizing the impact of potential failures.

CI/CD and Automation

Continuous integration and continuous delivery (CI/CD) are integral to building resilient systems. CI/CD practices automate the process of integrating, testing, and deploying code changes, fostering a culture of rapid iteration and continuous improvement. This streamlined approach minimizes human error, accelerates the delivery of new features and fixes, and enables swift identification and resolution of issues, reducing potential vulnerabilities that could lead to outages.

The standardized and repeatable nature of CI/CD processes eliminates variability and potential errors associated with manual processes. This consistency ensures reliable and predictable deployments across environments, reducing the risk of configuration drift and unexpected failures. CI/CD is more than just tools and processes; it's a mindset prioritizing continuous value delivery while maintaining system stability. By fostering collaboration, automation, and continuous improvement, CI/CD empowers organizations to build resilient systems that adapt to changing requirements, withstand disruptions, and deliver a seamless user experience.

Consider these best practices to maximize the benefits of CI/CD in building resilient systems. Encourage developers to commit code changes frequently, ideally multiple times a day. Committing code often reduces the risk of merge conflicts and makes isolating and fixing issues easier. Implement a comprehensive suite of automated tests covering your application's various aspects, including unit, integration, and end-to-end tests. Automated testing ensures that code changes don't introduce new bugs or regressions. Additionally, it provides rapid feedback to developers on the results of their code changes, enabling them to address issues promptly and maintain the quality of the codebase.

Treat your infrastructure as code and use immutable patterns. Instead of modifying existing infrastructure, create new instances for each deployment, ensuring consistency and reducing the risk of configuration drift. Implement monitoring and observability tools to gain real-time insights into your applications' performance and health. Observability lets you quickly detect and respond to issues, minimizing their impact.

Automate the deployment process to reduce human error and ensure consistent deployments across different environments. Have well-defined rollback strategies to quickly revert to a previous stable version of your application if a deployment fails or causes issues. Finally, integrate security testing into your CI/CD pipeline to identify and address security vulnerabilities early in development, reducing the risk of security breaches.

By implementing these best practices, you can leverage CI/CD to build more resilient systems that quickly adapt to changes, recover from failures, and deliver a reliable and consistent user experience.

Continuous Resilience

Continuous resilience involves a commitment to strengthening organizational capabilities, processes, and systems to withstand and recover from various disruptions.

Unlike traditional approaches, continuous resilience emphasizes a proactive and iterative approach to resilience building. It focuses on ongoing analysis, refinement, and optimization of applications and processes to ensure that resilience goals remain efficient, effective, and aligned with evolving business needs.

Creating a culture of continuous resilience can be challenging for organizations. It requires a shift in mindset from reactive to proactive resilience management, and buy-in from executives and stakeholders. By embracing continuous resilience, you can build software systems that are functional, adaptable, and capable of handling disruptions effectively. This proactive approach minimizes downtime, ensures business continuity, and contributes to overall business success.

Remember, resilience is a journey, not a sprint. The word "continuous" is used throughout this book to emphasize the ongoing nature of resilience building. It requires a sustained commitment to learning, adaptation, and improvement to ensure that your systems remain resilient in the face of ever-changing challenges.

Summary

This chapter has provided you with a comprehensive understanding of the multifaceted nature of building resilient systems. You've learned that resilience goes beyond technology, encompassing people, processes, and a Shared Responsibility Model between AWS and you, the customer.

You've firmly grasped the importance of setting clear resilience goals, conducting business impact analysis, and assessing risks to identify critical vulnerabilities. This understanding lets you appreciate the significance of defining recovery objectives like RTO, RPO, and downtime tolerance. You've also explored the concept of BRT and the relevance of MTBF, MTTD, and MTTR in setting realistic resilience targets.

Furthermore, you've delved into the AWS Resilience Analysis Framework and the AWS Well-Architected Framework, gaining valuable insights into how these frameworks can guide you in designing and implementing resilient workloads on AWS. You've also recognized the critical importance of high availability strategies in minimizing downtime during minor disruptions, and which disaster recovery strategies to employ to recover from significant impairments within your recovery time frames.

Additionally, you've explored the considerations and trade-offs involved in multi-region deployments, emphasizing the importance of aligning technical decisions with your business strategies.

You've learned about the nuances of networking in the AWS Shared Responsibility Model and the importance of effective quota management. You now understand the critical role of change management, failure management, and observability in building resilient systems. You've also recognized the significance of continuous testing and chaos engineering, including the benefits of using AWS Fault Injection Service to identify and address vulnerabilities proactively.

You've learned about the importance of CI/CD and automation in streamlining development and deployment processes, minimizing errors, and ensuring consistency. Finally, you've been introduced to continuous resilience, emphasizing the ongoing nature of resilience building and the need for a proactive and iterative approach to adapting to evolving challenges.

Armed with this foundational knowledge, you're now ready to embark on your resilience journey. In the next chapter, we will guide you through setting up your hands-on environment, and then you can start applying these concepts firsthand in the hands-on exercises and begin building resilient systems on AWS.

## CHAPTER 2

Prepare Your Working Environment

In Chapter 1, you were introduced to resilience in the AWS cloud, highlighting the frameworks and the resilience mental model for anticipating, observing, and mitigating failure modes in complex systems. In this chapter, you'll prepare yourself and your software development working environment for a series of hands-on resilience lessons. The hands-on lessons in this book walk you through building resilient components of the fictitious electronic trading application, AvailableTrade. This chapter focuses on installing and configuring the tools you need to run the lessons. If you intend to work through the hands-on examples, which we feel is the best way to learn, start by installing each of the tools listed. If you don't already have them installed or don't understand how to install them when you need them, links are provided to public documentation for each tool.

The resilience patterns demonstrated throughout the lessons in this book span industries and use cases beyond the AvailableTrade application and the financial services industry. However, using a financial services model helps us mentally align the importance of the use cases and lessons demonstrated in this book to real-world scenarios we are familiar with. Critical systems that require your intentional focus on resilience include systems like customer-facing applications that provide the brand and face of a company, payment systems that move money in real time, and systems that perform core business functions. These systems generate revenue, cause reputation risk when not available, and sometimes must comply with regulatory requirements for availability and business continuity.

Imagine you have decided to disrupt the stock trading market with a new online stock trading portal. You have a disruptive idea, the right team in place, and you know how to build your application securely. In addition, because your platform must be up and running to make money, and because the financial services industry regulates resiliency, your team needs to learn how to build your platform to meet your availability goals. You've completed a business impact assessment on your system and defined your RTO and RPO; now you'll continually use risk assessments as you build to meet those goals.

Hands-on Learning with Microservices

Throughout this book, you'll be presented with hands-on resilience lessons bounded by a domain problem and services that communicate over HTTP; these components are designed as microservices. Consider each chapter a customer journey—for example, opening a new brokerage account. This journey provides a bounded context for the application, data storage, and interaction with other components. Each chapter builds capabilities out as separate microservices. These services can be combined into a functional client-facing stock trading application. See Figure 2-1 for an example of the user journeys and microservices that you'll explore in this book.

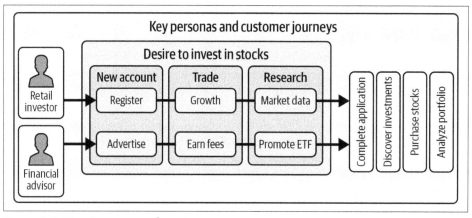

Figure 2-1. User journeys and services

Why did we choose to use the microservices design? When building an application, you need to make some up-front design choices. A monolithic application can typically communicate between modules faster using inter-process communication (IPC). Whether your component communication is one-to-one or one-to-many could be one driver for your decision. Another driver can be whether your communication is synchronous or asynchronous. In your stock trading application, you're going to choose a "microservices first" approach because of some key up-front benefits:

- Microservices architectures create fault isolation boundaries between components.

- Microservices can be scaled, deployed, and managed independently.

Martin Fowler defines microservices as an approach to developing a single application as a suite of small services:

> In short, the microservice architectural style is an approach to developing a single application as a suite of small services, each running in its own process and communicating with lightweight mechanisms, often an HTTP resource API. These services are built around business capabilities and [are] independently deployable by fully automated deployment machinery. There is a bare minimum of centralized management of these services, which may be written in different programming languages and use different data storage technologies.

You can read more about what a microservice is on Martin Fowler's website (*https://oreil.ly/GXP0O*).

You'll continually weigh performance and latency requirements as you decide how coarse-grained or fine-grained your services are, and keep in mind the specific ways that your microservice architecture can achieve your resilience goals as you build your components. Fault isolation boundaries restrict problems to a well-defined blast radius that contains the impact of a fault. When your workload has thoughtful segmentation between components, you have created fault isolation boundaries along with the ability to scale resources independently. Loosely coupled services can be built and maintained by separate teams that can choose technologies independently and focus on specific business outcomes. Your business domain model is expressed in bounded contexts defined with API contracts so that implementation changes within a particular service do not require changes and retesting of another service that interfaces with it. While API contracts are enforced natively in protocols like the Simple Object Access Protocol (SOAP) and GraphQL by way of schema-based object definition, the services in this book use the REpresentational State Transfer (REST) protocol. You'll leverage JSON schemas in your API producers to enforce your RESTful contracts expressed in JSON.

With a microservices architecture established for your application, you will apply resilience patterns both within each service and between these services at their integration boundary. In the following chapters, you'll get hands-on experience with some of these patterns, such as rate limiting, retries, timeouts, idempotency, and stateless design.

Bear in mind that while the brokerage application examples are not meant as a production-worthy solution that you can deploy to start your next business venture, the examples demonstrate how to analyze, design, and test for real-world resilience. You may read the rest of this book without executing examples, but you will get the most benefit if you deploy and work through the lessons that improve upon the resilience of each microservice. You'll build out a stock trading portal, including a UI, microservices for opening accounts and trading stocks, and an active-passive multi-region disaster recovery strategy. You'll also think through microservices for ingesting market data, analytics from screen-scraped news content, and disaster recovery for streaming services.

From a system design standpoint, the examples cover several modern application technologies, including serverless, containers, streaming data, NoSQL, relational databases, analytics tools, and caching. While you do not need to be an expert in each technology used, you must install the tools outlined in this chapter to deploy and work through the examples. This is not a beginner-level book, as system design requires some understanding of web development technologies, business strategy, and design patterns.

It helps to have a basic working knowledge of the Python programming language, database technologies, and the AWS cloud. Additionally, technical maturity means keeping a keen eye on creating successful systems aligned with business goals. Each lesson in the book describes a business use case and the reasoning for the architecture chosen to solve it. The chapters also provide context on the tools and frameworks used as you work through the lessons. Let's get started!

AWS Account and Permissions

Your first step is to ensure you have an AWS account with adequate Identity Access Management (IAM) permissions. If you don't already have an AWS account, it's a good idea to pause and create one now (*https://aws.amazon.com/free*).

 Setting up an AWS account is free, but running workloads on AWS can accrue charges. The lessons in this book have been designed to keep costs within the free tier when possible. However, it is your responsibility to practice good cloud financial management. This means you'll want to delete AWS resources in your account when you no longer need them to keep your costs to a minimum.

Now, with your AWS account ready, you can log in with an IAM principal; a principal is an IAM identity that has the required permissions to create the resources for each chapter. If you have a federation capability, use an IAM role; otherwise, create an IAM user. Then enable your federated role or user with the AWS-managed roles AdministratorAccess or PowerUserAccess. If you choose PowerUserAccess, you'll need the addition of policies to allow you to create, delete, and modify IAM roles and policies and attach policies to roles.

See the AWS documentation (*https://docs.aws.amazon.com*) for a high-level overview of the services used throughout the book. If you don't already have an administrative federated role or user setup, follow the public user guide for creating an administrative user (*https://oreil.ly/zidQ2*) in the AWS IAM documentation. The examples in this book have been tested using the AWS-managed role AdministratorAccess.

AWS and the authors recommend that you not use your root user credentials for the lessons in this book or any development work. The root user is created when you create your account. This user is meant to be reserved for managing specialized account-level settings like billing information. It is a best practice (*https://oreil.ly/ Bbpmu*) to enable MFA authentication for your root user and safeguard your credentials.

Choosing a Development OS and IDE

The examples in this book were developed and tested on macOS and Linux. The CLI commands and scripts follow GNU Bash syntax and will also run in the ZSH shell. The authors performed work on their local machines using a mix of PyCharm and Visual Studio Code; however, you can use the IDE of your choice. If you'd prefer not to install the tooling required to run the lessons on your workstation, you can set up a cloud VDI like Amazon Workspaces. You can also use AWS CloudShell to run AWS CLI command examples, but you will need knowledge of a shell-based text editor like Vim if you plan to edit files in CloudShell. You should be able to run any of the lessons on Windows as long as your version supports the Bash shell environment, which can be enabled with the Windows Subsystem for Linux (WSL) (*https://oreil.ly/icUo4*). You may have to make small adjustments to some commands for Windows compatibility.

From this point onward, you'll begin actively setting up your environment.

Git and Code Samples Repository

Open a terminal window to determine whether the Git CLI is already installed on your system. At the command prompt, type the command **git --version**. The version on my Macbook at the time of this writing is `git version 2.39.3 (Apple Git-146)`, though older and newer versions should work fine. You should see similar output if Git is installed on your system. If not, you will need to install the Git CLI or download the repository content as a ZIP file that you can unpack for a working project directory. You can download the installer for your system from git-scm for macOS, Windows, and Linux/Unix (*https://git-scm.com/downloads*). Follow the instructions provided to install the CLI utility.

Once installed, you can clone the project repository as shown, then move on to Python environment setup:

```
git clone git@github.com:engineering-resilient-systems-on-aws/AvailableTrade.git
cd AvailableTrade
```

Python Environment

The application code and infrastructure as code (IaC) that make up the examples in this book use Python 3. At a terminal, you can run **python3 --version** to determine whether you have Python 3 installed. Output will look similar to this:

```
> $ python3 --version
Python 3.9.16
```

If you don't have Python 3.9 or greater installed, you'll need to install it.

 Installation instructions (*https://realpython.com/installing-python*) vary by system and personal preference. To simply your life, if you don't already have Python installed or familiarity with how to set it up, use CloudShell.

Python has a useful feature called a "virtual environment," which helps you avoid compatibility issues when loading dependencies for a project. We suggest using a Python virtual environment with the projects for this book to avoid "dependency collisions" where other Python projects you may be working on require different dependency versions. In the project directory *AvailableTrade*, run the following command to create a virtual environment:

```
cd ~/environment/AvailableTrade
python3 -m venv .venv
```

Once your environment has been created, you can activate it with the following command. Any time you plan to work on lessons in this book, your first step should be to activate your virtual environment:

```
> $ source .venv/bin/activate
(.venv) > $
```

Notice that once your virtual environment has been activated, you'll see a visual indicator where the line begins with (.venv) at your terminal prompt. Once your virtual environment has been loaded, you can execute python or the Python package manager pip without suffixing 3 on the commands. See the following commands to verify this on your system:

```
(.venv) > $ python --version
Python 3.9.16
(.venv) > $ pip --version
pip 21.3.1
```

Finally, you'll want to make sure your IDE PYTHONPATH is configured to point to your .venv Python binaries instead of the path of Python installed at the OS level. This way, as you install dependencies in projects with pip, your IDE's typeahead code completion will be aware of the packages you've installed. Note that these steps are IDE specific; if you use another IDE, follow your IDE-specific instructions.

NPM and Node.js

You'll need to install the Node.js package manager to install or update the CDK to install packages, and test the web portal that will be introduced in later lessons.

To check currently installed versions, run **node --version** and **npm --version**. Go ahead and update them to the latest versions by running **npm install -g npm**.

 You can update to the latest or install Node.js and npm for your OS by visiting the node and npm site (*https://oreil.ly/8FP_y*).

If you have not used Node.js and npm before, the file that configures dependencies and commands is the *package.json* file. When you are working in a project directory with a *package.json* file, the command npm install will install the dependencies defined for that project. Additionally, in the file, you'll see a section called scripts. These are commands you can run for the project. Common examples are npm run dev to run a development server or npm run build to package an application for deployment.

AWS CDK

The AWS Cloud Development Kit (CDK) helps you build IaC in your familiar programming language. You'll use Python for the CDK examples in this book. To get started, you'll need to install the CDK CLI tooling. CloudShell already has the CDK installed; you can use the following command to install it on your Mac or Linux system, or follow instructions in the public documentation:

```
npm install -g aws-cdk
cdk --version
```

Before you can deploy a CDK solution, you'll need to ensure the CDK has been bootstrapped for your target account and region. First, activate the Python virtual environment, make a copy of the *env.template.sh* file by renaming it to *env.sh*, and then load your *env.sh* file. The following code snippet shows how the *env.sh* file sets your AWS account, primary, and secondary region environment variables. Before you run the CDK commands, you'll need to have your AWS CLI environment configured for your role or user profile.

If you don't know how to configure your CLI for AWS, use CloudShell. The CDK applications in this book use these to configure the deployment environment:

```
# contents of env.sh
export AWS_ACCOUNT_ID=$(aws sts get-caller-identity --query 'Account' \
  --output text)
export AWS_PRIMARY_REGION=us-east-2
export AWS_SECONDARY_REGION=us-west-1

export PYTHONPATH=$PYTHONPATH:`pwd`

export AWS_DOMAIN_NAME="your-domain"

export JSII_SILENCE_WARNING_UNTESTED_NODE_VERSION=1
```

In your terminal, **cd** into the main project directory, *AvailableTrade*, then run the following commands to activate your Python virtual environment and set the environment configuration. Prepare your terminal by running these two commands anytime you plan to deploy resources with the CDK in this book:

```
cp env.template.sh env.sh
source .venv/bin/activate
source env.sh
```

Now, with your terminal environment prepared, you can **cd** into the sample CDK application directory, load your requirements, run **cdk bootstrap** to bootstrap the CDK in your account, then deploy the sample application with these commands:

```
cd src/environment-setup
pip install -r requirements.txt
cdk bootstrap --force $AWS_ACCOUNT_ID/$AWS_PRIMARY_REGION \
  $AWS_ACCOUNT_ID/$AWS_SECONDARY_REGION
cdk deploy --require-approval never
```

You bootstrapped the CDK in your primary and secondary regions, and used the `--force` flag to upgrade the bootstrap in case you had an older CDK Toolkit installed for AWS CloudFormation in your environment. You only need to boostrap one time. Once the deployments have completed, you'll see a CloudFormation output parameter called `HelloResilienceStack.HelloResilienceEndpoint` in your terminal, similar to this:

```
HelloResilienceStack.HelloResilienceEndpoint =
  https://1d2hhzfjn4.execute-api.us-east-2.amazonaws.com/prod/getHello/
```

Now open the `HelloResilienceEndpoint` in your browser, or make a request with **curl** to see output from your deployed CDK application:

```
curl https://1d2hhzfjn4.execute-api.us-east-2.amazonaws.com/prod/getHello/
Hello, Resilience! You have hit /getHello/
```

Look at the sample Hello World project to understand a CDK app stack:

```
import os
import aws_cdk as cdk
from stacks.hello_resilience_stack import HelloResilienceStack

account = os.getenv('AWS_ACCOUNT_ID')
primary_region = os.getenv('AWS_PRIMARY_REGION')

app = cdk.App()
HelloResilienceStack(
    app, "HelloResilienceStack",
    env=cdk.Environment(account=account, region=primary_region))
app.synth()
```

Open and review the file *AvailableTrade/src/environemnt-setup/app.py*. You will see that cdk.App() is the entry point for any CDK application. You add CDK stacks to the application, HelloResilienceStack in this case, and each stack defines a set of AWS cloud resources. A CDK stack requires a configured AWS account and AWS Region to deploy; recall that you load the *env.sh* file to consistently configure the resilience lessons environment.

Now review the HelloResilienceStack in the file *hello_resilience_stack.py*:

```
from aws_cdk import (
    Stack,
    aws_lambda as _lambda,
    aws_apigateway as apigateway
)
import aws_cdk as cdk
from constructs import Construct


class HelloResilienceStack(Stack):
    def __init__(self, scope: Construct, construct_id: str, **kwargs) -> None:
        super().__init__(scope, construct_id, **kwargs)

        hello_resilience = _lambda.Function(
            self, "HelloResilience",
            runtime=_lambda.Runtime.PYTHON_3_9,
            code=_lambda.Code.from_asset("lambda"),
            handler='hello_resilience.handler'
        )

        hello_resilience_api = apigateway.RestApi(
            self, "HelloResilienceApi",
            deploy_options=apigateway.StageOptions(
                data_trace_enabled=True,
                tracing_enabled=True
            ))

        hello_resilience_endpoint = hello_resilience_api.root.add_resource(
                                                        "getHello")

        hello_resilience_endpoint.add_method(
```

```
    "GET",
    apigateway.LambdaIntegration(hello_resilience))

cdk.CfnOutput(self, "HelloResilienceEndpoint",
              value=hello_resilience_api.url_for_path("/getHello/"))
```

Once the class `HelloResilienceStack` is defined and initialized, you can start defin-ing the infrastructure resources that make up your stack. The first resource is an AWS Lambda function defined as a `_lambda.Function` CDK construct. CDK constructs are the objects that represent AWS infrastructure as code. The Lambda code is in the *environment-setup/lambda/hello_resilience.py* file.

> Learning the CDK is beyond the scope of this book, but you can use the CDK Developer Guide (*https://oreil.ly/1mssL*) to get started if you're new to the CDK. You can also reference the Python API docs (*https://oreil.ly/fleTU*) for details on the API constructs employed throughout the lessons.

After the Lambda function, an AWS API Gateway is configured with the CDK construct `apigateway.RestApi`. Next, an API endpoint is added with an integration to the Lambda function. Finally, an output is configured to print the API endpoint you tested with. All the sample projects in the book follow this structure, allowing a repeatable and automated way to configure and deploy your AWS resources.

Additional Software

If you plan to run the microservice resilience lessons in this book, you'll need several other third-party software frameworks. Those include Python packages, which will be installed in your virtual environment so that they will not affect other projects you may be running. Additionally, you'll need a few other command-line tools to run the lessons from your terminal.

AWS CLI

You'll install the AWS CLI using your operating system's package management sys-tem. The CLI commands in this book are written for AWS CLI version 2.

> The documentation page for AWS CLI V2 provides instructions for installing the AWS CLI on Linux, macOS, or Windows (*https://oreil.ly/SWscT*).

If you're using CloudShell, the AWS CLI is already installed on your system. To install the latest version, first remove the existing version with the following command:

```
sudo yum remove awscli
```

After answering **y** to the `Is this ok [y/N]:` prompt, you are ready to install the latest update for version 2 with this command:

```
curl "https://awscli.amazonaws.com/awscli-exe-linux-x86_64.zip" \
  -o "awscliv2.zip"
unzip awscliv2.zip
sudo ./aws/install
```

Finally, verify your installation:

```
(.venv) > $ aws --version
aws-cli/2.15.27 Python/3.11.8 Linux/6.1.77-99.164.amzn2023.x86_64
```

Python Packages

Typically, when developing microservices, each team owning a service can take a polyglot approach; they can choose the programming language and tools of choice. This means that creating a Python virtual environment would be done on a per-service basis. To simplify working through the lessons in this book, create your virtual environment at the root of the book project. This will make it easier to jump around between chapters once you've activated your virtual environment. However, if you'd like to create separate virtual environments for each module, feel free to do so. Either route you take, to get started, update pip to the latest version, like this:

```
python -m pip install --upgrade pip
```

Once you've updated pip, as you work through each lesson module, your first step will be to install the requirements for that module. Use pip for that, as well as the module-specific *requirements.txt* file:

```
pip install -r requirements.txt
```

Vue.js and Vite

The brokerage single-page web application (SPA) is built with the popular open source responsive web framework Vue.js. The lessons use Vite for local testing and packaging your web application for deployment. The Vite tooling will be installed when you run npm install, via the *package.json* dependencies you'll install with npm in the frontend chapters.

You can learn more about Vite from the public documentation (*https://vitejs.dev*).

Bootstrap CSS

The brokerage web application is styled to work both in a desktop browser and in a mobile phone browser. We chose Bootstrap to simplify CSS styling, building forms, and designing standard UI components. You can choose to install Bootstrap locally with npm; however, for simplicity and to keep the application light, we reference Bootstrap over a public CDN link. Bootstrap uses a grid layout system, so you'll see HTML <div> to build page structures, and there are many other features to help you quickly style and build your UI.

See the Bootstrap public documentation (*https://getbootstrap.com*) to learn more about installing Bootstrap and using the responsive components and grid layout.

Artillery.io

One key area where applications fail is when they are exposed to an excessive load. We have chosen to use Artillery.io, a load testing framework that is focused on HTTP endpoints and is straightforward to configure and install. An alternative Python open source load testing tool we like is Locust.io. Artillery.io tests are defined in a YAML file, and any load tests you need to run in the lessons in this book have already been defined for you. You need to ensure that you've installed Artillery.io so that they run correctly:

```
npm install -g artillery
```

Visit Artillery.io (*https://www.artillery.io*) to learn more about load testing with Artillery.io.

You can run **artillery --version** to confirm your installation:

```
(.venv) > $ npm install -g artillery
npm WARN deprecated querystring@00.2.0: The querystring API is considered Legacy.
new code should use the URLSearchParams API instead.

added 626 packages in 2m
```

```
76 packages are looking for funding
  run `npm fund` for details
(.venv) > $ artillery --version
```

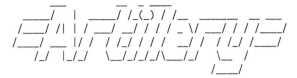

```
VERSION INFO:
Artillery: 2.0.16
Node.js:   v22.3.0
OS:        darwin
```

curl and watch

As you build HTTP APIs, you will need to test them. The examples in this book use the curl CLI utility. The curl utility is free and comes installed on most modern systems by default, including Windows 10 and greater. You should be able to run any of the supplied curl commands without modification and without installing any additional software.

Visit the curl page (*https://curl.se*) to learn more about curl.

The watch CLI utility from the procps library is used in combination with curl. The watch utility provides a simple way to run commands repeatedly at a given time interval. Examples use watch to create steady load and observe intermittent issues. The watch command is not available by default on Windows. We've tried to limit the use of watch to examples that use a Linux test client you'll access with the AWS Systems Manager Session Manager. So, you can still run the examples even if you decide to work through the book examples on your Windows machine.

Visit the procps page (*https://gitlab.com/procps-ng/procps*), which includes both source code and man pages to learn more about procps and watch.

Boto3

The `boto3` library is the AWS SDK for Python. You can generally find an SDK equivalent for any AWS CLI command. From a resilience standpoint, `boto3` and other AWS SDKs (for your language of choice) allow you to configure sensible defaults for things like connect and read timeouts, maximum retries, and more. The defaults are used for the lessons in this book, though you may need to customize the settings for your production projects.

> You can learn more about configuring `boto3` in the public documentation (*https://oreil.ly/wmLBR*).

PostgreSQL

Multiple chapters require interacting with an Amazon Aurora PostgreSQL relational database. To simplify interactions with these databases, each chapter lesson with PostgreSQL leverages the open source `psql` CLI tool for PostgreSQL. This allows examples to be scripted so that you can copy and paste them when loading data, defining a schema, or querying.

> You can learn more about `psql` from the public documentation (*https://oreil.ly/PGBTg*).

Lambda Powertools

Powertools for AWS Lambda (Python) is a developer toolkit to help you implement serverless best practices and increase developer velocity. From a resilience standpoint, using Powertools helps implement observability patterns, idempotency, and Lambda event typing to make programming simpler and more reliable.

> Visit the public documentation (*https://oreil.ly/bcP3c*) to learn more about Python Powertools for Lambda.

Docker Desktop

If you are using Linux, on some systems the Docker CLI is already installed. If you are working from your laptop, you'll need Docker Desktop to build and publish container images.

> Visit the Docker website (*https://oreil.ly/1o3-E*) to learn more about installing Docker Desktop on your machine.

Custom Domain and Route 53 Hosted Zone

When you build AWS applications with public endpoints, AWS will configure and deploy regional endpoints with service-specific Amazon Route 53 DNS names for you. For this book, when you deploy the disaster recovery architectures in Chapter 7 that can failover from one region to another, you'll need to configure and manage custom DNS routing. This means that to work through the Chapter 7 disaster recovery scenario examples, you will need a custom domain name and a third-party certificate for that domain. In AWS, domains are hosted in Route 53 in a hosted zone; for the lessons in this book, you'll need a public hosted zone. Within your public hosted zone, you create DNS records that point to regional endpoints. For an active-passive architecture, you'll create failover records that determine which region to route traffic to by checking the status of regional health checks.

You can stop here if you already have a domain hosted in AWS with a public hosted zone. You are all set to follow lesson-specific steps to create disaster recovery mechanisms. If you don't already have a domain, or you purchased one from another DNS provider, you will need to configure Route 53 before you can deploy and work through the DR lessons. Before you start these lessons, go ahead and create a new domain in Route 53, or transfer your domain over. Alternatively, you can read through the lessons without deploying them.

> The detailed steps for registering a new domain or transferring an existing domain are out of the scope of this book. You can follow the Route 53 documentation (*https://oreil.ly/JhAic*) to set up or transfer your domain.

Security

A strong resilience posture relies on both security practices and operational excellence. While we do address security where applicable in the configuration of the examples in this book, we do not address all aspects of security for the microservice components of each lesson.

We have focused on IAM permissions using CDK grants and generated policies to apply the principle of least-required privilege. As an example, we do not use or advocate global permissions with an asterisk (*) to define all principals, resources, or actions in IAM policies; however, we may, at times, take advantage of managed policies that may define broader permissions than suit your security requirements.

We will not cover security-specific topics and configurations in the lessons, but you should absolutely implement security best practices in your workloads.

Encryption in Transit

Encryption in transit is a secure best practice for keeping data private and mitigating data theft attacks like man in the middle. When you configure Transport Layer Security (TLS) in your services, be mindful that certificate expiration is a common resilience threat. When a certificate expires, connections can fail as browser, web service clients, and database clients can refuse a connection, resulting in service outages. Plan for and implement automated certificate rotation and certificate lifecycle management using tools like the AWS Certificate Manager or third-party tools.

Throughout the lessons in this book, when you access AWS service–managed API endpoints, AWS service–vended certificates are used for encryption in transit. Examples of this are API Gateway and connections to databases (DynamoDB, Aurora PostgreSQL). For simplicity, in some cases in the examples you'll use plain HTTP integration between application services built in containers that run in a private isolated VPC.

Encryption at Rest

Using cloud services makes applying encryption at rest easy. This book's examples take advantage of AWS Key Management Service (KMS) default keys. It is a best practice to configure and apply KMS Customer Managed Keys (CMK) in your workloads. In addition, those keys should have the principle of least private key policies configured to limit access and use.

Authentication and Authorization for API Endpoints

The custom API examples in this book do not include an authentication or authorization solution. When building APIs in AWS, you'll often choose Amazon Cognito for its integration with other AWS services; however, at the time of this writing, Cognito does not support a multi-region identity store. Reference implementations exist for exporting identity information, excluding passwords, and importing them to another region. Cognito also supports passwordless authentication with techniques like touch ID, which are an option for multi-region.

In the authors' opinion, a resilient and accessible multi-region Cognito implementation involves Route 53 in front of Cognito APIs to achieve a multi-region solution with front-door routing. This approach typically involves federating Cognito with a highly available identity provider and managing regional application IDs. The build-out and configuration of a robust multi-region federated solution for Cognito is beyond the scope of this book, but something well worth your time before you deploy applications into production.

Tokenization

Sensitive data should be strongly protected. This protection goes beyond encryption and can require need-to-know privilege. One approach is to use tokenization of sensitive data to achieve regulatory compliance for programs like the Payment Card Industry Data Security Standard (PCI DSS). Personally identifiable information (PII) can be protected with techniques like format-preserving encryption (FPE). While this book cannot be considered an authoritative source on compliance, the authors acknowledge that tokenization is a strong tool for security in the lens of customer data protection. Bear in mind that a tokenization service can also become a hard dependency for transactions and a single point of failure. If you go down the tokenization road, ensure the reliability of your tokenization solution meets your SLA.

Code Scanning

Vulnerabilities in your code or third-party code used by your application allow for breaches that affect the availability of your system or, even worse, could allow privilege escalation. Make sure that you have a comprehensive code scanning and Common Vulnerabilities and Exposures (CVE) remediation program in place. You can choose AWS services like AWS Inspector, or there are many third-party and open source solutions to choose from.

Cleaning Up

Deployed AWS resources accrue costs. The samples in this book are focused on serverless components to keep billing to a minimum and take advantage of the free tier. If you leave them running, you will accrue charges. Each chapter has instructions describing how to clean up and delete all resources. Follow the steps at the end of each chapter to avoid creating a bill you did not expect.

You can delete the Hello World application from this chapter by running **cdk destroy hello_world**.

Be aware of log retention settings for any CloudWatch log groups created in each chapter. Manually delete log streams and log groups to remove potential storage charges. When databases are created in a chapter, understand the backup settings and delete leftover backups and snapshots.

Summary

This chapter has equipped you with the essential tools and knowledge to set up your working environment for the hands-on resilience lessons that follow. You've learned about setting up an AWS account with the necessary permissions for the exercises, and explored options for choosing and configuring a development environment. This included the option to use AWS CloudShell where applicable to limit local tool installations.

You've walked through the process of installing and configuring required tools such as Git, Python, Node.js, npm, and the AWS CDK. These form the foundation of your development toolkit for building resilient systems on AWS. Additionally, you've set up supplementary software, including the AWS CLI, Vue.js, Vite, Artillery.io for load testing, and database tools like PostgreSQL, each playing a vital role in the upcoming exercises.

The chapter emphasized the importance of a custom domain and Route 53 hosted zone, particularly for the disaster recovery scenarios you'll encounter later. You've also gained insights into key security considerations, including encryption in transit and at rest, authentication and authorization for API endpoints, and the critical nature of code scanning in maintaining a resilient system.

Throughout the setup process, you've been introduced to the microservices architecture that will form the backbone of the AvailableTrade application. This architecture will allow you to explore various resilience patterns and strategies in a realistic context, providing practical experience in engineering resilient systems.

Importantly, you've learned about the significance of proper resource cleanup to manage costs effectively when working with AWS resources. This knowledge will help you maintain control over your AWS environment as you progress through the book's exercises.

With your environment now prepared, you're ready to dive into the practical aspects of engineering resilient systems on AWS. In the coming chapters, you'll apply this setup to build, test, and improve the resilience of various microservices, putting into practice the concepts and tools you've just configured. The journey ahead promises hands-on experience in creating robust, fault-tolerant systems that can withstand the challenges of modern cloud computing environments.

Reliable Trading Portal

In Part II, you'll embark on the journey into reliable system architectures, building a comprehensive trading portal for a brokerage company. This includes developing both the microservices backend and a resilient frontend web application. You'll assess foundational components for building mission-critical websites, balancing costs for varying levels of criticality (e.g., external customer-facing site versus internal employee portal). This section includes three core examples:

- A global customer-facing site with a focus on optimizing the frontend web application for performance, scalability, and resilience.

- An account open microservice, ensuring a seamless and secure onboarding process for new customers.

- A stock trading microservice, capable of handling high-volume transactions with low latency and robust error handling.

You'll plan, implement, and validate resiliency patterns across the entire application stack, leveraging AWS managed services to streamline development and enhance reliability.

## CHAPTER 3

Frontend Web Application

In today's technology-driven landscape, online applications are your essential tools, whether you're an individual or a business. Any disruption or performance hiccup can cause significant frustration for your users, potentially leading to financial losses and damage to your organization's reputation and customer base.

As technology has advanced, so too have user expectations for seamless, uninterrupted service. This rising tide of technological progress has elevated the baseline for system uptime across the board, creating an environment where users anticipate near-constant availability. You'll discover that meeting these heightened expectations isn't just about user satisfaction—it's a critical factor that can significantly impact your organization's bottom line and reputation. When your services falter, even briefly, the consequences can be severe. Customer dissatisfaction can translate directly into financial losses and erosion of brand value, underscoring the importance of resilience in your application design and operation.

The frontend of your application is the face of your product and a critical factor in shaping user experience. A resilient frontend should incorporate strategies like caching, throttling, and graceful degradation to ensure a seamless experience even during unexpected disruptions. By proactively integrating these resilience patterns, you can directly influence user satisfaction and foster confidence in your application's reliability.

By understanding the critical role resilience plays in software development and delivery, you'll be equipped to elevate the standards of your user experience. This knowledge will empower you to prioritize resilience in your work, ensuring your applications remain robust and performant even when faced with challenges.

As you delve deeper into this chapter, you'll explore the creation of the frontend for AvailableTrade. This hands-on approach will allow you to encounter and address various failure scenarios, implementing patterns and best practices to enhance your frontend's resilience. Through this process, you'll gain invaluable insights into building applications that are not only functional but also robust and reliable under diverse conditions.

After deployment, you'll explore various failure scenarios and learn to implement patterns and best practices to make your frontend more resilient. This hands-on approach will equip you with the tools and knowledge to build applications that are not only functional but also resilient and reliable, ultimately delivering a consistently delightful user experience.

Technical Requirements

In almost every interaction with a frontend application, a user will initiate a request through their web browser or mobile app. This request needs to find its way to the location where the website's content is hosted. The typical flow of this request is shown in Figure 3-1.

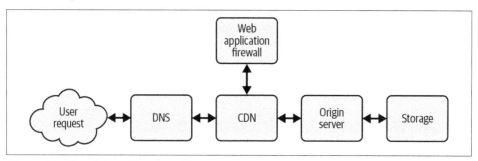

Figure 3-1. User interaction flow diagram

Let's break down this request:

1. *User's browser*

   The user enters a website's URL (e.g., *www.example.com*) into their browser.

2. *DNS resolver*

   The browser queries a DNS resolver (often provided by the user's ISP or local network) to translate the domain name into an IP address.

3. DNS server
The DNS resolver contacts the authoritative DNS server for the domain, which provides the IP address of the website's content delivery network (CDN) (or origin server if no CDN is used).

4. CDN edge server
The request is routed to the nearest CDN edge server based on the user's location. If the requested content is cached on the CDN, it's delivered directly to the user.

5. Web application firewall
The request is inspected for malicious activity or security threats before proceeding.

6. Origin server
If the content is not cached on the CDN, or if the request requires dynamic content, it's forwarded to the origin server.

7. Storage
The origin server retrieves the necessary data from storage (database, filesystem, etc.) to generate the web page.

8. Origin server (response)
The origin server prepares the response (HTML, CSS, JavaScript, etc.).

9. Web application firewall (response filtering)
The response is filtered by the web application firewall again to ensure no security risks are introduced before it's sent back to the user.

10. CDN edge server (caching)
The CDN edge server caches the response for future requests.

11. User's browser (receives content)
The user's browser receives the web page content and renders it for the user.

Architecture Overview

Let's take the flow diagram we just discussed and map it to the AWS services you'll use for your frontend application, as illustrated in Figure 3-2. This architecture represents a standard and effective setup for modern web application frontends. In the next chapter, you'll shift your focus and explore how to implement the backend architecture to complement your frontend.

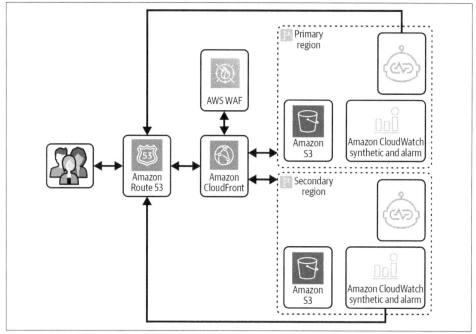

Figure 3-2. Architecture mapping the user interaction flow diagram to AWS services

Let's review the AWS services you'll be using:

Amazon Route 53
> This highly available and scalable Domain Name System (DNS) web service will be used to create an alias record that points to your Amazon CloudFront distribution. The DNS record will only be created if you have a domain name ready for use, as discussed in Chapter 2.

Amazon CloudFront
> This CDN will cache your content at edge locations closer to your users, reducing retrieval time and improving their experience. You'll configure Amazon Cloud-Front to use multiple Amazon S3 buckets as the origin for your website's static assets (images, videos, CSS, JavaScript). This redundancy helps avoid a single point of failure.

AWS Web Application Firewall (WAF)
By integrating AWS WAF with Amazon CloudFront, you'll be able to inspect incoming requests at the edge locations. AWS WAF will check requests against your predefined rules and conditions, ensuring that only legitimate requests are forwarded.

Amazon S3 Cross-Region Replication (CRR)
You'll use CRR to replicate data between your primary and secondary Amazon S3 buckets. This ensures that objects in your primary bucket are asynchronously copied to the secondary bucket, adding another layer of redundancy for your website content, which includes a Vue application.

Amazon CloudWatch Synthetics canaries
These canaries will proactively monitor your website. By integrating them with CloudWatch alarms, you can set thresholds and receive notifications when those thresholds are breached. This allows you to quickly investigate and address any issues that arise.

Deploying the AWS CDK Application

To begin, deploy your frontend application with the following components:

- An Amazon Route 53 Alias DNS record
- An Amazon CloudFront distribution
- An AWS WAF
- Two Amazon Simple Storage Service (S3) buckets, one in your primary region and one in your secondary region, with a Cross-Region Replication rule configured
- Two Amazon CloudWatch Synthetics and alarms, one in your primary region and one in your secondary region

If you have an Amazon Route 53 domain name that you configured in Chapter 2, an Amazon Route 53 alias DNS record will be created for you as part of the deployment, along with a certificate via AWS Certificate Manager (ACM). If you don't have an Amazon Route 53 domain name, make sure to follow the steps in "Using an Amazon CloudFront Domain" on page 58.

An Amazon Route 53 hosted zone is a container for DNS records that define how internet traffic is routed to resources such as websites and web applications. It is a central management point for configuring DNS settings. It allows users to define and associate domain names with specific IP addresses or AWS resources like Amazon EC2 instances, Amazon CloudFront distributions, or Amazon S3 buckets.

You will need an Amazon Route 53 domain for the hands-on exercises in Chapter 7.

To deploy these components, activate your Python virtual environment and set environment variables for the CDK solution. Before doing so, be sure to review the *env.sh* file for the primary and secondary regions you've selected. You must also enter your domain name (if you have one), confirm that you have the required permissions, and use the correct AWS account.

Run the following commands:

```
cd AvailableTrade
source .venv/bin/activate
source env.sh
cd AvailableTrade/src/frontend/website
npm install
npm run build
```

Next, deploy the stack that will create the Amazon S3 bucket in your secondary region. Run the following commands:

```
cd AvailableTrade/src/frontend
cdk deploy FrontEnd-BucketStack-Secondary --require-approval never
```

Once that has completed, you can deploy the remaining stacks and run the following command:

```
cdk deploy FrontEnd-CanaryStack-Secondary FrontEnd-CanaryStack-Primary \
FrontEnd-WebsiteStack FrontEnd-RumStack --require-approval never
```

When you first deploy the application, prepare for a deployment process that spans several minutes. During this time, you'll witness the creation of infrastructure and the deployment of your application. To gain insight into the configuration of these stacks, you'll want to examine the top-level CDK application file located at *AvailableTrade/src/frontend/app.py*. This CDK app serves as the orchestrator, meticulously configuring the stacks by passing essential configuration inputs to each one.

You'll find that the account number, AWS Region names, and credential variables have been conveniently exported into your local CLI environment from the *env.sh* file.

After the declaration of each stack, you'll observe how the app file applies grants to the resources created by these stacks. This is where you'll appreciate the power of the CDK. It's advantageous to delegate IAM policy and role creation to the CDK constructs whenever possible. Many of these constructs will generate access policies and roles based on the resource associations and grants you define in your code. This approach not only simplifies your job but also ensures that permissions are appropriately scoped to resources, limiting their access to only what is necessary for your application.

As you progress through the deployment process, you'll notice that the stacks are evaluated in a carefully planned dependency order. This intentional sequencing is crucial because as resources are created from one stack, they often become inputs to subsequent stacks. This interdependency ensures a smooth and logical flow in the creation and configuration of your infrastructure.

By understanding this process, you'll gain valuable insights into how the CDK orchestrates the deployment of your application, from the initial infrastructure creation to the final application deployment. This knowledge will empower you to make informed decisions about your application's architecture and deployment strategy, ultimately leading to more resilient and efficient cloud-based solutions.

Before testing the application, it is beneficial to understand the resources that each stack creates and review how resources are partitioned into different stacks.

Navigate to your primary region AWS CloudFormation dashboard and verify that the stacks shown in Figure 3-3 show a status of CREATE_COMPLETE.

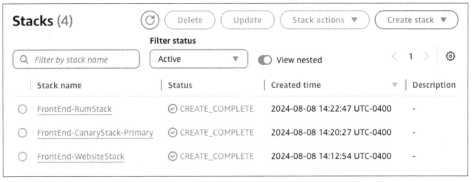

Figure 3-3. Amazon CloudFormation primary region stack successful

In the top right, change your region to your secondary region. Verify that the stacks shown in Figure 3-4 show a status of CREATE_COMPLETE.

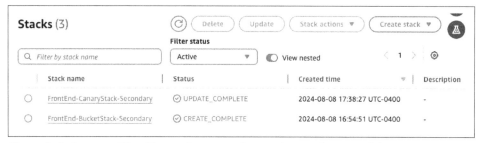

Figure 3-4. Amazon CloudFormation secondary region stack successful

Using an Amazon CloudFront Domain

If you don't want to register a domain name with Amazon Route 53, you can use your Amazon CloudFront domain. Once an Amazon CloudFront distribution is created, Amazon CloudFront will provide you with a unique domain name that serves as your public endpoint.

To use the Amazon CloudFront domain name in your deployment, you will need to update the AWS_DOMAIN_NAME value in your *env.sh* file. You can find your Amazon CloudFront domain name in the AWS CloudFormation dashboard's Output tab with the Key equal to CloudFrontDomainName.

Once your *env.sh* file has been updated to reflect the new Amazon CloudFront domain name as the AWS_DOMAIN_NAME value, you can run the following commands:

```
cd AvailableTrade
source env.sh
cd AvailableTrade/src/frontend
cdk deploy FrontEnd-CanaryStack-Secondary FrontEnd-CanaryStack-Primary \
FrontEnd-WebsiteStack FrontEnd-RumStack --require-approval never
```

Let's inspect the deployed resources in more detail. To do so, you can use the Resources tab in the AWS CloudFormation dashboard to navigate directly.

Amazon CloudFront

Navigate to Amazon CloudFront and review the distribution configuration (Figure 3-5).

Figure 3-5. Amazon CloudFront dashboard

Amazon Simple Storage Service

Navigate to Amazon S3 and review the buckets. You should see two buckets whose names start with *website-* configured in your primary and secondary regions, as shown in Figure 3-6.

Figure 3-6. Amazon S3 buckets

You will see the Vue application code if you click into either bucket. The code is available in both buckets because a Cross-Region Replication rule is configured on the primary bucket to replicate to the secondary bucket. To review the replication rules settings, click into the primary bucket, navigate to the Management tab, and scroll down to the Replication rules section. Click the "View replication configuration" link to see more details about the rule's implementation, as shown in Figure 3-7.

Figure 3-7. Amazon S3 primary bucket CRR rule configuration

From the Amazon S3 dashboard, navigate to the Permissions tab for your primary region Amazon S3 bucket and scroll down to see that a Bucket Policy has been set up to only allow access to the bucket to the Amazon CloudFront distribution via the Origin Access Control. This is known as the principle of least privilege (PoLP), a cybersecurity practice that limits access to the minimum level necessary for success. You will set up the same policy on the secondary region Amazon S3 bucket in "Addressing Single Points of Failure" on page 77.

Amazon Route 53

You will only see the routing record deployed if you provided a custom domain name during deployment. If you provided an Amazon CloudFront domain name, then no Amazon Route 53 DNS record will be deployed.

If you navigate to Amazon Route 53 Hosted Zone, you should see a Type A record that was created, as shown in Figure 3-8, with routing to your Amazon CloudFront distribution.

Figure 3-8. Amazon Route 53 Type A record

OK, now that you have reviewed the detailed resources that make up our application, let's make sure our website is available. Open your favorite browser, type your domain name, and you should see what is shown in Figure 3-9.

Figure 3-9. Frontend website

Success!!

Implementing Observability

In this chapter, you will also use synthetic monitoring to build proactive monitoring. Alarms can be configured to notify you when thresholds are being met, helping you quickly identify a failure so investigation or mitigation mechanisms can be started.

Synthetic monitoring is a proactive approach to application health that emulates user interactions and transactions to assess system performance. By simulating real-world scenarios, synthetic monitoring can identify potential issues before they impact actual users. These simulated transactions provide valuable insights into your application's responsiveness, reliability, and overall health across various endpoints and environments.

Synthetic monitoring can provide the following benefits:

Differential observability
> This refers to the practice of analyzing the discrepancies between how a system perceives its own health and how users actually experience it. Traditional system monitoring focuses on technical metrics (e.g., CPU usage, memory), but these may not always align with the user experience. Synthetic monitoring bridges this gap by simulating user journeys, revealing discrepancies between system-reported health and what your users actually encounter.

Proactive issue detection
> Failures are rarely binary. Synthetic monitoring helps you detect subtle performance degradations, errors, and anomalies that might not trigger traditional alerts. This allows you to address issues proactively before they escalate and impact users.

Resilient infrastructure
> Deploying synthetic monitoring across multiple regions (primary and secondary) ensures continuous monitoring even during regional impairments. This redundancy safeguards application availability and minimizes potential downtime.

Validation of changes
> Before rolling out software updates, infrastructure changes, or new features, synthetic monitoring allows you to test them in a controlled environment. This helps ensure a seamless user experience upon deployment.

With synthetic monitoring in place, you gain a multilayered and proactive approach to application health, minimizing downtime and ensuring a smooth, reliable user experience. By identifying and addressing performance issues early on, you can proactively improve the overall stability and reliability of your application. Synthetic monitoring helps you uncover vulnerabilities and areas for improvement, reducing the risk of unexpected disruptions. Ideally, this approach empowers you to shift from reactive troubleshooting to proactive optimization, ensuring your application remains resilient, high performing, and consistently aligned with user expectations.

Navigate to your primary or secondary region's AWS CloudWatch Synthetics canaries dashboard. You should see your canary starting with *canary-web*. Your canary should (hopefully) show a success of 100%, as shown in Figure 3-10.

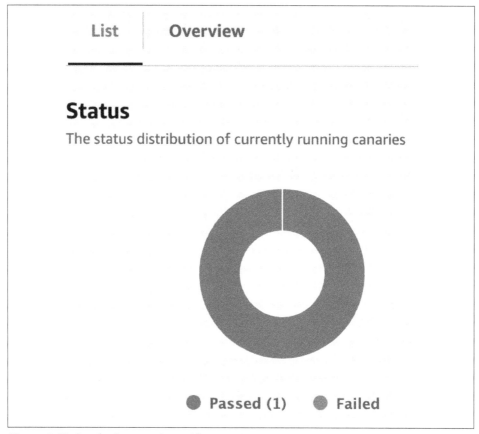

Figure 3-10. Synthetics overview with canaries passing

Click on your canary's name and navigate to the Configuration tab. You will see the alarm associated with it in the Alarms section. This is a best practice and you should always associate an alarm with a notification, such as an Amazon SNS topic, so your team can be notified if the alarm is triggered.

Amazon SNS is a managed messaging service offered by AWS. It acts as a central communication hub that allows you to send notifications (messages) to many subscribers in a flexible and scalable way. You can effectively configure an Amazon SNS topic to manage your notification needs and keep subscribers informed about important updates within your AWS environment.

Injecting Failure Modes

To ensure a seamless and positive user experience on your AvailableTrade application, you'll need to address potential points of failure that could lead to customer dissatisfaction and potential loss of business to competitors. By proactively identifying and mitigating these risks, you can bolster your application's resilience and retain your valuable customer base.

Let's delve into specific failure modes that can disrupt the user experience and explore how resilient design patterns can help you prevent them.

You will focus on three key areas:

Excessive load
> When user traffic overwhelms your system's capacity, it can cause slowdowns, errors, and even complete outages. You'll examine how to design your frontend to handle spikes in demand gracefully.

Excessive latency
> Delays in response times can frustrate users and drive them away. You'll explore strategies to minimize latency and ensure a responsive user interface.

Single points of failure
> A single component failure can bring down your entire system. You'll look at how to implement redundancy and failover mechanisms to prevent this.

For each failure mode, you'll follow these steps:

1. Introduce the fault. You'll simulate the specific failure to understand how it affects your frontend application.

2. Implement a resilient design pattern. You'll apply a proven best practice to mitigate the impact of the failure.

3. Validate success. You'll thoroughly test the implemented pattern to ensure it effectively prevents or mitigates the identified failure mode.

By systematically addressing these potential vulnerabilities, you'll create a more robust and reliable AvailableTrade application that delivers a superior user experience and keeps your customers satisfied.

Introducing Excessive Load

In your first experiment, you will intentionally subject the application to excessive load, a critical test of any application's resilience. Overwhelming the system with an influx of requests can strain, and ultimately break, even the most well-designed architectures. This stress test aims to expose vulnerabilities and assess how the application handles extreme demand.

Here's what could happen when your application faces excessive load:

Performance degradation
> You might notice slower response times, increased latency, and an overall sluggishness in completing tasks.

Service disruptions
> Your application could experience intermittent failures, errors, and become unable to handle user requests effectively.

Complete downtime
> In the worst-case scenario, excessive load could cause your entire application to become unavailable.

Now, you might think, "My architecture is designed to be resilient! It should handle this." And that's the goal. Resilient architectures are built to withstand fluctuations in traffic and scale up as needed. However, when the load exceeds your application's capacity, or if your scaling mechanisms can't react quickly enough, the system can become overloaded. This can lead to several issues:

Dropped requests
> Your application might not be able to process all the incoming requests, causing some to be dropped or ignored.

Increased error rates
> Errors may become more frequent as the system struggles to keep up with demand.

Degraded performance
> Even if your application keeps running, overall performance will suffer, impacting the user experience.

Excessive load can also expose hidden weaknesses or bottlenecks within the application's infrastructure. Database limitations, storage constraints, network congestion, or insufficient computing power can all become amplified under stress, leading to cascading failures and a breakdown of the system's resilience.

By deliberately simulating excessive load conditions, you can identify these vulnerabilities, assess the effectiveness of scaling mechanisms, and gain valuable insights into how the application responds under extreme stress. This allows you to proactively address potential issues and strengthen the application's resilience against future load spikes.

The current load demonstration is designed to showcase a potential method for introducing load into your system, but it's not intended to push your infrastructure to its limits. There are numerous tools and techniques available for load testing, and it's crucial to select the one that best aligns with your specific requirements and budget.

Keep in mind that load testing can incur additional costs due to increased resource usage. To ensure you're optimizing your approach and minimizing unnecessary expenses, we strongly recommend following AWS Prescriptive Guidance on load testing (*https://oreil.ly/YMKR4*). This resource offers valuable insights and best practices to help you conduct efficient and cost-effective load tests on your AWS infrastructure.

Preventing excessive load with rate limiting

WAFs can significantly enhance your web application's resilience. WAFs act as a shield, filtering and monitoring incoming traffic to protect against malicious attacks and excessive load. AWS WAF offers a robust set of features to bolster this resilience, one of them being rate limiting.

Rate limiting is a proactive measure you can employ using AWS WAF to mitigate the risk of abuse or exploitation of your web application. It works by restricting the rate of incoming requests, preventing sudden spikes in traffic from overwhelming your system.

Within AWS WAF, you have the flexibility to configure rate-limiting rules to define thresholds based on various criteria, such as:

- Number of requests per IP address
- Rate of requests per minute
- Specific patterns in request headers or payloads

When these thresholds are exceeded, AWS WAF can take predefined actions, such as:

- Blocking the excessive requests
- Redirecting them to a less critical endpoint
- Triggering alerts for further investigation

Implementing rate limiting is a straightforward process:

1. Create rate-based rulesets tailored to your specific requirements and risk tolerance levels.

2. Associate these rulesets with web access control lists (ACLs) or your Amazon CloudFront distributions.

By effectively leveraging rate limiting in AWS WAF, you fortify the resilience of your web applications, ensuring they maintain consistent performance and availability, even during unexpected traffic surges or malicious activities. This proactive approach safeguards your applications and the valuable user experiences they provide.

Injecting excessive load

You will use Artillery.io (*https://artillery.io*) as the tool to inject load into your website. You will run these from the *tests* directory. The load test prepared for this workload runs an Artillery.io scenario. If you still need to install Artillery.io, return to Chapter 2 and install it.

Open and review the file *AvailableTrade/src/frontend/tests/frontend-website-load-test.yml* and review the configuration. This simple test runs three load phases: a warm-up for initial scaling, a ramp-up to steady state, and a spike phase. Load phases are defined in the config phase of the YAML file. The scenario phase executes HTTP GET requests against your website.

To execute this test, run the following commands:

```
cd AvailableTrade/src/frontend/tests
python3 onboarding_test_client.py --test 1
```

The test client will issue the `artillery run` command and use the URL provided by the output parameter `WebsiteURL` from your AWS CloudFormation stack to run the load test. The test client code snippet is:

```
if test == 1:
c = "artillery run website-load-test.yml --variables '{ \"url\": \"{url}\" }'"
    .replace("{url}", get_url())
print(c)
os.system(c)
```

Once your load test has been completed, navigate to the AWS WAF Web ACLs dashboard. Before you can see your web ACL, ensure you've switched to the global region in the AWS console. After clicking on the Web ACL name, go to the "All traffic" tab. Your output should look similar to Figure 3-11.

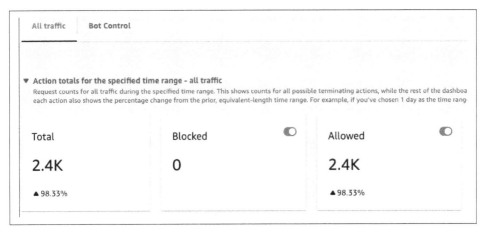

Figure 3-11. AWS WAF traffic dashboard before implementing rate limiting

The dashboard confirms that no requests have been blocked.

Implement AWS Web Application Firewall with rate limiting

In this section, you'll learn how to implement rate limiting using AWS Web Application Firewall (AWS WAF). Rate limiting is a crucial technique for protecting your application from potential abuse by restricting the number of requests from individual IP addresses. A RateLimitRuleGroup has been preconfigured for you. Within this rule group, you'll find a rule called RateLimitRule. This rule is designed to block requests that exceed 100 per second from the same source IP address.

To associate RateLimitRuleGroup with your AWS WAF ACL:

1. Navigate to the AWS WAF Web ACLs dashboard and ensure that you've switched to the global region.
2. Click on the Web ACL.
3. In the Rules tab, create a new rule:
   a. Click "Add rules."
   b. Select "Add my own rules and rule groups."
   c. Set "Rule group" as the Rule type.
   d. Enter a rule name.
   e. Select RateLimitRuleGroup as the Rule group.
   f. Save the changes.

When adding the AWS WAF rule, refer to the example configuration in Figure 3-12. If your configuration differs, carefully review the previous instructions to ensure accuracy.

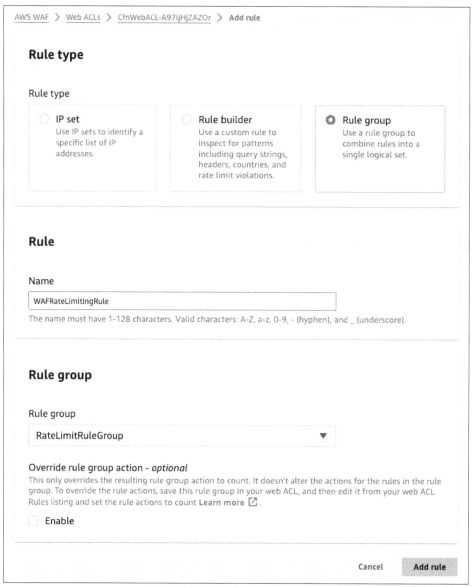

Figure 3-12. AWS WAF add a new rule

By implementing this rate-limiting rule, you're adding a targeted layer of protection to your application which allows you to maintain service for the majority of your users while mitigating potential abuse from specific sources.

Rerun excessive load experiment

You will execute the load test again with the new AWS WAF rate-limiting rule implemented.

To execute this test, run the following command:

```
python3 onboarding_test_client.py --test 1
```

You do not need to wait for your load test to finish this time.

Observe successful mitigation

As part of deploying the AWS WAF rate-limiting rule, an Amazon CloudWatch alarm was also configured. Setting alarms on your metrics is a best practice, as it allows you to stay ahead of potential issues. When a metric exceeds your predefined threshold, the alarm will send you a notification, enabling you to investigate and take corrective action as needed. You can even set up automatic remediation for certain situations, such as triggering AWS Lambda functions to execute specific code when an alarm is triggered.

Now that you've implemented the AWS WAF rate-limiting rule and rerun your load test, navigate to the Amazon CloudWatch Alarms dashboard to check the results. Depending on how long after you run the load test you navigate to the dashboard, the alarm could show a status of "Insufficient data" or "In alarm," as shown in Figure 3-13. You may have to wait a few minutes for the alarm to move from "Insufficient data" to the "In alarm" state.

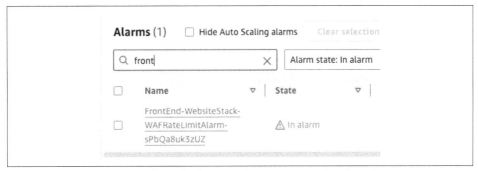

Figure 3-13. Amazon CloudWatch showing the test state as "In alarm"

Navigate to the "All alarms" dashboard and locate the alarm that starts with "FrontEnd-WebsiteStack." The graph shown in Figure 3-14 illustrates the spike in load that exceeded the alarm's threshold, triggering an alert. You'll also notice that the load subsequently decreased after the load test concluded.

Figure 3-14. Amazon CloudWatch alarm graph

Navigate back to the AWS WAF Web ACLs dashboard. In the "All traffic" tab, your output should look similar to Figure 3-15, which shows the number of blocked requests.

Figure 3-15. AWS WAF traffic dashboard after implementing rate limiting

You've successfully implemented safeguards to protect your AvailableTrade frontend application from excessive traffic originating from a single IP address. In Chapter 4, we'll delve into the concept of load shedding, a design pattern employed by high-performance web services to gracefully manage and respond to traffic congestion. *Load shedding* strategically identifies which requests to prioritize and serve when your system is overwhelmed by a sudden surge in traffic or encounters issues with dependent services. This proactive approach prevents a cascading failure effect across your distributed systems.

To gain a deeper understanding of load shedding and how it can be applied to safeguard your systems, we recommend exploring the Amazon Builder's Library article titled "Using load shedding to avoid overload" (*https://oreil.ly/2c1xF*). This insightful resource details the strategies and techniques used by Amazon's Service Frameworks team to effectively address overload issues.

Introducing Excessive Latency

In your second experiment, you'll deliberately introduce excessive latency into your application. *Latency*, the delay between a user's request and the application's response, can significantly impact your system's resilience when it exceeds acceptable thresholds. You'll discover how this seemingly simple issue can cascade into complex problems, affecting your application's performance and stability.

Increased latency that is prolonged can cause the following issues:

Timeout breaches
> As response times grow, requests start exceeding predefined timeout limits. This direct consequence of high latency can lead to failed operations and unhappy users.

Snowball effect
> Initial delays can be compounded, triggering a chain reaction. Slower responses lead to more concurrent requests, consuming additional resources and further degrading performance. This vicious cycle can quickly spiral out of control.

Resource exhaustion
> Prolonged latency issues strain your system's capacity. As more resources are tied up handling delayed requests, your application's ability to process new incoming requests diminishes.

Recovery challenges
> High latency can impair your application's ability to bounce back from errors or disruptions. Sluggish response times hinder effective error handling and recovery processes.

Even a well-designed system can struggle when faced with excessive delays. As latency is introduced to a system, there will be an increase in request concurrency. This surge in simultaneous operations, rather than just the extended processing time, often lies at the heart of performance degradation. Heightened concurrency can push your infrastructure to its limits, potentially triggering cascading failures during high traffic periods.

By deliberately pushing your system to its breaking point, you'll uncover valuable lessons about its behavior under stress. This knowledge will prove invaluable as you develop strategies to mitigate latency-related risks and enhance your application's overall resilience. Remember, the goal isn't just to observe problems, but to understand their root causes and impacts.

Balancing caching and resilience for consistent latency

Caching is a technique you can leverage to enhance the performance and resilience of your web applications, but it's not without its complexities and potential pitfalls. While caching can help reduce average latency, its true value in resilience lies in its ability to ensure consistent latency, even at the tail end of your request distribution.

When implementing caching, you'll store copies of frequently accessed content closer to your users. This approach can significantly reduce the load on your origin servers and minimize average latency. However, it's crucial to understand that reducing average latency alone isn't necessarily a resilience play.

The real challenge lies in maintaining consistent performance, even during peak loads or when facing unexpected issues. Caching can help you achieve this by:

- Alleviating pressure on your origin servers during traffic spikes
- Providing a buffer against network disruptions or origin server issues
- Ensuring more predictable response times across different geographical locations

However, caching also introduces its own set of challenges that can potentially undermine your application's resilience if not carefully managed:

Cache dependency
  Your application might become overly reliant on the cache, leading to performance degradation or even failure if the cache becomes unavailable.

Inconsistent behavior
  Cached and uncached requests can exhibit significantly different performance characteristics, leading to unpredictable user experiences.

Stale data
  Serving outdated information from the cache can lead to errors, user confusion, and potential system failures.

Cache stampede
> When cached data expires, a flood of requests to the origin can overwhelm your systems, causing a temporary but severe performance hit.

To leverage caching effectively for resilience, consider the following strategies:

Implement fallback mechanisms
> Design your system to gracefully handle cache misses or cache unavailability. This might involve falling back to the origin server, using a secondary cache, or serving slightly stale data with a warning.

Use the soft TTL/hard TTL pattern
> Implement two expiration times for cached items. Attempt to refresh based on the soft TTL, but continue using existing cache data until the hard TTL if the origin is unavailable.

Employ request coalescing
> Prevent the "thundering herd" problem by ensuring only one request is sent to the origin for an uncached resource, even if multiple clients request it simultaneously.

Monitor cache performance
> Set up comprehensive monitoring for your cache, including hit rates, error rates, and latency distributions. This will help you identify and address issues before they impact your users.

Implement circuit breakers
> Use circuit breakers to prevent cascading failures when your origin server or other dependencies start to fail.

Practice cache warming
> For predictable high-traffic events, consider prepopulating your cache to ensure consistent performance from the start.

Amazon CloudFront, AWS's CDN service, offers features that can help you implement these strategies. It provides a global network of edge locations to cache and serve your content, along with features like origin failover and real-time logs for monitoring.

When configuring Amazon CloudFront, you'll need to carefully consider your caching behaviors. Set appropriate TTLs based on your content's nature and how frequently it changes. Implement cache invalidation strategies to ensure that your cached content stays up-to-date without overwhelming your origin during updates.

Remember, the goal isn't just to reduce average latency, but to ensure consistent, predictable performance across all requests. This means paying special attention to the tail latency—those slower requests that can disproportionately impact user experience.

By thoughtfully implementing caching with these considerations in mind, you can enhance your application's resilience, providing a more consistent and reliable experience for your users, even in the face of unexpected challenges or high-load situations.

 To dive deeper into caching best practices, challenges, and strategies, refer to this Amazon Builder's Library article on "Caching challenges and strategies" (*https://oreil.ly/wgbjq*). It provides valuable insights into the complexities of caching and how to navigate them effectively.

Injecting excessive latency

In this experiment, you'll explore the impact of excessive latency on your application's performance. To simulate real-world scenarios where users access your content from various geographical locations, you'll use AWS CloudShell to execute commands from a region different from your primary one.

AWS CloudShell is a browser-based shell that provides you with a convenient way to run command-line operations in the AWS environment. It comes preconfigured with AWS CLI and other tools, making it an ideal choice for running quick commands without the need for local setup.

First, you'll upload a large movie file to your Amazon S3 primary region bucket. This step will be performed using your local AWS CLI. If you haven't installed the AWS CLI yet, take a moment to revisit Chapter 2 and complete the installation process. Once you're ready, navigate to the project directory and execute the following command:

```
cd AvailableTrade/src/frontend
aws s3 cp AdobeStock_4k.mov s3://<your-bucket-name>
```

Replace <your-bucket-name> with your Amazon S3 bucket name in your primary region. It should start with website-. After successful execution, you'll see a confirmation message indicating that your object has been uploaded.

Now, here's where things get interesting. To simulate latency that users might experience when accessing your content from distant locations, you'll switch to a different AWS Region.

Look at the top-right corner of your AWS dashboard. You'll see a drop-down menu showing your current region (Figure 3-16). Click on it and select a region that's different from your primary one. The further away from your primary region, the more noticeable the latency will be.

Figure 3-16. Change AWS Region

In this new region, navigate to and launch AWS CloudShell. You'll see a new browser window open up, presenting you with a command-line interface. Let's begin by making an initial request to retrieve the large movie file you uploaded earlier. This first attempt will likely result in a cache miss, as the content hasn't been cached yet. Open your AWS CloudShell and run the following command:

```
curl -v https://{replace with your domain name}/AdobeStock_4k.mov \
    --output AdobeStock_4k.mov
```

By executing this command from a region different from your primary one, you're introducing additional latency. The further the AWS CloudShell region is from your Amazon S3 bucket's primary region, the longer it will take to retrieve the object. This simulates the real-world scenario of users accessing your content from various global locations.

As you run this experiment, pay close attention to the time it takes for the download to complete. You might notice significant delays compared to accessing the same file from a closer region. This exercise will give you valuable insights into how geographical distance can impact your application's performance and user experience.

Observing excessive latency

Since you've enabled the -verbose flag, the output will be quite detailed. The line x-cache: Miss from cloudfront indicates that the requested file was not found in the cache and had to be retrieved from the origin server. Make a note of the retrieval time:

```
< HTTP/2 200
< content-type: video/quicktime
< content-length: 225054176
< date: Tue, 09 Apr 2024 20:22:36 GMT
< last-modified: Tue, 09 Apr 2024 20:15:49 GMT
```

```
< etag: "af05d0ff65b13de229938e41eeb95022-14"
< x-amz-server-side-encryption: AES256
< accept-ranges: bytes
< server: AmazonS3
< x-cache: Miss from cloudfront
< via: 1.1 8dbfaf7df256a75768461d934659b6b2.cloudfront.net (CloudFront)
< x-amz-cf-pop: HIO50-C1
< x-amz-cf-id: Y-0rNXp3P1iHhXHHyRpaUb_CfFyY8go6dEhOl4zTkdG1BclFHATGUQ==
<
{ [16026 bytes data]
100 214M 100 214M 0 0 46.1M 0 0:00:04 0:00:04 --:--:-- 51.7M
```

Rerun excessive latency experiment

Run the command again:

```
curl -v https://{replace with your domain name}/AdobeStock_4k.mov \
  --output AdobeStock_4k.mov
```

Observing the impact of caching on resilience

This time, you should see output similar to this:

```
< HTTP/2 200
< content-type: video/quicktime
< content-length: 225054176
< date: Tue, 09 Apr 2024 20:22:36 GMT
< last-modified: Tue, 09 Apr 2024 20:15:49 GMT
< etag: "af05d0ff65b13de229938e41eeb95022-14"
< x-amz-server-side-encryption: AES256
< accept-ranges: bytes
< server: AmazonS3
< x-cache: Hit from cloudfront
< via: 1.1 efe54e8b68e074d39b2ecd249f85100a.cloudfront.net (CloudFront)
< x-amz-cf-pop: HIO50-C1
< x-amz-cf-id: RWzgobXN9GJBvGFbV-yPegbwsfmBwRKwbNeUB9oN5Qroa5BI7lpPbg==
< age: 13

{ [32387 bytes data]
100 214M 100 214M 0 0 183M 0 0:00:01 0:00:01 --:--:-- 183M
```

Observe the key distinction: x-cache: Hit from cloudfront. This signifies that
Amazon CloudFront successfully delivered the file directly from its cache. Even if
your origin server (the Amazon S3 bucket) became temporarily inaccessible, your
users would still be able to retrieve the file. Pay close attention to the retrieval time
when the file is served from the cache—it's notably faster, showcasing a significant
performance improvement.

This experiment illustrates a fundamental aspect of resilience: your application
remains functional and continues serving content even when the origin may be
unavailable. By caching content at the edge, Amazon CloudFront acts as a buffer

---

against origin failures, substantially bolstering your application's ability to withstand disruptions.

It's crucial to recognize that while caching significantly enhances resilience, it's not a silver bullet. You'll still need to address the root cause of any origin outages and incorporate additional resilience strategies for a holistic approach to fault tolerance. You will learn how to address origin outages in the next section. Caching is a powerful tool, but it's just one component of a comprehensive resilience toolkit.

As you analyze this experiment, consider how you can extend similar caching strategies to other areas of your application. Could caching shield against failures in database queries, API calls, or other backend services? How can you strike the optimal balance between data freshness and the resilience advantages of caching? These are the critical questions that will guide you in building truly resilient systems.

Addressing Single Points of Failure

In your final experiment, you'll explore the concept of a *single point of failure* (SPOF) and how to mitigate its impact on your application. A SPOF is a component or service in your architecture that does not have redundancy or fault tolerance. When unavailable, a SPOF can cause significant impact to your application if it's a hard dependency.

Here's what could happen if your application has a SPOF:

Service downtime
    A complete interruption of service could occur when the SPOF fails.

Degraded performance
    Even if your application remains partially functional, its performance may suffer significantly.

Data loss
    Depending on the nature of the SPOF, there's a risk of data loss or corruption if it fails unexpectedly.

By identifying and addressing SPOFs, you can enhance your application's resilience and its ability to maintain availability, reliability, and performance under adverse conditions.

As you progress in your understanding of resilience, challenge yourself to think creatively about different failure modes and how to simulate them in your systems. This creative thinking is crucial for comprehensive resilience testing and improvement.

Enhancing resilience through redundancy and fault tolerance

To mitigate the risks associated with SPOFs, you can implement redundancy and fault tolerance mechanisms. By providing redundant spares of critical components, you create alternative pathways or backups that can seamlessly take over if primary elements fail. This approach safeguards service availability and continuity, protecting against widespread service disruptions or downtime.

Redundancy also enhances fault tolerance. By distributing workloads or resources across multiple components or fault isolation boundaries, you reduce the risk of overload or bottlenecks arising from a single point of failure. This distributed approach improves system reliability, scalability, and performance as redundant components share the load and handle increased demand more effectively.

Amazon S3 offers Cross-Region Replication (CRR), a feature that enables you to automatically replicate objects between Amazon S3 buckets in different AWS Regions. To implement CRR, you create a replication rule and define replication parameters for your source bucket. Once enabled, Amazon S3 replicates new objects, modifications, or deletions to existing objects asynchronously, ensuring minimal impact on your application's performance and latency.

Replication Time Control (RTC) is an additional feature of CRR that provides an SLA of 99.99% of objects being replicated within 15 minutes. This feature is valuable if you have stringent data replication timeliness and reliability requirements, such as those in regulated industries or mission-critical services.

Simulating a single point of failure

To simulate a SPOF scenario, you'll deliberately make your primary Amazon S3 bucket inaccessible. This is achieved by adjusting the bucket policy to deny access from your Amazon CloudFront distribution. This method effectively replicates the unavailability of your origin server (the S3 bucket) in a controlled environment, allowing you to test the resilience of your system.

Follow these steps to remove access to your Amazon S3 primary bucket:

1. Navigate to the Amazon S3 console and locate your primary region Amazon S3 bucket. It should start with `website-`.
2. Go to the Permissions tab and edit the bucket policy.
3. Locate the section of the policy that allows access to your Amazon CloudFront distribution's origin access control, which should look similar to this:

```
{
"Effect": "Allow",
"Principal": {
        "Service": "cloudfront.amazonaws.com"
    },
```

```
    "Action": "s3:GetObject",
    "Resource": "arn:aws:s3:::<your-bucket-name>/*",
    "Condition": {
        "StringEquals": {
          "AWS:SourceArn":
        "arn:aws:cloudfront::<AWS_ACCOUNT_ID>:distribution/<DISTRIBUTION_ID>"
        }
    }
},
```

4. Change the Effect from Allow to Deny and save your changes.

This change will make your primary Amazon S3 bucket inaccessible to Amazon CloudFront, simulating a failure scenario.

To ensure that Amazon CloudFront doesn't serve cached content during our experiment, let's invalidate the cache for the distribution.

Run the following command:

```
aws cloudfront create-invalidation \
  --distribution-id $(aws cloudformation describe-stacks \
    --stack-name FrontEnd-WebsiteStack \
    --query \
    'Stacks[0].Outputs[?OutputKey==`CloudFrontDistributionID`].OutputValue' \
    --output text) \
  --paths '/*'
```

As you become more experienced with resilience testing, consider automating these tests to prevent human error and ensure all required steps are consistently executed.

Observing the single point of failure

After modifying the bucket policy, access your website using a different browser or an incognito window to ensure you're not viewing cached content.

You should expect to see an error due to the intentional inaccessibility of the origin server:

```
---
<Error>
<Code>AccessDenied</Code>
<Message>Access Denied</Message>
<RequestId>9T0GVX1HPW03Y5H9</RequestId>
<HostId>
WtAsXUI4AcYznfVxNz2KmpXqK83wL7TrFWIrEH3H4j2cd1s4V9CODWrfwX/6fbAwmyuOlHYnaJQ=
</HostId>
</Error>
---
```

To verify the impact of this simulated impact, let's turn to your Amazon CloudWatch Synthetics monitoring. Navigate to the CloudWatch Synthetics Canaries dashboard and closely examine the "Canary runs" graph. Your output should look similar to Figure 3-17.

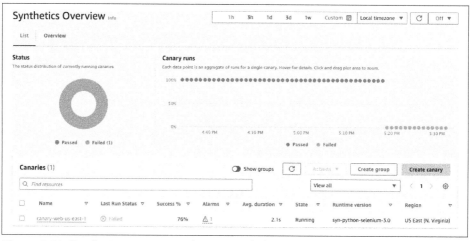

Figure 3-17. Synthetics overview with canaries failing

These failures are expected to have triggered an alarm. To confirm, proceed to the CloudWatch Alarms dashboard and locate the alarm named "Synthetics-Alarm-canary-web." The graph associated with this alarm should display "In alarm" metrics, as shown in Figure 3-18, indicating that the simulated outage has been successfully detected.

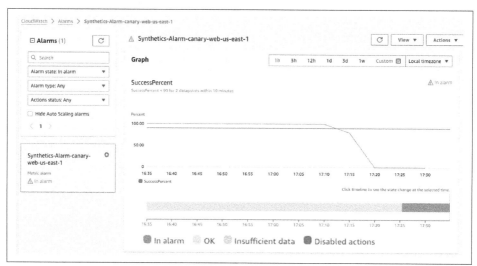

Figure 3-18. Amazon CloudWatch synthetics alarming

Implementing Amazon CloudFront origin failover

Amazon CloudFront origin failover is a feature that can help mitigate disruptions caused by origin failures. It allows you to automatically reroute requests to an alternate origin server if your primary origin becomes unavailable. However, it's important to note that Amazon CloudFront will only failover for specific HTTP error responses and only for GET, HEAD, or OPTIONS requests. To implement Amazon CloudFront origin failover you will create a secondary origin, create an origin group, and update the default behavior to use the new origin group.

To create a secondary origin:

1. Navigate to the Amazon CloudFront dashboard and select your distribution.

2. In the Origins tab, create a new origin for your secondary region Amazon S3 bucket:

   a. Click "Create origin."

   b. Select the domain name of your secondary region Amazon S3 bucket.

   c. Select "Origin access control settings (recommended)."

   d. Create a new Origin access control.

   e. Copy the provided Amazon S3 bucket policy and apply it to your secondary region bucket.

   f. Save the changes.

When adding the Amazon CloudFront origin, refer to the example configuration in Figure 3-19. If your configuration differs, carefully review these instructions to ensure accuracy.

In Step 2c, ensure you're configuring *Origin Access Control* (OAC), a crucial Amazon CloudFront security feature that safeguards your content origins, like Amazon S3 buckets or AWS Elemental MediaPackage. By enabling OAC, you effectively restrict access to your origins, ensuring that only authorized Amazon CloudFront distributions can retrieve your content. This prevents unauthorized parties from directly accessing your origin, significantly enhancing security and mitigating the risk of unauthorized access or data breaches.

OAC leverages AWS Signature Version 4 (SigV4), a robust cryptographic authentication mechanism, to validate that requests originate from trusted Amazon CloudFront distributions. This adds a strong layer of defense against potential threats, making it difficult for malicious actors to bypass Amazon CloudFront and directly access your sensitive content.

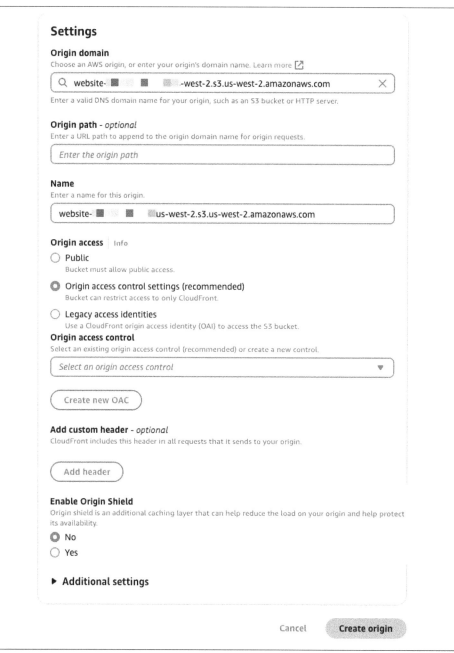

Figure 3-19. Amazon CloudFront add new origin

Follow these steps to create an origin group:

1. In the Amazon CloudFront console, go to the "Origin groups" section.
2. Click "Create origin group."
3. Select your primary origin as the first origin to add.
4. Select your secondary origin as the failover origin to add.
5. Enter an origin group name.
6. Set the failover criteria by selecting all of the HTTP status codes.
7. Save the changes.

When adding the Amazon CloudFront origin group, refer to the example configuration in Figure 3-20. If your configuration differs, carefully review the instructions to ensure accuracy.

Follow these steps to update behavior:

1. Go to the Behaviors tab in your Amazon CloudFront distribution.
2. Select the default behavior and click Edit.
3. In the "Origin and origin groups" drop-down, select your newly created origin group.
4. Save the changes.

 Amazon CloudFront origin failover prioritizes routing requests to the primary origin, even if it's experiencing consistent unavailability. This can introduce latency as Amazon CloudFront attempts to access the primary origin before switching to the secondary. This behavior should be factored into your resilience strategy when designing a highly available and responsive system.

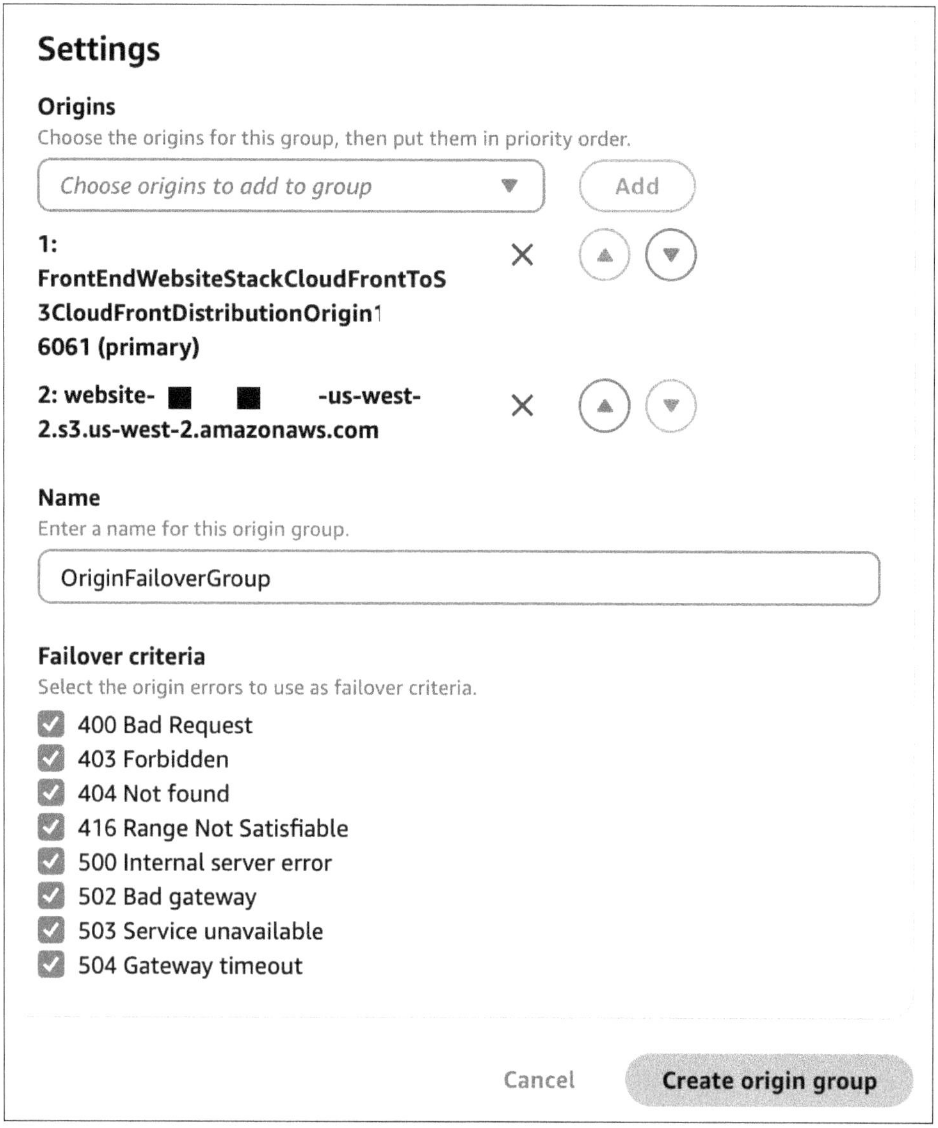

Settings

Origins

Choose the origins for this group, then put them in priority order.

| Choose origins to add to group ▼ | Add |

1:
FrontEndWebsiteStackCloudFrontToS
3CloudFrontDistributionOrigin1
6061 (primary)   ✕ ▲ ▼

2: website- ■ ■ **-us-west-**
2.s3.us-west-2.amazonaws.com   ✕ ▲ ▼

Name

Enter a name for this origin group.

OriginFailoverGroup

Failover criteria

Select the origin errors to use as failover criteria.

- ☑ 400 Bad Request
- ☑ 403 Forbidden
- ☑ 404 Not found
- ☑ 416 Range Not Satisfiable
- ☑ 500 Internal server error
- ☑ 502 Bad gateway
- ☑ 503 Service unavailable
- ☑ 504 Gateway timeout

Cancel   **Create origin group**

Figure 3-20. Amazon CloudFront add new origin group

When updating the Amazon CloudFront behaviors, refer to the example configuration in Figure 3-21. If your configuration differs, carefully review the instructions to ensure accuracy.

Be aware that users might experience different performance characteristics between cached and uncached requests. This variability is an important consideration when implementing caching as part of your resilience strategy.

Figure 3-21. Amazon CloudFront edit default behavior

Observing successful mitigation

After your Amazon CloudFront distribution finishes updating, refresh your browser. Your website should now be available (Figure 3-22).

If you encounter an Access Denied error, ensure your secondary region Amazon S3 bucket policy is correctly configured to allow access from your Amazon CloudFront distribution.

Figure 3-22. Frontend website successfully loading

By implementing origin failover, you've added a layer of resilience to your application. While this approach can mitigate certain types of failures, it's important to consider other resilience strategies as part of a comprehensive approach to fault tolerance and high availability.

Remember that once your primary origin becomes available again, Amazon CloudFront will automatically transition back to it, restoring normal operations without manual intervention. This smooth transition helps maintain consistent performance over time.

As you continue to develop your resilience strategies, keep in mind that different approaches may be better suited for different types of outages or performance issues.

Always consider your specific business requirements and the nature of potential failures when designing your resilience solutions.

Cleaning Up

The resources you created in this chapter accrue charges when services are invoked and for data storage. If you plan to work through each chapter in Part II, you can leave this stack installed and continue until you have worked through Chapters 2–7. Be aware that if you stop working through the lessons and leave your infrastructure running, you will be charged for it.

To avoid costs, remove the applications and data you've created. Delete all AWS CloudFormation stacks by running the following command:

```
cdk destroy --all
```

Your Amazon S3 buckets should be deleted when your Amazon CloudFormation stacks are deleted. However, ancillary buckets are created for log files, and so on, and you should go into your Amazon S3 bucket dashboard to do manual cleanup if necessary.

Summary

In this chapter, you successfully configured a resilient frontend web application and implemented various resilient design patterns. You put your application to the test by injecting failure modes and observing its behavior, and then you applied best practices and patterns to prevent or mitigate those failures.

You also learned the importance of identifying key metrics and setting resilience thresholds. By monitoring these metrics and utilizing alarms and notifications, you can proactively investigate potential issues before they escalate into major problems.

Throughout your implementation of AWS services and features like AWS WAF, Amazon CloudFront, Amazon S3 Cross-Region Replication, and Amazon CloudFront origin failover, you gained valuable insights into mitigating common risks to application resilience:

AWS WAF
    You effectively managed excessive load by implementing rate-limiting rules and load shedding, ensuring that incoming traffic remains within manageable thresholds to safeguard your application's performance and availability.

Amazon CloudFront
    By leveraging Amazon CloudFront to cache content closer to your end users, you significantly reduced latency and enhanced the overall responsiveness of your application.

Amazon S3 Cross-Region Replication

Employing multiple Amazon S3 buckets allowed you to mitigate single points of failure, ensuring high availability and reliability of your data storage across multiple regions.

Amazon CloudFront origin failover

By implementing origin failover, you ensured continuous content delivery even in the event of origin failures, providing a seamless experience for your users.

These lessons underscore the importance of strategically leveraging resilient design patterns and AWS services to enhance your application's resilience and effectively mitigate various risks.

In the following chapters, you'll take the next step in building a robust and resilient application by building and integrating backend APIs into your frontend web application.

CHAPTER 4
Serverless Account Open API

A useful frontend user interface is often backed by transactional services that bring the user experience to life. As you explore the Account Open service, imagine it as part of a complete brokerage platform, which you'll fully assemble by Chapter 6. A brokerage customer's goal is to open a new account easily and reliably, so that they can start investing in stocks. Bear in mind that opening new brokerage accounts is a lower volume activity than the higher frequency trading activity that takes place once an account has been opened. In addition, while some accounts can be opened in a straight through processing mode, some require offline steps like proof of identity in a branch location, human approval, or handling of processing or data entry errors. To optimize reliability, the Account Open service is asynchronous and built with AWS serverless services that optimize resource usage and costs.

You can think of the Account Open service as your control plane. It creates the infrastructure, a brokerage account, which a customer needs to trade. Trading is the data plane, it is transactional, real time, and once created no longer has a dependency on the operation of the control plane to operate.

To simplify deployment and resilience test scenarios, this service performs only one business function, persistence to a NoSQL database. In the real world, a brokerage Account Open service would orchestrate a workflow that includes steps like compliance checks, customer validation, legal document generation, document vaulting, and persistence to a trading system of record. After this chapter, you will gain the knowledge needed to extrapolate resilience concepts to more complex serverless and event-driven workflows.

In this chapter, you will deploy and test an asynchronous microservice that reliably opens a new brokerage account on the AvailableTrade application. After deploying a prebuilt solution and test client, you will explore native AWS serverless resilience features and design patterns that help deal with:

- Handling invalid input
- Duplicate submissions
- Queued message processing failures
- Unanticipated load spikes
- Poison pills
- Regional impairment
- Blue-green code deployments

Working through test scenarios, you'll learn to mitigate common failure modes by inducing failures and then recovering. You'll gain a thorough understanding of built-in serverless resilience features as well as design patterns.

Technical Requirements

In almost all web-enabled business scenarios, user-initiated activity begins with an HTTP request to an API. The request is first received by an HTTP listener that forwards the request to a processing component that performs work on request data and then provides a response. We can visualize this as a synchronous request flow (Figure 4-1) where the requestor waits until all processing is complete before receiving a response. A synchronous flow depends on external components to be available and operating within latency constraints to succeed. If there is a failure in any hard dependency, the response cannot be delivered to the customer. An error is returned, and the customer may need to reenter and resubmit the request later when the system is working. That is, if they don't decide to go to another financial institution and open an account with a competitor instead.

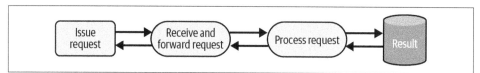

Figure 4-1. A synchronous request flow

Synchronous request/response flows are appropriate for data plane operations. Examples of operations are adding an item to a shopping cart, credit card purchase transactions, or trading stocks. Account openings are typically complex, multistep, and potentially long-running workflows that in some cases have human review or approval activities. In these scenarios, it's useful to apply asynchronous strategies. You can provide extremely fast API responses by introducing reliable queue-based messaging components that decouple the HTTP forwarder and the processing component. Applying this *Fire-and-Forget* (*https://oreil.ly/Zd4Kg*) pattern returns the response to the customer as soon as the request is reliably queued (Figure 4-2).

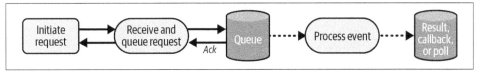

Figure 4-2. An asynchronous request flow

Then you can apply event-driven architectures to do further work and either use a callback or polling mechanism to notify the customer that the control plane operation is complete, their account is open. When implementing an asynchronous strategy, you'll need to ensure both highly reliable message capture and success of the offline downstream processes. In addition, simple techniques like endpoint canaries are not enough to ensure the system is online. You'll need to measure and monitor the end-to-end workflow, including queues, intermediate steps, and completion. Let's start understanding the architecture and AWS serverless services to achieve a resilient asynchronous API.

Architecture Overview: An AWS Serverless Approach

When you use AWS serverless services, you offload infrastructure management tasks like provisioning capacity, managing servers, operating system (OS) patching, and OS version upgrades. AWS serverless provides ways to run code, store and manipulate data, and integrate applications. In the case of Amazon SQS and AWS Lambda, you can focus on application logic, and let AWS handle dynamically scaling up or down in response to load. For your Account Open use case, serverless is a great choice to optimize costs, simplify development, and build customer trust with a reliable system.

> This chapter will help you explore the resiliency responsibilities you can offload to AWS using serverless versus implementing patterns. If you make alternate architectural trade-offs by selecting different services in your design, the same high-level resilience strategies covered in this chapter still apply. However, your level of responsibility will vary depending on your AWS service choices.

Review the logical architecture diagram in Figure 4-3 for an overview of the AWS serverless services you'll deploy and how data flows through the new Account Open service. Each AWS serverless service is an AWS regional service (*https://oreil.ly/GzHvH*). As discussed in "AWS Responsibility" on page 6, AWS Regions are made up of Availability Zones. Availability Zones can contain one or more data centers. Serverless services spread work across AZs to provide high availability so that you usually don't need to think about or configure the service beyond choosing an AWS Region. Multizonal high availability is built in.

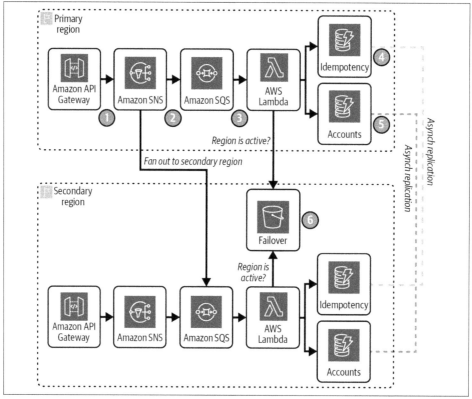

Figure 4-3. New Account Open AWS serverless architecture

The Account Open microservice is invoked with an HTTP request event from a web or mobile client, then passes the event to a queue with a notification. With a valid response from the event notifier, a response is returned to the client, and the message is queued before downstream processes consume it, and the new account record is finally stored in a NoSQL database. After persistence, or any other workflow steps you might build into your system, a customer can be notified that their account is ready. For this exercise, you'll confirm completion by querying your database and observing metrics:

1. Amazon API Gateway is configured with a REST API that validates the request structure against a JSON schema, then POSTs an event to SNS.

2. Amazon Simple Notification Service (SNS) returns an HTTP 200 code to the API Gateway to confirm message receipt. SNS delivers the new account message out

to an Amazon Simple Queue Service (SQS) queue residing both in the active primary AWS Region and in the secondary region.

3. AWS Lambda is configured with an event source mapping (ESM) that polls the SQS queue and runs custom code to process the Account Open message. The autoscaling Lambda adjusts capacity based on queue depth, processes messages, and includes logic to ensure idempotency. Once a new account is created in DynamoDB, the message is deleted from the primary and recovery AWS Region queues.

4. The idempotency feature of Powertools for AWS Lambda (*https://oreil.ly/C-Eht*) ensures that multiple attempts to process the same record result in a single outcome, and always return the same response. Idempotency is managed through an Amazon DynamoDB Global tables persistent store. In this service, the persistent store synchronizes idempotency data across the primary and secondary region. There is additional logic built into the Lambda function to ensure accounts are only processed once and only removed from both regional queues once the account is created successfully.

5. New account records are created in an Amazon DynamoDB global table and are replicated across regions. The table has point-in-time recovery (PITR) backups enabled, so backups are available at per-second granularity for the past 35 days.

6. Site switching is controlled with an indicator file placed in an S3 bucket. The regional Lambda function behaves in active or passive mode according to the indicator.

Deploying the AWS CDK Application

To deploy this application, start by activating your Python virtual environment and setting environment variables for the CDK solution. Be sure that you have reviewed the *env.sh* file for the primary and secondary regions you've selected, and that you have the required permissions and are using the correct AWS account.

Note that the commands in this chapter have been tested on Mac and Linux in the Bash and ZSH shells. Some commands may require slight changes to work on Windows. Ensure you are in the main project directory, *AvailableTrade*, and run the following commands:

```
cd AvailableTrade
source .venv/bin/activate
source env.sh
cd AvailableTrade/src/account_open
cdk deploy --all --require-approval never
```

The first time you deploy the application, the deployment will run for several minutes as infrastructure is created and the application is deployed. This CDK application deploys two stacks in your primary region, and two stacks in your secondary region.

Once deployed, your regional CloudFormation consoles should look like Figures 4-4 and 4-5.

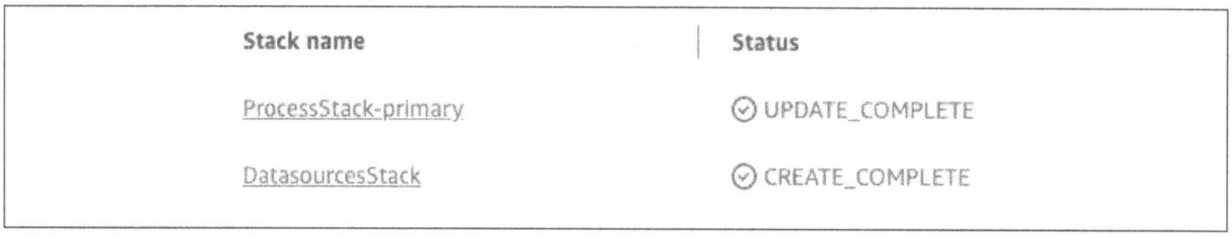

Stack name	Status
ProcessStack-primary	⊘ UPDATE_COMPLETE
DatasourcesStack	⊘ CREATE_COMPLETE

Figure 4-4. Primary AWS Region stacks

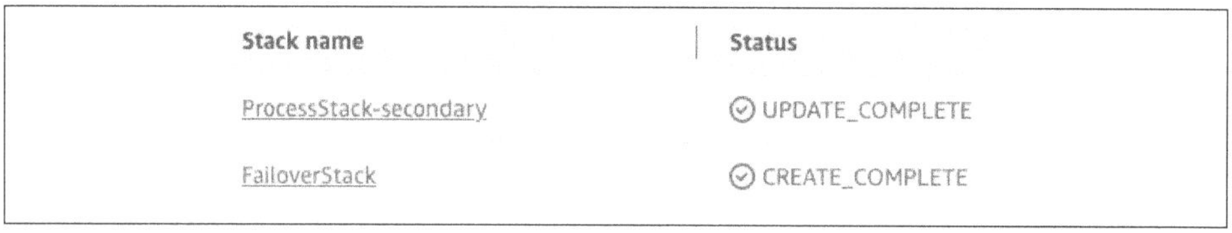

Stack name	Status
ProcessStack-secondary	⊘ UPDATE_COMPLETE
FailoverStack	⊘ CREATE_COMPLETE

Figure 4-5. Secondary AWS Region stacks

To understand how these stacks are configured, reference the top-level CDK application file, *AvailableTrade/src/account_open/app.py*. The CDK application orchestrates the stacks, passing configuration inputs to them. The account number, AWS Region names, and credential variables were exported into your local CLI environment from *env.sh*. Constants are defined for table names that are reused across stacks as they are executed. Before testing the application, it is beneficial to understand the resources that each stack creates, and review how resources are partitioned into different stacks:

FailoverStack

The FailoverStack creates an S3 bucket in the secondary AWS Region that you'll use to indicate if the app should process requests in the primary or secondary region. Site switching is controlled from the secondary region, so you can be sure you'll be able to force a switch when the primary AWS Region is impaired.

DatasourcesStack

The DatasourcesStack is installed in the primary region. It configures two global DynamoDB tables: one is the persistent store for Lambda Powertools idempotency and the other is the NoSQL database for brokerage accounts. Global tables are multiactive and replicate changes in either region. DynamoDB replication is asynchronous and can be monitored in CloudWatch metrics under the path All → DynamoDB → ReceivingRegion → ReplicationLatency. It is not uncommon for this latency to be 1–2 seconds, so it is important to consider the implications of eventual consistency on a multi-region workload.

ProcessStack

The ProcessStack is installed in both the primary and secondary regions. This stack builds the data processing for the Account Open API, so the same infrastructure resources are needed in both regions. The resources in the process stack include an API Gateway, an SNS topic, an SQS standard queue with a *dead-letter queue* (DLQ), and a Lambda function with logic to process requests and interact with SQS, DynamoDB, and S3.

The Lambda function actively processes messages in the active region, while the passive region verifies the results of active region processing before purging messages from the secondary queue.

New Account service test client

Testing is a critical aspect of any modern software application. Many product teams have adopted unit testing practices like test-driven development (TDD) or behavior-driven development (BDD). The testing pyramid (*https://oreil.ly/073ey*), coined by Mike Cohn in his book *Succeeding with Agile* (Addison-Wesley), helps you rationalize how to balance the amount of unit versus integration versus end-to-end UI testing. Repeatability and speed drive us to automate many of these tests and integrate them with our CI/CD processes. In the resilience world, we learn to apply resilience and chaos engineering (*https://oreil.ly/yeqKq*) where we design and test hypothesis about how our systems handle failure. See Figure 4-6 to understand how resilience fits within the test pyramid.

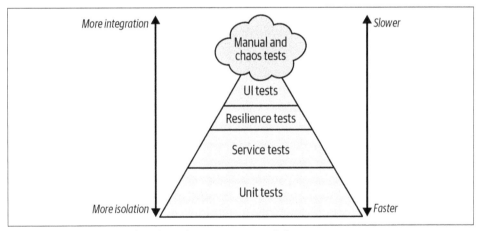

Figure 4-6. Test pyramid with resilience testing and chaos engineering

Resilience and chaos experiments both serve to validate and improve the resilience of your system. Resilience tests are deterministic tests that quickly validate self-healing capabilities of your system; they are similar to service integration tests and should be included in your CI/CD pipelines. Resilience tests are gating, and failures should stop a deployment to ensure your system can be relied on to tolerate faults that have been thought through and validated, either manually or with automation.

Chaos engineering experiments can be more time-consuming and can require research and analysis while the test is running. Due to this exploratory nature, these tests are aligned with the manual tests that reside in the cloud at the top of the pyramid. The name "chaos," and infamous ideas about chaos testing in production, can scare IT teams and leaders away from giving serious consideration to the importance of chaos engineering. It is perfectly acceptable to perform chaos testing in preproduction environments.

As you design and build mission-critical systems, it's imperative to reason about the failure modes of the system. Once you have identified potential failure modes, you can improve resiliency by embedding failure mode testing into your change management process.

Many of the scenarios that are validated in the following sections are manual and require you to investigate the deployment and understand how it works. In your real-world systems, the validations can and should be automated and enforced with assertions. The tests that execute quickly can be integrated into CI/CD pipelines, and when more complex, can be scheduled to run as a standalone job once or twice per day.

In the following lessons, you'll use a command-line client built to assist you with validating resilience engineering scenarios. The following sections outline hands-on scenarios that apply common failure modes and resilience to them. While the set of scenarios is not exhaustive, it covers common scenarios that apply to real-world applications. The scenarios are intended to provide a hands-on foundation for resilience engineering so that you can effectively think about and validate resilience to mitigate failure in your systems. After working through the following lessons, you'll gain confidence that the serverless applications you build can operate reliably when faced with common failure modes.

Sunny Day Scenario

When thinking about failure and validate failure modes, it goes without saying that you need to first understand your normal modes of operation. To that end, start with a sunny day scenario that submits a well-formed, successful request. This will help you get familiar with your application components and behaviors. You'll use the provided test client to issue a PUT request to the Account Open service and create a new account. Once you've validated a successful request, you'll learn where to look to see logs and data so that you can more easily navigate and explore the resilience engineering scenarios that follow. Review the provided client located at *Available-Trade/src/account_open/tests/onboarding_test_client.py*. You can read the source code, or you can run the client with the -h argument to see the help files that list scenarios the client supports. At your CLI, run **python onboarding_test_client.py -h**:

```
(.venv) > $ python onboarding_test_client.py -h                    [±main ●●●]
usage: Account Open Test Client [-h] --test TEST
                                [--request_token REQUEST_TOKEN]
                                [--user_id USER_ID]

Test Account Open Resiliency

optional arguments:
  -h, --help            show this help message and exit
  --test TEST           Choose a test to run
                            1/ Submit a valid request.
                            2/ Submit a invalid request missing account_type.
                            3/ Retries - see text, use CDK deployments.
                            4/ Switch to secondary region.
                            5/ Switch back to primary.
                            6/ Test load throttling.
                            7/ Poison pill, test DLQ.
                            8/ Test in recovery/green region.
  --request_token REQUEST_TOKEN
                        Use specified request token instead of generating at
                        random. Good for idempotency testing.
  --user_id USER_ID     Create accounts for specified user_id instead of
                        randomly generating a user_id.
```

The test client supports both valid and invalid requests. It also supports retries, switching to and back from the primary region, load, and poison pills. The client is a useful way to demonstrate examples, but you'll want to develop your tests in a standard framework with assertions for your automation.

Time to dive in. Send a valid request by specifying option value 1 to the --test argument flag. Note that the --test argument is always required, and the test client will complain if you try to run it without specifying a valid test number. At your CLI, type the command **onboarding_test_client.py --test 1** to produce a valid response:

```
(.venv) > $ python onboarding_test_client.py --test 1
<Response [200]>
```

The HTTP 200 response code confirms your submission was accepted as allowable. This confirms that the API Gateway was able to successfully submit the response to the SNS topic. You need to look deeper to determine if an account has actually been created/opened.

Sign in to your AWS account and navigate to the DynamoDB console → Tables → Explore items. Here you will find that both of your DynamoDB tables now contain a record. Make a note of the generated request_token in the brokerage_accounts table because we will use it again in scenario 3. In the menu bar of the AWS console, select the caret next to your current AWS Region and switch from the primary to the secondary region. You'll see that the record is present in the brokerage_accounts table in both AWS Regions because DynamoDB is globally replicating the records. Refer to Figures 4-7 and 4-8 to see how your idempotency and brokerage_accounts records should look in the DynamoDB console. If needed, you can run a query and filter by user_id.

Figure 4-7. Idempotency record

Figure 4-8. Brokerage account record

Now navigate to the CloudWatch console and choose LogGroups from the lefthand menu. You will see a number of log groups that have been created with your API deployment and your Lambda function. SQS and SNS logs have not been enabled as they are not needed to debug this application, but logging is supported for both if you need it.

Look for the log group named */aws/apigateway/welcome*. If you explore the log stream within this log group, you'll find a message indicating that logs are enabled for this API Gateway in this region. This log group is enabled when you initially provide API Gateway with a role containing permissions for CloudWatch.

Next, you will see a log group containing a random string of characters specific to your installation (denoted by Xs) called */aws/lambda/ProcessStack-primary-NewAccountXXXXXXXXX-XXXXXXXXX*. This string maps to the generated name for your Lambda function, and the log group contains streams for your Lambda executions. You can change the log level on your Lambda with the environment variable LOG_LEVEL defined in the *AvailableTrade/src/account_open/stacks/process_stack.py* file.

The *API-Gateway-Execution-Logs_xxxxxx/prod*, followed by the API ID and stage name, contain the request and response details and payloads for each API request. You may not want to log full request/response data in production to protect sensitive data and save space. In lower environments, this log helps to understand the interactions between the API Gateway with the HTTP client and the downstream request to SNS.

Finally, *ProcessStack-primary-NewAccountApiLogsXXXXXXXXX-XXXXXXXXX* contains API Gateway log entries that contain a single line for each request. These include the timestamp, requesting client IP address, and other high-level request data, including the response code. These logs are similar to web server access logs and are stored in JSON format so that you can query them or create metric filters. From a resilience standpoint, make sure you understand each log from your application so that you can effectively research issues. Being able to research issues in your application effectively helps you reduce your mean time to detect (MTTD) and mean time to recovery (MTTR). Your goal is to reduce MTTD and MTTR, while you increase the mean time between failures (MTBF).

 Learn more in the whitepaper "Availability and Beyond: Understanding and Improving the Resilience of Distributed Systems on AWS" (*https://oreil.ly/O2Psj*).

In your secondary region, there are no API Gateway logs. This is because the test client only sent requests to the primary region. The client should only send requests to the API Gateway endpoint when you perform a regional failover. You'll explore this further in "STOP: Business Continuity Regional Switchover" on page 115.

However, if you inspect the Lambda log streams by changing regions and navigating to the log group */aws/lambda/ProcessStack-secondary-NewAccountXXXXXXXXX-XXXXXXXXX*, observe that the Lambda function was invoked in the secondary region. When your SNS topic received a message from the primary API Gateway, the subscriptions pushed messages to your SQS queue in both regions, and each corresponding regional Lambda function consumed them. Review the log messages to see that the recovery AWS Region function waited until the brokerage_accounts record had been replicated to the recovery AWS Region brokerage_accounts table. Then it safely purged the message from the secondary region queue. This wait-for-success approach ensures that if the primary AWS Region fails to process a message, the message will be available in the secondary region. If enough time passes, the message may have been moved to the DLQ, but it will be available for redrive in the case of a site switch recovery strategy. There's more on this in "Self-Healing with Message Queue Retries" on page 106.

You won't run out of storage for logs in the cloud, but you will accrue costs for log storage. Set a reasonable retention period (*https://oreil.ly/_Xttz*) for log groups in both regions. I've set mine to 5 days to avoid clutter and log storage charges.

In a production environment, you should configure a retention that supports both your business data retention requirements and operational support needs.

Explore the log statements of your Lambda processing logs in CloudWatch in both regions to see the log statements from the function execution. With this multi-region queue, your application needs the intelligence to handle a single request idempotent across regions.

In the active region, your primary, the Lambda ESM for SQS, polls for and pulls a message from the queue, sets the visibility timeout, and if it is the first to process it, creates a new account. If another Lambda is also processing the message, an idempotent response is returned; then the function execution exits.

By default, when Lambda encounters an error during a batch, all messages in that batch become visible in the queue again after the visibility timeout expires. Batch item failure is enabled in the Account Open service to address this. Lambda event source mappings still process messages "at least once," and duplicate processing of records can still occur; so you must make your code idempotent. Learn more in the public documentation for "Using Lambda with Amazon SQS" (*https://oreil.ly/XTqM_*).

Review the log events shown in Figure 4-9 where the current AWS Region is active. The message is processed and finally stored in the brokerage_accounts table. With successful account creation, the function publishes a custom CloudWatch metric NewAccountOpened, a business-centric service-level indicator (SLI). On the last line in Figure 4-9, you'll see the CloudWatch embedded metric format (EMF), which is used by default with Lambda Powertools. The EMF allows you to generate custom metrics asynchronously in the form of logs, allowing you to query and find detailed log event data for deeper insights.

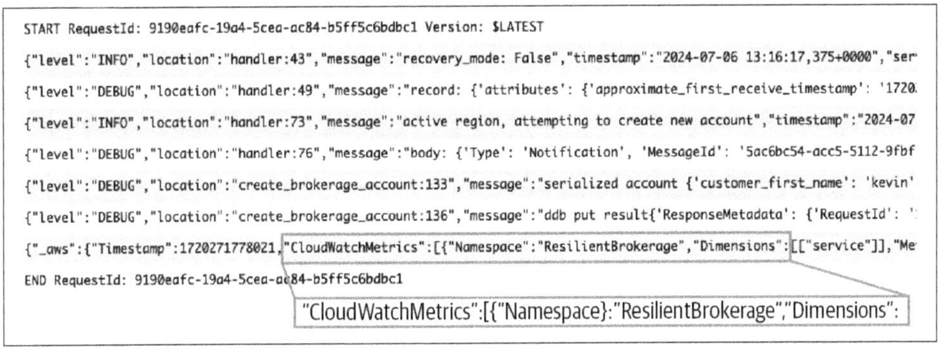

START RequestId: 9190eafc-19a4-5cea-ac84-b5ff5c6bdbc1 Version: $LATEST

{"level":"INFO","location":"handler:43","message":"recovery_mode: False","timestamp":"2024-07-06 13:16:17,375+0000","ser

{"level":"DEBUG","location":"handler:49","message":"record: {'attributes': {'approximate_first_receive_timestamp': '1720.

{"level":"INFO","location":"handler:73","message":"active region, attempting to create new account","timestamp":"2024-07

{"level":"DEBUG","location":"handler:76","message":"body: {'Type': 'Notification', 'MessageId': '5ac6bc54-acc5-5112-9fbf

{"level":"DEBUG","location":"create_brokerage_account:133","message":"serialized account {'customer_first_name': 'kevin'

{"level":"DEBUG","location":"create_brokerage_account:136","message":"ddb put result{'ResponseMetadata': {'RequestId': '

{"_aws":{"Timestamp":1720271778021,"CloudWatchMetrics":[{"Namespace":"ResilientBrokerage","Dimensions":[["service"]],"Me

END RequestId: 9190eafc-19a4-5cea-ac84-b5ff5c6bdbc1

"CloudWatchMetrics":[{"Namespace}:"ResilientBrokerage","Dimensions":

Figure 4-9. Active AWS Region successful processing logs

In the recovery AWS Region while in recovery mode, the message is still processed by Lambda, but it does not create a new account. The recovery mode is read, observed as False, and the Lambda knows it is in the secondary region. The function code skips the create_brokerage_account method, which is wrapped with an idempotency check, and instead checks for a record in the brokerage_accounts table. It looks this record up using the global secondary index which does not require an account account_id. Instead, it searches based on user_id and request_token, which are values in the unprocessed request. Once the record is found, the secondary region Lambda will purge the message from the queue, as reflected in Figure 4-10.

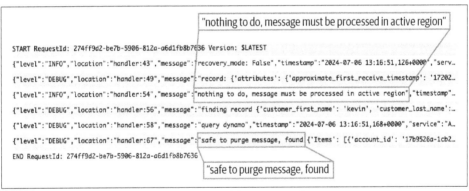

"nothing to do, message must be processed in active region"

START RequestId: 274ff9d2-be7b-5906-812a-a6d1fb8b7636 Version: $LATEST

{"level":"INFO","location":"handler:43","message":"recovery_mode: False","timestamp":"2024-07-06 13:16:51,126+0000","serv…

{"level":"DEBUG","location":"handler:49","message":"record: {'attributes': {'approximate_first_receive_timestamp': '17202…

{"level":"INFO","location":"handler:54","message":"nothing to do, message must be processed in active region","timestamp"…

{"level":"DEBUG","location":"handler:56","message":"finding record {'customer_first_name': 'kevin', 'customer_last_name':…

{"level":"DEBUG","location":"handler:58","message":"query dynamo","timestamp":"2024-07-06 13:16:51,168+0000","service":"A…

{"level":"DEBUG","location":"handler:67","message":"safe to purge message, found {'Items': [{'account_id': '17b9526a-1cb2…

END RequestId: 274ff9d2-be7b-5906-812a-a6d1fb8b7636

"safe to purge message, found

Figure 4-10. Recovery AWS Region successful processing logs

Congratulations. You've successfully followed a request moving through the Account Open system components. You learned about the logs emitted by different components of this system, and how active and recovery modes drive processing in the Lambda function. You are now ready to work through failure scenarios and recovery mechanisms.

Strongly Typed Service Contracts

One of the easiest ways to make a request fail to process is by inputting invalid data. This aligns to the adage "garbage in, garbage out." The type of failure illustrated in this scenario is from incomplete or poorly formed requests due to invalid data. One of the simplest ways to be resilient to invalid input is to block it at the front door. A well-defined API interface will reject nonconforming requests up front with an HTTP error.

In API Gateway we use JSON Schema. This approach is simple, declarative, and stops requests that are not well-formed up front, even if UI validation did not require a correct value. In the process stack, a JSON Schema (*https://json-schema.org*) is configured for the API Gateway request model and then attached to the REST API for new accounts. This schema enforces the structure of the payload body, field data types, and the presence of required fields. If an incoming request does not confirm to the schema validation, the API returns an HTTP 400 code indicating a bad request.

To validate this scenario, at your CLI run **python onboarding_test_client.py --test 2** to send an invalid request. This request is missing the required account_type field, and you see a 400 error when you run the test:

```
(.venv) > $ python onboarding_test_client.py --test 2
<Response [400]>
```

This request was rejected at the API layer before it could reach SNS and the SQS queues. The approach quickly informs the calling client of a bad request. It also avoids consuming application resources with work that is destined to fail. This work would otherwise backlog your queues, increase costs, and needlessly consume compute resources that could otherwise complete valid work. In your primary region, you can compare the API Gateway execution logs under the log group *API-Gateway-Execution-Logs_xxxxxx/prod* to see how a valid API request confirms delivery to SNS in Figure 4-11, as opposed to an invalid request rejected by the API validator in Figure 4-12.

A valid 200 response requires that API Gateway was able to transmit a message to SNS and receive a 200 from SNS. This asynchronous response success code confirms the message reached the SNS queue, but provides no insight into downstream processing. The important feedback to the customer relies on the fact that the message has been durably captured by your backend, and Account Open work will begin. API Gateway returns a 200 response to the client.

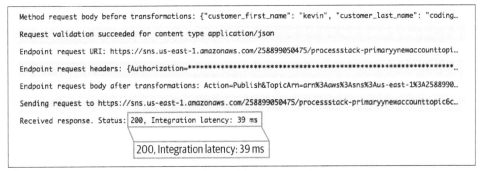

```
Method request body before transformations: {"customer_first_name": "kevin", "customer_last_name": "coding...

Request validation succeeded for content type application/json

Endpoint request URI: https://sns.us-east-1.amazonaws.com/258899050475/processstack-primaryynewaccounttopi...

Endpoint request headers: {Authorization=*****************************************************************...

Endpoint request body after transformations: Action=Publish&TopicArn=arn%3Aaws%3Asns%3Aus-east-1%3A2588990...

Sending request to https://sns.us-east-1.amazonaws.com/258899050475/processstack-primaryynewaccounttopic6c...

Received response. Status: 200, Integration latency: 39 ms

                                         200, Integration latency: 39 ms
```

Figure 4-11. A valid API request confirms delivery to SNS

On the other hand, you can see a 400 returned with a validation reason, missing the account type, when the request does not adhere to the JSON schema. API Gateway does not make a call to SNS in this case; the request is immediately rejected.

> You can learn more about how the best practice of providing service contracts per API improves resilience by visiting the AWS resilience Well-Architected whitepaper "Provide Service Contracts Per API" (*https://oreil.ly/AJ8sX*).

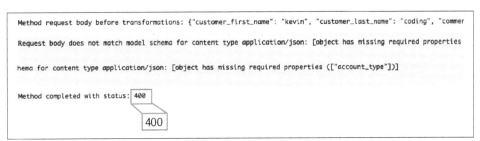

```
Method request body before transformations: {"customer_first_name": "kevin", "customer_last_name": "coding", "commer

Request body does not match model schema for content type application/json: [object has missing required properties

hema for content type application/json: [object has missing required properties (["account_type"])]

Method completed with status: 400

                                          400
```

Figure 4-12. An invalid API request is rejected by the request validator

Idempotent Responses

When customers place web requests for new accounts or stock purchases, they expect to receive a single account or single charge. Multiple accounts being opened could result in customer frustration and confusion, or worse yet an overcharge. A duplicated outcome impacts a company's reputation and needs to be avoided; therefore, responses need to be idempotent. A service that creates a single and repeatable outcome, even when the same request is submitted multiple times, demonstrates idempotency or is idempotent. The Account Open microservice can be relied on to return the same result even if the same call is made multiple times within the idempotency period.

You can learn how the best practice of making all responses idempotent improves resilience by visiting the AWS resilience Well-Architected whitepaper "Make All Responses Idempotent" (*https://oreil.ly/CI2u7*).

In the process stack, the API for creating new accounts is configured to respond to HTTP PUT requests. Using PUT communicates to API consumers that they should expect an idempotent outcome (*https://oreil.ly/YVSxb*) as defined in the HTTP specification that outlines the HTTP safe verbs. It is important to be aware that a standard SQS queue guarantees at least once processing; however, it could send a message to a consumer more than once. An SQS FIFO queue supports exactly once processing, and the best effort ordering of a standard queue is acceptable; a standard queue has been selected in this use case because the standard queue API calls are priced slightly less. In addition, retries on the client side might send the same request more than once if they receive an error on a first request. Client-side duplicate submissions are problematic and arise in scenarios where a service accepts and processes a request, but a network-related or other rare glitch causes a response failure prompting a client to retry.

The idempotent implementation in this application relies on a client assigning a universally unique identifier (UUID) for the request_token field of the request payload. In the *AvailableTrade/src/account_open/functions/new_account.py* file, the Lambda Powertools idempotency library is used, along with custom logic for handling our multi-region design to enforce idempotency in and across regions.

In this implementation, the Powertools idempotency logic is exercised in the currently active AWS Region as follows. First, the IdempotencyConfig for Powertools is made aware that it should check the request_token to identify a unique request, as shown in the following code:

```
persistence_store = DynamoDBPersistenceLayer(table_name=idempotency_table)
config = IdempotencyConfig(event_key_jmespath="request_token",
                           expires_after_seconds=60 * 60 * 3)
```

When a message is processed, Powertools maintains and verifies request processing state in the idempotency table in DynamoDB for an entry with a matching request_token. If found, the cached prior response is returned, skipping execution of the idempotent create_brokerage_account function, as shown in the following code snippet. The idempotency expires_after_seconds lasts for 3 hours, or 60 * 60 * 3 seconds, by setting a DynamoDB time-to-live (TTL) on the record:

```
@idempotent_function(
    data_keyword_argument='account_event',
    config=config, persistence_store=persistence_store,
    output_serializer=DataclassSerializer
```

```
)
def create_brokerage_account(account_event: dict) -> Account:
```

It is important to recognize that due to the eventual consistency of cross-region database synchronization, idempotency is only reliable within a region. You should include the DynamoDB `ReplicationLatency` and `PendingReplicationCount` metrics explained in monitoring global tables (*https://oreil.ly/dKtE_*) as part of your observability strategy for global tables.

 You can learn more about capabilities provided by Lambda Power-tools (*https://oreil.ly/FuYP2*), including idempotency, logging, custom metrics, and event sources. Each of these features is used in the Account Open Lambda function of this application.

To validate the idempotency of the service, send a request that reuses an already used `request_token`. First, run the client with the test argument of 1, which tells the service to send a valid request. In this case, you will provide a predefined `request_token`, and the client will use your existing value instead of generating a new UUID. The code will not publish an additional increment to the `NewAccountOpened` metric, as it skips the `create_brokerage_account` execution to achieve idempotency. As you can see in the following command sample, a 200 success response is returned:

```
(.venv) > $ python onboarding_test_client.py --test 1 \
   --request_token <replace_with_your_token>
<Response [200]>
```

Once the request is processed, validate that the record has not been duplicated in DynamoDB. You can also inspect the CloudWatch logs to see that log statements from the `create_brokerage_account` function were not emitted into the logs during function execution. You can also validate this in the AWS DynamoDB console, or with this CLI query:

```
> $ aws dynamodb query --table-name brokerage_accounts \
   --index-name user_request \
   --key-condition-expression "user_id = :u AND request_token = :r" \
   --expression-attribute-values \
   '{":u":{"S":"user169"}, ":r":{"S":"b267cc11-90df-426f-bd22-d9e0090d341a"} }' \
   --projection-expression "id" --region $AWS_PRIMARY_REGION | jq .Count

1
```

Be sure to replace `:u` and `:r` values in the `expression-attribute-values` parameter with the values from your request. The output should be 1, as shown on the last line; a duplicate account was not created as long as you tried the second account within 3 hours of creating the first.

Self-Healing with Message Queue Retries

Impairments to the Lambda function of the Account Open service could cause processing of Account Open requests to fail. Impairments can come in the form of a code or configuration error, or even a cloud service impairment. If a failed request is not retried with success, a customer will not receive the account they applied for, or feedback about why it may not have been possible to open the account. Failing to open a requested account is a sure way to lose business.

When you use SQS as the event trigger for your Lambda function, you can configure built-in retry capabilities. Set the `max_receive_count` to the number or times a message should be retried when code or throttling issues cause message processing to fail. As failures necessitate retries, the likelihood of success improves when you provide small but increasing windows of time between retries for the system to recover. This is called retrying with backoff. The Lambda documentation explains the backoff strategy for message queue retries (*https://oreil.ly/fQN63*).

In this lesson, you'll create a failure in Lambda, forcing SQS messages to be retried. You configure Lambda retries by setting the `visibilityTimeout` which controls how long a message is invisible in a queue while a consumer, the Lambda function, processes it. In the case of the Account Open service, messages are read off the queue in batches to improve throughput. For batch processing, batch item failure reporting allows you to report partial success when processing queued messages in batches of up to 10 instead of failing an entire batch. For SQS, the Lambda best practice is to set the `visibilityTimeout` to 6 times the Lambda function `timeout` when `report_batch_item_failures` is set to `True`. You can see the Lambda event source mapping configuration for SQS in the following lines from the process stack:

```
self.queue = sqs.Queue(self, "NewAccountQueue",
    dead_letter_queue=dead_letter_queue,
    encryption=sqs.QueueEncryption.UNENCRYPTED,
    visibility_timeout=cdk.Duration.seconds(6 * function_timeout_seconds)
)
...
self.new_account_function.add_event_source(eventsources.SqsEventSource(
    self.queue,
    batch_size=10,
    max_concurrency=15,
    report_batch_item_failures=True,
    max_batching_window=cdk.Duration.seconds(1))
)
```

Batching requires your Lambda function to format the SQS batch response as a list of any failed SQS message IDs. These messages will not be purged from the queue like the successful ones are, and they will be retried once the `visibilityTimeout` expires and the ESM poller finds them in the queue again. The following code shows a `try/except` collecting message IDs for failures:

```
batch_item_failures = []
sqs_batch_response = {}

if active_in_recovery or passive_in_primary:
# don't process, code omitted from example else:
for record in event.records:
try:
    body=json.loads(record["body"]) account: Account=create_brokerage_account(
        account_event=json.loads(body['Message'])
    )
except Exception as exc:
    batch_item_failures.append({"itemIdentifier": record.message_id})
    sqs_batch_response["batchItemFailures"] = batch_item_failures

return sqs_batch_response
```

To run this test scenario, temporarily introduce a failure into the Lambda function code in the active primary region. Open the file *AvailableTrade/src/account_open/functions/new_account.py* in your editor. Locate this code block within the body of the for loop that processes new account records:

```
try:
    # raise Exception("kaboom!!!") # forced failure
    logger.debug(f'body: {body}')
    account: Account = create_brokerage_account(account_event=message)
```

Uncomment the `raise Exception` line by removing the leading # which will force a failure for any Account Open. In a real-world impairment, you'll need observability in the form of metrics and alarms to drive your decision. Your code should now look like this:

```
try:
    raise Exception("kaboom!!!") # forced failure
    logger.debug(f'body: {body}')
    account: Account = create_brokerage_account(account_event=message)
```

Save your changes and deploy the updated function code to the primary region by running the command **cdk deploy ProcessStack-primary**. Make sure you are in the *AvailableTrade/src/account_open* directory to run the CDK commands, and in *AvailableTrade/src/account_open/tests* when you run tests. Using two shells can simplify this. Once the deployment is complete, run a valid account scenario with your test client by executing **python onboarding_test_client.py --test 1**. Check your CloudWatch logs, and you should see errors with the text `Arguments: (Exception("kaboom!!!")`. Query your SQS queue to verify that there is a message retained in the queue. The queue attribute `ApproximateNumberOfMessagesNotVisible` displays the count of messages currently invisible. Messages remain invisible and are skipped by ESM polling for the duration of the visibility timeout, 30 seconds in this application. You can run this CLI command to verify the value of `Approximate NumberOfMessagesNotVisible`:

```
export queue_url=$( \
  aws sqs list-queues --region us-east-2 | jq -r '.QueueUrls[1]')
  aws sqs get-queue-attributes --attribute-names \
  ApproximateNumberOfMessagesNotVisible --region $AWS_PRIMARY_REGION \
  --queue-url $queue_url | jq .Attributes.ApproximateNumberOfMessagesNotVisible
"1"
```

In your logs you'll also see log lines indicating repeated failures as the message is being retried. Now, replace the # to comment out the forced failure in your function code, then save and redeploy with **cdk deploy ProcessStack-primary**. Once the updated code is in place, the message will be picked up and processed successfully. Rerun the CLI command as follows to verify that ApproximateNumberOfMessagesNotVisible is now 0, and you can check your logs to validate processing success:

```
aws sqs get-queue-attributes \
  --attribute-names ApproximateNumberOfMessagesNotVisible \
  --region $AWS_PRIMARY_REGION --queue-url $queue_url \
  | jq .Attributes.ApproximateNumberOfMessagesNotVisible
"0"
```

Recall that following best practices (*https://oreil.ly/VFkHK*), the visibility timeout is set to 6 times the Lambda function timeout of 5 seconds which is 30 seconds. You'll have a window of 7–8 minutes of backing off with retries to fix and redeploy your code during this lesson. After this, Lambda will stop retrying your message and move it to the DLQ, causing false negatives when you check the queue for invisible messages. If a message does move to the DLQ, you can use dead-letter queue redrive to push it back to the main queue after deploying your fixed code to complete your test.

Rate Limiting: Throttle Unanticipated Load

Turn up the heat and attempt to stress your application with a burst of higher traffic rates than planned for. Spikes in traffic may originate from valid sources like a marketing promotion or news coverage, generating increased interest. Alternatively, traffic spikes can originate from nefarious sources like bot farms, scammers creating fake accounts for fraudulent purposes, or distributed denial of service attacks.

When websites experience sudden bursts of unanticipated traffic, that traffic can rapidly consume and exhaust resources. This can cause an application to fail, or in the case of serverless cloud applications, scale out and run up costs. Amazon API Gateway has account-level quotas, per region, (*https://oreil.ly/B_i86*) for requests per second (RPS). Setting throttle limits on a per API or API stage basis ensures that a single API cannot consume the account-level quota, impacting other APIs in the account.

A variety of approaches are used to shed unauthentic traffic. For example, you could use a captcha or a web application firewall (WAF) with rules to block robots and rate-limit IPs originating high volumes of traffic, as demonstrated in Chapter 3. Another load-shedding mitigation technique is API Gateway request throttling. Throttling is a practice where requests are counted against planned-for capacity. If the planned capacity is exceeded, a burst over capacity may be absorbed for a short time, but ultimately, overcapacity traffic will be rejected.

In this application, the throttle rate is set to 100 concurrent requests with a throttle burst rate of 25. API Gateway uses a token bucket algorithm to implement throttling. See Figure 4-13 which illustrates how each request takes a token from the bucket while tokens are refilled at the throttle rate per second.

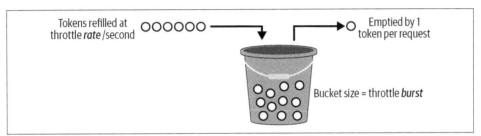

Figure 4-13. Tokens are refilled at the throttle rate

If the bucket is emptied faster than it is filled, requests will be throttled once the bucket is empty. As traffic subsides, the bucket fills up again.

 You can learn more about how to apply the throttle request best practice to improve your resilience by visiting the AWS resilience Well-Architected whitepaper "Throttle requests" (*https://oreil.ly/ y8b8M*).

To run this scenario, first, confirm that your primary AWS Region is active by issuing a switch to the primary AWS Region with your test client:

```
(.venv) > $ python onboarding_test_client.py --test 5
Primary AWS region is already active
```

The load test prepared for this workload runs an Artillery.io scenario. There are many options for load testing tools. AWS provides a ready-to-use solution (*https://oreil.ly/ QPZkd*) that relies on Taurus (*https://gettaurus.org*). Taurus helps you automate common open source testing tools (Apache JMeter, Selenium, Gatling, and many others), and once deployed to Amazon Elastic Container Service (ECS) on Fargate, supports large-scale distributed test automation. Artillery was selected for this lesson because of the ease of use for small-scale local CLI testing.

If you haven't already installed Artillery with npm, do it now by running the command `npm install -g artillery@latest`. Once installed, you can confirm your installation with the `--version` flag, as follows:

```
> $ artillery --version


    ___   |   ___/ /_(_) / /_      _____   __ __
   /__/  /| | / __/ _// / / / _ \/ __/ / / /__/
  /__/ __ |/ / / /_/ / / /  _/ / / / /_/ /__/
     /_/  |_/_/  \_/_/_/_/\__/_/   \_  /
                            /___/
```

```
VERSION INFO:
Artillery: 2.0.16
Node.js:   v22.3.0
OS:        darwin
```

Open the file *AvailableTrade/src/account_open/tests/new-account-load-test.yml* and review the configuration. This is a simple test inspired by the Artillery.io first test example. The test runs three phases of load, including warm-up for initial scaling, ramp-up to steady state, and finally a spike phase. Load phases are defined in the config phase of the YAML file.

The scenario phase executes HTTP PUT requests against the Account Open service endpoint with a valid payload. Built-in random number generators are used for creating mostly unique user_id and reqeust_token pairs. Overlap is OK for this test, so these random generators suffice and keep the test simple to create and maintain. For more rigorous tests, you can extend Artillery by adding UUID generators or other customizations you may need either with existing plug-ins or by writing your own.

To run this test, you'll issue the **artillery run** command and provide the YAML configuration file as a parameter via the test client: python onboarding_test_client.py --test 4. The test client will capture the URL of your service in the primary AWS Region and pass it to Artillery, which will then run your test scenario through the traffic phases:

```
elif test == '6':
  command =
    "artillery run account-load-test.yml --variables '{ \"url\": \"{url}\" }'"
    .replace("{url}", get_url())
  print(command)
  os.system(command)
```

Rather than focus on the details of interpreting Artillery output, instead we'll dive into how the Account Open service behaves. When API Gateway throttles requests, it returns HTTP 429 `Too Many Requests` errors. In a production system, it is a good idea to configure a metric over the API Gateway access logs on 429 errors, and monitor with alerting on throttle breaches so you can handle them appropriately. Navigate to the CloudWatch Logs Insights console in your primary region. Choose the *ProcessStack-primary-NewAccountApiLogsXXXXXXXXX-XXXXXXXXX*, then paste in and run the following query. Your output should look like Figure 4-14.

```
filter @message like /429/
    | stats count(*) as rateLimitCount by bin(15s)
    | sort rateLimitCount desc
```

CloudWatch Logs Insights enables you to query logs with SQL-like syntax to retrieve by keywords or field values, perform aggregation, and sort output. The results of the load test are shown in Figure 4-15, grouped by increments of 15 seconds. You can see how the throttles increase as load increases, and then finally clear out as the token bucket is refilled when traffic subsides. This test ran for about 3 minutes.

Figure 4-14. Run a CloudWatch Logs Insights query

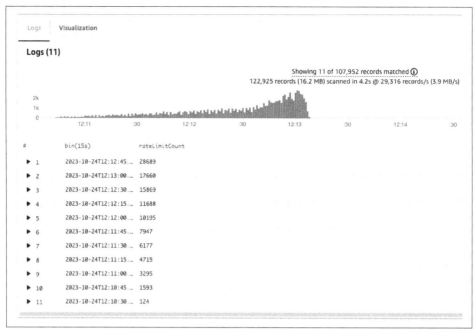

Figure 4-15. Access logs 429 throttling results

When running your analysis on logs to research errors, be aware that access logs have the least data—one line per request. It is less expensive to scan and query these logs than scan the contents of the API Gateway execution logs that include validation, request, response, and integration details. CloudWatch Insights queries are billed by the amount of data scanned. Monitor access log HTTP response codes for common API Gateway errors that reject requests like 403 and 429. For more complex errors that can happen in your Lambda function, monitor your application logs.

Finally, take notice of the queue metrics shown in Figure 4-16, a screenshot of the SQS monitoring tab. You'll see that as traffic ramped up, messages started to back up in the Account Open queue.

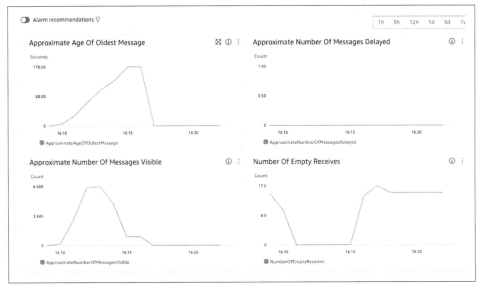

Figure 4-16. SQS load tests backlogging

The speed at which Lambda consumes this backlog is proportionate to the max number of concurrent Lambdas. The `max_concurrency` is configured in the event source mapping for SQS, and in this application it is set to 15. The `max_concurrency` limits Lambda queue consumption to 15 concurrent executions:

```
self.new_account_function.add_event_source(
    eventsources.SqsEventSource(
        self.queue,
        batch_size=10,
        max_concurrency=15,
        report_batch_item_failures=True,
        max_batching_window=cdk.Duration.seconds(1)
))
```

In this type of architecture, you can experiment with throttle limits and concurrency to understand how your system will perform under load. How quickly you scale and consume the messages often depends on the amount of account concurrency you need to reserve for other Lambda functions servicing other operations. Consider whether your queues can face backlog situations like those demonstrated here, and think about what you'd do to handle a large queue backlog. You just learned how to shed requests based on an API Gateway throttle; other options include bounding your queue length, shedding requests once the queue grows to a certain length, or creating and moving messages to a sideline queue. With a sideline queue, new inbound work is not held up behind a backlog.

Surviving a Poison Pill

In messaging systems, a *poison pill* is a message that cannot be processed due to a code defect or invalid data that causes processing failure. The effect of this could be Lambda execution failure if the payload causes an unhandled exception. Lambda execution failures that cause repeated message retries can result in reduced servicing of valid requests and increased Lambda billing costs, with no productive work being completed. If too many erroneous messages occur, and they continue to pile up, they will begin to consume your Lambda concurrency. Too many poison pills can cause queues to backlog, and account delivery to customers can be delayed. Based on the size of the backlog and resulting latency, the reputation of your business can be affected.

If ordering is important, and you use a FIFO queue, this problem becomes acute more quickly. Fortunately, the Account Open service does not require strict ordering. The *poison pill* scenario where invalid messages get stuck in a queue can be partially mitigated with a dead-letter queue (DLQ). In SQS a DLQ is not a default, but if you configure one, SQS will move poisoned messages that cannot be processed into another queue.

In this test, processing of your test request will pass API Gateway validation, but will fail in Lambda execution because it's missing the required beneficiaries list. The beneficiaries list was not defined as required in your JSON schema, but it is required in the Python dataclasses code (*https://oreil.ly/JLMgm*) running in your Lambda that serializes content into JSON, then saves the JSON data to DynamoDB.

Test number 5 issues the poison pill. To get started run **python onboard ing_test_client.py --test 5** to issue a PUT request. This message will propagate from SNS to SQS, but the Lambda execution fails when processing the message. Looking into the CloudWatch log group */aws/lambda/ProcessStack-primary-NewAccountXXXXXXXXX-XXXXXXXXX* for the Lambda function, you'll see stack traces with this error text: TypeError("__init__() missing 1 required posi tional argument: 'beneficiaries'"). The message will be retried until the configured three attempts, as specified in the DLQ's max_receive_count, are exhausted, and then it will be moved to a DLQ. This is defined in the process stack, as shown in the following code snippet:

```
dead_letter_queue = sqs.DeadLetterQueue(max_receive_count=3, queue=dlq)
```

After a few moments, you'll be able to see the poison pill message moved to the DLQ. Once retries have expired, you can run the following command to verify the message in the DLQ, or you can validate this by looking into the SQS console. If the message has not yet been moved to the DLQ, the command will output 0:

```
export queue_url=$(aws sqs list-queues --region us-east-2 | \
  jq -r '.QueueUrls[0]')
```

```
aws sqs get-queue-attributes --attribute-names ApproximateNumberOfMessages \
  --region $AWS_PRIMARY_REGION --queue-url $queue_url \
  | jq .Attributes.ApproximateNumberOfMessages
"1"
```

You just learned how consuming messages from SQS with Lambda and a DLQ allows your system to sideline poison pills, either due to message content or code defects, to a DLQ. Without a Lambda and using the SQS SDK clients, it is more challenging to deal with poison pills. Lambda's ability to scale and batch messages with the ESM simplify this resilience pattern. Instead of backing up your queue, poison pill messages are preserved for operational research, after which they can be addressed.

As an operational process for your system, you can:

- Fix the message contents and resubmit using the SQS API.
- Discard it from the queue by purging it.
- Update your code and redrive messages, which pushes the message back into the main queue.

A redrive on this lesson's test messages will fail again due to missing beneficiaries, so it can be purged. A redrive is often more suited to address reprocessing of intermittent errors, like a bad code deployment that was subsequently rolled back.

STOP: Business Continuity Regional Switchover

During the rare event that you are unable to open new accounts in the primary region, you can maintain business continuity by switching your application to the secondary region. A switchover can be necessitated in the unusual event that an AWS serverless service like Lambda suffers a temporary impairment. More commonly, a switchover is performed during continuity testing, or in response to a failure event that is not easily understood or quickly rolled back due to code or configuration changes to be able to achieve a bounded recovery.

In this lesson, to emulate a regional outage, you will temporarily break your Lambda function again, and again only in the primary region. Open the file *Available-Trade/src/account_open/functions/new_account.py* in your editor. Once again, locate this code block within the body of the for loop that processes Account Open records:

```
try:
    # raise Exception("kaboom!!!") # forced failure
    logger.debug(f'body: {body}')
    account: Account = create_brokerage_account(account_event=message)
```

Uncomment the `raise Exception` line by removing the leading #, and save your changes. In a real-world impairment, you'll need observability in the form of metrics and alarms to drive your decision. You can see in the except clause that Account

Open failures are tracked with a metric that you can use to send an alarm to your support team. Your code should now look like this (the except block did not change):

```
try:
    raise Exception("kaboom!!!") # forced failure
    logger.debug(f'body: {body}')
    account: Account = create_brokerage_account(account_event=message)
except Exception as exc:
    logger.error('failed to create account', exc)
    batch_item_failures.append({"itemIdentifier": record.message_id})
    metrics.add_metric(name="NewAccountFailure", unit=MetricUnit.Count, value=1)
```

Now, deploy the process stack in the primary AWS Region by running the command **cdk deploy ProcessStack-primary** and then push a new request with **python onboarding_test_client.py --test 1**. The Lambda function code will fail and begin the process of retrying. If you are observing logs in CloudWatch, you'll see the following log error lines in your primary AWS Region log:

```
Exception: kaboom!!!
...
Message: 'failed to create account'
```

Instead of fixing the code this time, you'll recover by switching regions. You can issue a site switch by running test 6 with your test client:

```
(.venv) > $ python onboarding_test_client.py --test 6
failover-bucket-us-west-1-998541053034
Switched to secondary region
```

This command will upload the *AvailableTrade/src/account_open/tests/failures.txt* file to your recovery AWS Region failover S3 bucket, as well as emit the bucket name and a message confirming switchover. Look into your S3 bucket to confirm the placement of the indicator file. To list files in the bucket with your CLI, use the following command or validate in the S3 console:

```
> $ aws s3 ls failover-bucket-$AWS_SECONDARY_REGION-$AWS_ACCOUNT_ID
2023-10-21 15:41:23        103 failover.txt
```

As the Lambda function processes each message in a batch, it checks for the presence of the *failover.txt* file to determine if it is currently running in an active or passive region, as shown in this code:

```
def in_recovery_mode():
    objects = s3_client.list_objects_v2(Bucket=failover_bucket)
    for obj in objects.get('Contents', []):
        if 'failover.txt' in obj['Key']:
            return True
    return False
```

Whenever the Account Open function determines it is running in an inactive region, Lambda will run in recovery mode. In this mode, Lambda will query the brokerage_accounts table using a global secondary index (GSI) with a partition_key of user_id, the sort_key of request_token. Only once the broker age_account record is found will it purge the account request message from the SQS queue. This ensures that a new account is created for a valid request, even if the primary (not active) AWS Region continues to accept Account Open requests but fails to process them.

Check the Lambda logs in the primary AWS Region again, and you'll find an entry like the following log excerpt. The brokerage_account record has been found. The recovery AWS Region still had a copy of the request in its SQS queue. When you activated recovery mode, the recovery AWS Region became the active region. Lambda processed the Account Open, then the primary AWS Region Lambda ran in recovery mode and purged the message from its queue:

```
{
    "level": "DEBUG",
    "location": "handler:66",
    "message": "safe to purge message, found {'Items': [{'account_id':
    '6a3f7722-04b5-466a-8e0d-7f7b32aeeb76'}], 'Count': 1, 'ScannedCount': 1,
    'ResponseMetadata': {'RequestId':
    'C0JKC8U06JT73FLF5QMA7N2393VV4KQNSO5AEMVJF66Q9ASUAAJG', 'HTTPStatusCode':
    200, 'HTTPHeaders': {'server': 'Server', 'date': 'Mon, 23 Oct 2023 21:05:10
    GMT', 'content-type': 'application/x-amz-json-1.0', 'content-length': '98',
    'connection': 'keep-alive', 'x-amzn-requestid':
    'C0JKC8U06JT73FLF5QMA7N2393VV4KQNSO5AEMVJF66Q9ASUAAJG', 'x-amz-crc32':
    '2383576647'}, 'RetryAttempts': 0}}",
    "timestamp": "2023-10-23 21:05:10,745+0000",
    "service": "AccountOpen",
    "xray_trace_id": "1-6536e006-feaaa67c99852e0822c1c4a2"
}
```

The pattern you just executed is called Standby Takes Over Primary (STOP). In this lesson, you manufactured a simple code-induced failure. Then you invoked recovery to observe how to switch your active region quickly and reliably with the STOP pattern. No matter which custom component or AWS service is not working properly in the primary AWS Region, the failure is mitigated by a data plane operation in the recovery AWS Region to drive the secondary region taking over as primary.

Returning to Business as Usual

It is important to make a business continuity decision and perform a regional switchover both to rehearse and to maintain business continuity in light of regional impairments. Performing an AWS Region switch does require some analysis and should be done with care. The same care should be applied when returning to your primary region. In both scenarios, ensure the target environment is healthy, and after switching, ensure that all messages have been processed from queues as expected.

To return to business as usual, you can comment out the exception line `# raise Exception("kaboom!!!")` in your Account Open Lambda function and redeploy to the primary AWS Region with **cdk deploy ProcessStack-primary**. For this test, run test 7 from the test client without needing to worry about any data cleanup:

```
(.venv) > $ python onboarding_test_client.py --test 7
failover-bucket-us-west-1-998541053034
Switched to primary region
```

Once you have switched back over, you can rerun the sunny day scenario to validate that processing accounts in the primary region, and your code is again operating normally, business as usual.

Blue-Green Testing

Changes to your code or infrastructure can lead to failures in your service when defects or misconfigurations are introduced. Blue-green testing is a way to test code deployments without exposing new changes to your end users until after you validate your new deployment with test users. In a deployment like the new Account Open service, it is relatively easy to demonstrate a blue-green test. The code is already written to find `greentest_` users and process them in the recovery AWS Region where you can deploy your changes. This allows the primary active AWS Region to continue processing real user traffic, while the secondary region mimics being active but only for `greentest_` users. Review the conditional clause in the *new_account.py* Lambda source code to understand the `greentest_` logic; the code snippet is shown here:

```
green_test = "greentest_" in message["user_id"]
if (active_in_recovery or passive_in_primary) and not green_test:
    ...
```

Put blue-green testing into action by introducing a simple change to your Lambda, API Gateway, or other component in the service. A simple change that is easy to validate is introducing or updating a log statement. This lesson leaves it up to you to think of and try out a change of your choice. Once your changes are ready, deploy them with the command **cdk deploy ProcessStack-secondary**. Once the deployment is complete, you can push a request to the API endpoint in the secondary region. Test 8 in the test client is configured to send a valid request to the secondary region. In Chapter 6, you'll configure a custom domain for the Account Open endpoint with failover routing, giving you control of which region your client applications route traffic to.

To validate your changes, run the command **python onboarding_test_client.py --test 8 --user_id greentest_1234**. Once your request has been published, use what you've learned in the previous scenarios to validate your changes. Once you are comfortable that your changes work as desired, you are safe to make your green environment blue:

1. Site-switch production traffic to the secondary region.

2. Deploy your code to the primary region, then validate the primary AWS Region with a test user.

3. Finally, switch back to the primary with your new code deployed.

Of course, if your changes did not work as expected, you can roll back deploy fixes and retest before exposing new features to real user traffic.

There are many more serverless patterns to explore as you continue your journey through resiliency. As you build more complex workloads and to support your business requirements, be sure to understand the features of each service you use. AWS Lambda supports function aliases that allow you to deploy multiple versions of a single function. API Gateway supports multiple stages, so you can deploy and support a multiple version of an API. Combining the two supports versioning strategies and single-region blue-green strategies. AWS Lambda supports provisioned concurrency that can prewarm your Lambda for a preset level of concurrency to more rapidly handle spikes without a cold-start induced latency. This can be effective for traffic spikes and emergency failover scenarios.

Cleaning Up

The resources you created in this chapter accrue charges when services are invoked and for data storage. To avoid costs, remove the applications and data you've created. If you plan to work through each chapter in Part II, you can leave this stack installed until you have worked through Chapters 2–7. But be aware that if you stop working through the lessons and leave your infrastructure running, you will be charged for it.

Before you delete your stacks with the CDK, delete resources protected by a `Deletion Policy`, including the DynamoDB tables, S3 bucket, and CloudWatch logs. This is the only chapter that uses a deletion policy to demonstrate another way to protect resources that contain data. For simplicity, all other chapters allow the CDK to automatically tear down data resources.

1. Navigate to the S3 console or use the CLI to delete your failover bucket. If your *failover.txt* file is in the bucket, switch back to primary using test 5 or manually delete the file.

2. Navigate to the CloudWatch LogGroups console in your primary region. Select the four LogGroups for this solution and delete them. Switch to the secondary AWS Region and repeat.

3. Navigate to the secondary AWS Region DynamoDB console. Choose both the brokerage accounts and the idempotency table. Remove deletion protection. Delete each table.

4. Navigate to the primary AWS Region DynamoDB console once the tables in your secondary AWS Region finish deleting.

   a. Ensure that both the brokerage accounts and idempotency table have completed updates.

   b. Select both tables and remove deletion protection.

   c. Delete both tables. If you encounter errors while turning off deletion protection on any tables, wait a few seconds and try again.

Finally, delete all remaining resources by running `cdk destroy --all` to delete the stacks.

Summary

In this chapter, you learned how to configure some built-in serverless resilience features and implement some serverless resilience design patterns. Strongly typed contracts and throttling at the API Gateway layer load-shed invalid messages or traffic spikes without invoking compute or backlogging message systems. You learned how to implement idempotency logic in your code to avoid duplicate processing both in a single AWS Region and across AWS Regions with SQS. The Lambda ESM facilitates retries and interacts with a dead-letter queue. When SQS and Lambda retries don't eventually succeed, like in the case of a poison pill, messages can be sidelined to allow valid messages to continue to be processed. You also learned the benefit of a blue-green multi-region strategy and how to use it to test out new code deployments. However, if you don't require a multi-region design, almost all the lessons in this chapter worked for a single region.

In the next chapter, the microservice architecture will focus on a stock trading API. You'll learn about resilience in a severless container API workload backed by a cloud native relational database. Code-level design patterns will demonstrate secret management and caching, credential rotation, circuit breakers, and retries. AWS service configuration features will include how to recover container tasks quickly, configure health checks, and induce rollbacks on bad deployments. Finally, you'll learn how to configure the API for an active-passive multi-region architecture, including both AWS regional failover at the HTTP API endpoint and the database.

CHAPTER 5

Containerized Trade Stock API

With a new AvailableTrade brokerage account open and funded, your investment customer is ready to start trading on your AvailableTrade application. Now you'll deploy the Trade Stock API that processes trade orders to buy or sell stocks. As with the Account Open API, the business owners of the AvailableTrade platform have requested an RPO of one hour and an RTO of four hours for the Trade Stock API. In addition, they have asked for a service-level agreement (SLA) specific to a trade latency of under 200 milliseconds from the point a request is received. The SLA does not include client-side processing or transmission over the internet, as those are both out of your control. Because stock prices change constantly during trading hours when the stock market is open, trades are executed at the bid/ask price at the time they are received by the brokerage. There can be minor fluctuations from the value the customer sees on the UI when they submit a trade until the time the trade is matched. The Trade Stock API is synchronous, so the frontend can report errors or transaction timeouts immediately back to the customer, so they are quickly aware if their trade was accepted or not.

To achieve these business requirements, this service first places an order with a third-party brokerage which will then confirm the trade and orchestrate matching and clearing with the National Securities Clearing Corporation (NSCC). To complete the trade, the service will persist trade details to an operational data store. This organization will match the customer transaction between buying and selling parties in preparation for T+1 activities, which include the settlement of funds and the electronic transfer of securities by the Depository Trust & Clearing Corporation (DTCC). The Trade Stock API will be simplified for learning purposes so it will leave out much of the complexity a real Trade Stock API may have and will not cover the orchestration of T+1 and T+2 activities.

You can learn more about the lifecycle of a trade on the DTCC website (*https://oreil.ly/q4cEY*).

In this chapter, you will deploy and test a synchronous microservice that reliably executes trades for the AvailableTrade application. After deploying the prebuilt service, you will incrementally apply native Amazon Elastic Container Service (Amazon ECS) and Amazon Aurora PostgreSQL resilience features, and apply software development resilience patterns. You'll be able to mitigate:

- Container deployment failures
- Database connection exhaustion
- Database password rotation login failures
- Database primary writer failures
- Dependency intermittent failures
- Detecting and handling Availability Zone issues
- Dependency outages

Working through these scenarios, you'll learn to identify and mitigate common failure modes. In each lesson, you'll induce distributed systems failures and then apply mitigations to either prevent failure modes or quickly self-heal and recover from them. You'll gain a thorough understanding of Amazon ECS and Amazon Aurora PostgreSQL built-in resilience features as well as how to implement code-level design patterns to achieve high availability.

Technical Requirements

There are a variety of trade order networks, such as order to the floor, electronic communications networks (ECNs), over-the-counter (OTC) networks, and more. The Trade Stock service is fictitious and simplified to demonstrate the lessons in this chapter. In addition, while you can place many order types like conditional, limit, and good-til-canceled, we'll be working with a pseudomarket order.

 If you are interested in learning more about the stock trade order execution, take a look at "What Is Order Execution?" on Investopedia (*https://oreil.ly/Gg3x-*).

The Trade Stock service will first receive a trade request from a trading customer using our brokerage portal. The first component of the microservice will receive and forward the request to a service that contains the logic to process the trade order. The processing of the trade order includes both recording the trade request in a pending state and sending the order to a third-party stock exchange service that will confirm and match the trade. Once the trade is confirmed and matched by the exchange, the order is filled, and acknowledgment is returned to the client.

When something goes wrong in the trade order process, the service returns an error to the trade order client; the order has not been filled. The dataflow diagram for the trade order service is shown in Figure 5-1.

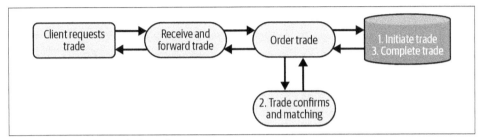

Figure 5-1. Trade Stock data flow

Architecture Overview

The architecture for the Trade Stock service will be implemented with AWS serverless containers with AWS Fargate with Amazon ECS fronted by an AWS Application Load Balancer (ALB). Data will be stored in the relational AWS Aurora PostgreSQL database. See Figure 5-2 for a high-level overview of the data flow through the AWS components supporting this microservice workload. Access to regional services like Amazon Elastic Container Registry (ECR), Amazon CloudWatch, AWS Systems Manager (SSM) Parameter Store, and AWS Secrets Manager is provided over AWS VPC PrivateLink endpoints, keeping VPC traffic private. While this is a multi-region architecture, you'll deploy and work in a single region for this chapter. You'll deploy the remaining infrastructure to the secondary region in Chapter 7.

Application logic is coded in the Trade Stock service, and the third-party exchange Trade Confirms service. Both are hosted as separate ECS services. To simplify the implementation and allow for resiliency experimentation with external service dependencies, the Trade Confirms service runs in your VPC. In the real world, this dependency would be external, so think of it as a black box for the lessons that follow. An AWS ALB fronts both ECS services for dynamic scaling based on system demand.

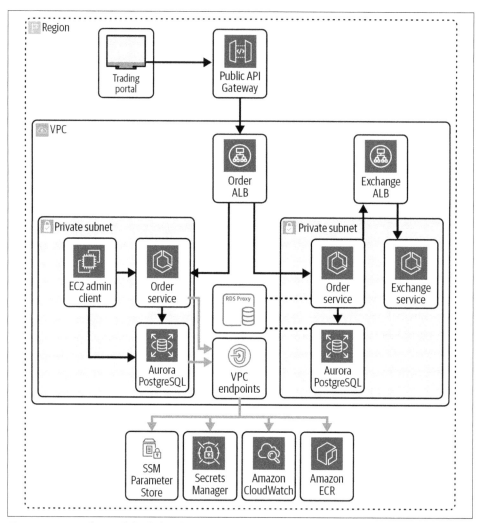

Figure 5-2. Trade Stock high-level architecture

Before jumping into the deployment process and stack composition, it will be helpful for you to understand the overall application and have a high-level familiarity with the libraries used. You can view the microservice code in the files *src/trade-stock/ order_api/order_api.py* and *src/trade-stock/confirms_api/confirms_api.py*. You'll notice several imported libraries that were selected to simplify coding as well as use more resilient and proven solutions. Utility functions have been designed to make the logic in the request handlers simple and clear.

Both the Trade Stock and the Trade Confirms APIs service requests with Flask (*https://oreil.ly/MFWeh*), the popular and easy-to-use micro web framework for

Python. The containers will run Flask with Gunicorn "Green Unicorn" (*https://guni corn.org*), the production-grade Python Web Server Gateway Interface (WSGI) HTTP server for Linux. The order service uses the AWS SDK for Python (Boto3) to interact with AWS services for configuration management. The AWS Secrets Manager and Parameter Store hold database credentials and service discovery values.

Interaction with the database relies on the Python object-relational mapper (ORM) SQLAlchemy database toolkit (*https://sqlalchemy.org*). You configure the SQLAlchemy database dialect with the popular Psycopg database adapter for PostgreSQL (*https://psycopg.org*). You can browse the ORM objects in the file *src/trade-stock/order_api/data_objects.py*. The order service uses the Python native `requests` library to interact with the Trade Confirms service over HTTP, as well as the `retry` and `circuitbreaker` libraries to implement resilience patterns.

For observability, CloudWatch APIs are used to push custom metrics, and log formatting is structured as JSON. JSON formatting facilitates structured queries with CloudWatch Logs Insights, the ability to create metric filters over log data like exceptions, and improved readability by reducing the number of lines.

Further enhancing observability in the order microservice, CloudWatch Container Insights are enabled for ECS, and CloudWatch Performance Insights are enabled for Aurora PostgreSQL. Both service insights capabilities are the AWS native solutions to observe infrastructure performance metrics, which you can view in the service or CloudWatch consoles. AWS X-Ray is not currently enabled for orders, but you should consider enabling it in a real-world solution, similar to the account open microservice.

Deploying the AWS CDK Application

To deploy this application, activate your Python virtual environment and set environment variables for the CDK solution. Ensure you have reviewed the *env.sh* file for the primary and secondary regions you've selected, that you have the required permissions, and that you are using the correct AWS account. While this service is a multi-region design, you will only need to deploy a single region for the lessons in this chapter, and you won't need the public endpoint. In Chapter 7, you'll deploy to the secondary region, including public regional API endpoints:

```
cd AvailableTrade
source .venv/bin/activate
source env.sh
cd AvailableTrade/src/trade_stock
# download xray sidecar image, create repo, tag and push to repo
export XRAY_REPO=$AWS_ACCOUNT_ID.dkr.ecr.$AWS_PRIMARY_REGION.amazonaws.com
docker pull amazon/aws-xray-daemon
aws ecr get-login-password --region $AWS_PRIMARY_REGION | \
docker login --username AWS --password-stdin $XRAY_REPO
```

```
aws ecr create-repository --repository-name xray-sidecar
docker tag amazon/aws-xray-daemon $XRAY_REPO/xray-sidecar:latest
docker push $XRAY_REPO/xray-sidecar:latest
# deploy CDK application in primary region
pip install -r requirements.txt
cdk deploy TradeVpcStackPrimary TradeDatabaseStackPrimary \
  TradeConfirmsStackPrimary TradeOrderStackPrimary \
  TradeStockApiGatewayStackPrimary --require-approval never
```

The first time you deploy the application, it will run for several minutes as infrastructure is created and the application microservices are deployed. Once the deployment completes, you will need to set up the database before you can interact with the microservices. While the application deploys, take a moment to understand each of the CDK stacks, and then you can jump into the admin client and database setup.

VpcStack

The VpcStack, source file *AvailableTrade/src/trade-stock/trade_stock/vpc_stack.py*, creates an Amazon Virtual Private Cloud (VPC), your application's private network. The subnets configured in this VPC restrict any ingress or egress using the Subnet Type.PRIVATE_ISOLATED, which means that there is no Internet Gateway (IGW) or NAT Gateway (NAT) configured. Any external access required to interact with AWS service endpoints is done through this stack's VPC interface endpoints. Network access to the publicly hosted Amazon Linux packages for PostgreSQL and Docker images from ECR is provided through a PrivateLink gateway endpoint for S3.

> In this stack, detailed VPC endpoint policies are not configured and rely on defaults; however, in a production implementation, it's a defense in-depth best practice to control and limit access to VPC endpoints with resource policies (*https://oreil.ly/-jY9m*).

TradeDatabaseStack

The TradeDatabaseStack, source file *AvailableTrade/src/trade-stock/trade_stock/trade_database.py*, manages the Aurora PostgreSQL database and deploys an Amazon Elastic Compute Cloud (EC2) admin client. You'll use your EC2 admin client running on Amazon Linux in one of your private VPC subnets. You can open a terminal session using AWS Session Manager to connect this admin client where you can then privately interact with the database, flask microservices, and AWS configuration management.

The Aurora configuration is serverless to keep costs to a minimum but automatically scales CPU, memory, storage, and TCP client session connections when more resources are needed.

You can read "How Aurora Serverless v2 Works" (*https://oreil.ly/xAb2Q*) to learn more about Aurora serverless.

A single primary writer is deployed to support read-write traffic, while multiple reader instances will service read-only traffic. These readers also provide an HA configuration; if the primary experiences a problem, one of them can be promoted to the primary writer. Database secrets are configured for admin and application access as well as SSM parameters for Amazon RDS Proxy endpoints.

Finally, IAM roles for the services and admin client are set up in this stack. Permission policies are narrowly scoped to allow access to the required AWS configuration management services, database access, and logs and metrics publishing.

The database is not encrypted because we have not configured a multi-region CMK, which is needed for the Aurora global database. Encrypt your database when you store real customer data.

TradeOrderStack

The `TradeOrderStack`, source file *AvailableTrade/src/trade-stock/trade_stock/trade_order_stack.py*, deploys the ECS service for the Trade Orders API. It stores the ALB endpoint in the parameter store for discovery. It also creates CloudWatch metric filters to track errors on database credentials access and connections.

ECS configuration is simplified using the ECS service extensions constructs for the CDK. While this library simplifies the configuration of ECS, it requires you to code your own extensions to accomplish more complex ECS configurations like running in private isolated VPCs. The `PrivateAlbExtension` in the file *src/trade-stock/trade_utils/private_lb_extension.py* is used to configure the private ALB for the service.

While enabling tracing is an observability best practice, X-Ray is currently not enabled due to a need for access to the public docker.io repository. You can build your own X-Ray sidecar with an ECR image or enable egress through an allow-listing web proxy configured to control and limit egress traffic. Enabling allow-listed egress traffic is beyond the scope of this chapter.

TradeConfirmsStack

The `TradeConfirmsStack`, source file *AvailableTrade/src/trade-stock/trade_stock/trade_confirms_stack.py*, deploys the ECS service for the Trade Confirms API. Like the `TradeOrderStack`, the `TradeConfirmsStack` uses the ECS service extensions and the same `PrivateAlbExtension`. Parameter store entries are created in the `TradeConfirmsStack` for service discovery and fault injection for chaos testing of external dependencies. Take notice that the Trade Confirms is a mock service, so it does not reach out to any third party or even leave the VPC. Faults will be coded directly into the mock service; however, this technique is only applied in the mock service and is not recommended in real application code.

Prepare the Database

Recall that this application runs in a private VPC that does not allow direct ingress or egress, and the admin client is the only principal configured with admin access to the PostgreSQL database. As the `TradeDatabaseStack` summary notes, an admin client has been deployed into the private subnet where the service runs. You'll log in to this admin client as you work through the resilience lessons for the stock trading microservice APIs and database. You will not be able to use SSH to access the admin client's Linux terminal, as the VPC doesn't support public ingress, and the security group of the admin client does not allow any inbound traffic. You'll need to rely on private traffic that securely flows through VPC endpoints and provide a path to the resources you need by connecting to the instance with the AWS Systems Manager.

Navigate to the EC2 console, select the admin client instance, then choose Connect with the connection method Session Manager. See Figure 5-3.

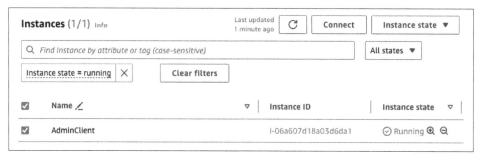

Figure 5-3. Open a secure terminal on the admin client with AWS Session Manager

 You can find more details on privately connecting to instances with Session Manager in the EC2 documentation topic about connecting with Session Manager for Linux instances (*https://oreil.ly/ZQnD_*).

Once you have connected and are at a terminal prompt, you'll need to set up the admin client with the tools you need to administer the database. Note that throughout these lessons, there are several blocks of shell commands that need to be run. You'll find these commands in the directory *src/trade-stock/shell_scripts/*. You can copy commands from these files and paste them into your terminal, or upload the directory to S3, then copy it from S3 to your admin client where you can run commands as scripts. Run the following commands from the file *src/trade-stock/shell_scripts/install_admin_client_packages.sh* to install the required tools on your admin client. Note that even though your admin client doesn't have access to the internet, it does have an S3 VPC gateway endpoint and the Amazon Linux repositories are hosted on S3, so the admin client can access and install available packages.

```
cd ~
bash
sudo yum update -y
sudo yum install jq -y
sudo amazon-linux-extras enable postgresql14

install parallel

sudo yum install postgresql-server -y
yum clean metadata
```

Next, you'll need to extract the information required from the AWS Secrets Manager to create your admin database connection. Your secret was configured in the TradeOrderStack which is in the file *src/trade-stock/trade_stock/trade_database.py*. Run the following block of commands to retrieve the secret value, then parse and export PostgreSQL environment variables (*https://oreil.ly/FLXA0*) to simplify connecting to the database. These commands are found in *src/trade-stock/shell_scripts/load_db_admin_session.sh*:

```
export ADMIN_SECRET_ID=$(aws ssm get-parameter --name trade_db_secret_id \
  --region us-east-1 | jq -r .Parameter.Value)
export ADMIN_SECRET=`aws secretsmanager get-secret-value \
  --secret-id $ADMIN_SECRET_ID --region us-east-1 | jq -r '.SecretString'`
export PGUSER="`echo $ADMIN_SECRET | jq -r '.username'`"
export PGPASSWORD="`echo $ADMIN_SECRET | jq -r '.password'`"
export PGHOST="`echo $ADMIN_SECRET | jq -r '.host'`"
export PGDATABASE="`echo $ADMIN_SECRET | jq -r '.dbname'`"
export PGPORT="`echo $ADMIN_SECRET | jq -r '.port'`"
psql -c "select version(),AURORA_VERSION();"
```

Once you've successfully connected to your database, you'll see the psql CLI output from the SQL statement select version(),AURORA_VERSION();, similar to the following:

```
version                                                    | aurora_version
-----------------------------------------------------------+----------------
PostgreSQL 15.4 on aarch64-unknown-linux-gnu 9.5.0 64-bit | 15.4.3
(1 row)
```

For the order service to successfully interact with the database, you will need to build out tables in the database schema and populate some data. The following database script creates enumerations, tables, and triggers to manage `created_on` and `updated_on` timestamps:

- The *customer* table contains registered portal users who can place trade orders.

- The *symbol* table contains OHLC data where the *close* price is equivalent to the current price when a trade is ordered.

- The *activity* table records Trade Stock activity records, one for each trade of a *symbol* by a *customer*.

See the entity relationship diagram (ERD) in Figure 5-4.

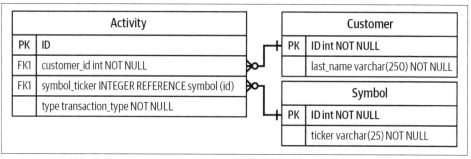

Figure 5-4. A trade activity represents a trade type made by a customer for a stock symbol

Back in your admin client CLI, you've already loaded the admin user by running the file *shell_scripts/load_db_admin_session.sh*. Enter the **psql** command to log in to your database, and issue the **SELECT CURRENT_ROLE;** statement to confirm that you are logged in as the `clusteradmin`. Your output should look like this:

```
[ssm-user@ip-10-0-0-45 ~]$ psql
psql (14.8, server 15.4)
WARNING: psql major version 14, server major version 15.
        Some psql features might not work.
SSL connection (protocol: TLSv1.2, cipher: AES128-SHA256, bits: 128,
    compression: off)
Type "help" for help.

trades=> SELECT CURRENT_ROLE;
 current_role
--------------
 clusteradmin
(1 row)

trades=>
```

After you have confirmed you are logged in to a `psql` session with the `clusteradmin` user, proceed to deploy your database schema by running the following code block from *src/trade-stock/sql_scripts/schema.sql* at the `trades=>` prompt of your `psql` session. Open the file, select all, copy, and then paste into your session:

```sql
CREATE TYPE trade_state AS ENUM ('submitted', 'pending', 'rejected', 'filled');
CREATE TYPE transaction_type AS ENUM ('buy', 'sell');

CREATE TABLE customer (
    id serial PRIMARY KEY,
    first_name VARCHAR ( 250 ) NOT NULL,
    last_name VARCHAR ( 250 ) NOT NULL,
    created_on TIMESTAMP DEFAULT CURRENT_TIMESTAMP NOT NULL,
    updated_on TIMESTAMP DEFAULT CURRENT_TIMESTAMP NOT NULL
);
CREATE TABLE symbol (
    id serial PRIMARY KEY,
    ticker VARCHAR ( 25 ) NOT NULL,
    open numeric NOT NULL CHECK (open > 0),
    high numeric NOT NULL CHECK (high > 0),
    low numeric NOT NULL CHECK (low > 0),
    close numeric NOT NULL CHECK (close > 0),
    volume integer NOT NULL CHECK (volume > 0),
    created_on TIMESTAMP DEFAULT CURRENT_TIMESTAMP NOT NULL,
    updated_on TIMESTAMP DEFAULT CURRENT_TIMESTAMP NOT NULL
);
CREATE TABLE activity (
    id serial PRIMARY KEY,
    request_id VARCHAR ( 40 ) UNIQUE NOT NULL,
    customer_id INTEGER REFERENCES customer (id),
    symbol_ticker INTEGER REFERENCES symbol (id),
    type transaction_type NOT NULL,
    current_price numeric NOT NULL CHECK (current_price > 0),
    share_count numeric NOT NULL CHECK (share_count > 0),
    status trade_state NOT NULL,
    created_on TIMESTAMP DEFAULT CURRENT_TIMESTAMP NOT NULL,
    updated_on TIMESTAMP DEFAULT CURRENT_TIMESTAMP NOT NULL
);

CREATE  FUNCTION update_updated_on()
RETURNS TRIGGER AS $$
BEGIN
    NEW.updated_on = now();
    RETURN NEW;
END;
$$ language plpgsql;

CREATE TRIGGER update_symbol_updated_on
    BEFORE UPDATE
    ON
        symbol
    FOR EACH ROW
EXECUTE PROCEDURE update_updated_on();
CREATE TRIGGER update_activity_updated_on
```

```
    BEFORE UPDATE
    ON
        activity
    FOR EACH ROW
EXECUTE PROCEDURE update_updated_on();
CREATE TRIGGER update_customer_updated_on
    BEFORE UPDATE
    ON
        customer
    FOR EACH ROW
EXECUTE PROCEDURE update_updated_on();
```

After your database objects have been created, you'll need to load two data files to see both the *customer* and *symbol* tables. In your project repository, you'll find two seed comma-separated values (CSV) files. You'll need to copy the contents of these files into files on your admin client before you can load them into the database with **psql**:

1. Type **\q** to quit your **psql** session.

2. Create a new directory for seed data with **mkdir ~/seed**.

3. Open a new file in edit mode by typing **vi ~/seed/stocks.csv** in your admin client terminal.

4. Type **i** once to enter edit mode, then paste the content of *AvailableTrade/src/ trade-stock/seed/stocks.csv* into the file.

5. Press the Esc key, type **:qw**, then press Enter to save the file.

6. Open another new file in edit mode by typing or pasting **vi ~/seed/custom ers.csv** in your admin client terminal.

7. Type **i** once to enter edit mode, then paste the content of *AvailableTrade/src/ trade-stock/seed/customer.csv* into the file.

8. Press the Esc key, type **:qw**, then press Enter to save the file.

Alternatively, you can upload the seed files to S3 through the S3 console and then use the AWS CLI to copy them from S3 into the *~/seed/* directory of your admin client. The upload shortcut requires some advanced AWS knowledge, as it will also require IAM changes. Explore this on your own.

Now, you're ready to load the files into the corresponding tables. Type **psql** to enter the database session and then copy and run the following commands from *src/trade-stock/sql_scripts/load_seed_data.sql*:

```
\COPY symbol(ticker,volume,open,close,high,low)
  FROM '~/seed/stocks.csv' DELIMITER ',' CSV HEADER;
\COPY customer(first_name,last_name)
  FROM '~/seed/customers.csv' DELIMITER ',' CSV HEADER;
```

Before jumping into the resilience lessons, you may want to take a few moments to get familiar with the dataset and tables. You can run some of these `psql` commands to explore the data:

- `\dt` describes the tables.
- `\du` or `\dg` describes user roles and grants.
- `select * from symbol limit 5;` returns five records from the table.
- `\q` quits and exits from a `psql` session.

In addition to the administrative database user created for the cluster, you'll need to create an application user named `order_api_user`. The AWS Secrets Manager has been configured with password rotation for the `order_api_user` but it cannot create the initial user, so you have to do it manually. The following block of commands from *src/trade-stock/shell_scripts/create_api_user.sh* will create your application user with the correct password and grants:

```
export API_SECRET_ID=$(aws ssm get-parameter --name trade_order_api_secret_id \
  --region us-east-1 | jq -r .Parameter.Value)
export API_SECRET=`aws secretsmanager get-secret-value \
  --secret-id $API_SECRET_ID --region us-east-1 | jq -r '.SecretString'`
export API_PASSWORD="`echo $API_SECRET | jq -r '.password'`"
export API_USER="`echo $API_SECRET | jq -r '.username'`"
psql -c "create user $API_USER with password '$API_PASSWORD';"
psql -c \
"grant select,insert,update,delete on all tables in schema public to $API_USER;"
psql -c \
"grant usage,select on all sequences in schema public to $API_USER;"
```

You can test the API user you just created with the following command block. Run the commands from *src/trade-stock/shell_scripts/load_db_order_api_session.sh*:

```
export API_SECRET_ID=$(aws ssm get-parameter --name trade_order_api_secret_id \
  --region us-east-1 | jq -r .Parameter.Value)
export API_SECRET=`aws secretsmanager get-secret-value \
  --secret-id $API_SECRET_ID --region us-east-1 | jq -r '.SecretString'`
export PGUSER="`echo $API_SECRET | jq -r '.username'`"
export PGPASSWORD="`echo $API_SECRET | jq -r '.password'`"
export PGHOST="`echo $API_SECRET | jq -r '.host'`"
export PGDATABASE="`echo $API_SECRET | jq -r '.dbname'`"
export PGPORT="`echo $API_SECRET | jq -r '.port'`"
psql -c "select version(),AURORA_VERSION();"
psql -c "select current_role;"
```

The final output of the commands will verify access for the `order_api_user`:

```
[ssm-user@ip-10-0-0-247 ~]$ psql -c "select current_role;"
  current_role
---------------
```

```
order_api_user
(1 row)
```

Now that the API user is verified, it's time to verify database connectivity from the Trade Stock API service.

You can interact with the Trade Stock API over HTTP using `curl` from the command line. You need the DNS endpoint of the Application Load Balancer which you can retrieve from the CDK or CloudFormation outputs, the EC2 Console, or the SSM parameter for the application. Examples in this chapter will pull values from the SSM Parameter Store when it's an option. Run the commands from *src/trade-stock/shell_scripts/curl_order_endpoint.sh* to query the *customer* table:

```
export ORDER_ENDPOINT=$(aws ssm get-parameter --name trade_order_endpoint \
  --region us-east-1 | jq -r .Parameter.Value)
curl $ORDER_ENDPOINT/db-health/
```

You should see a response like this:

```
{"created_on":"Mon, 01 Jan 2024 21:49:02 GMT","first_name":"kevin","id":4,
  "last_name":" schwarz","updated_on":"Mon, 01 Jan 2024 21:49:02 GMT"}
```

This response confirms that your service can access your database and return a record that you loaded from the *customers.csv* file. Your environment is set up correctly, and now you are ready to begin the resilience lessons.

Beware Expired Database Credentials

If it has been over a day since you created your Trade Stock API ECS service, the AWS Secrets Manager will have rotated the database password. This means that the cached value of the password in your container is wrong, and the service will return an HTTP 500 error with the message:

```
The server encountered an internal error and was unable
to complete your request. Either the server is overloaded
or there is an error in the application.
```

You see firsthand that your application requires some logic to handle password rotation gracefully.

To resolve this, implement the lessons as the ECS task will retrieve the updated password from the AWS Secrets Manager after deploying new service code updates. Or you can fix it immediately by navigating to the ECS console, the Order service, and then to Tasks. Select all the tasks and stop them, Fargate will spawn new tasks, and you can retest.

Container Deployment Failures

Before you work through the rest of these lessons, take a moment to understand how ECS handles container deployments. The CDK `DockerImageAsset` construct used in the `TradeOrderStack` and `TradeConfirmsStack` references a directory containing the assets for a container service, as shown below with the *order_api* path join to the current working directory. This construct builds your container image from the code in the *AvailableTrade/src/trade-stock/order_api* directory, tags and pushes the Docker image to ECR, and then provides the image to the `Container` construct where it's woven into your generated task definition:

```
trading_api_image = ecr.DockerImageAsset(self, 'order_api_image',
    directory=os.path.join(os.path.dirname('.'), 'order_api')
)
...
container = Container(cpu=256, memory_mib=512, traffic_port=80,
    image=ecs.ContainerImage.from_docker_image_asset(asset=trading_api_image)
)
```

These CDK constructs and the ECS Service extensions make it simple to configure and deploy containers on ECS. But debugging deployments can be confusing if ECS doesn't successfully start tasks from your image. Tasks can fail to start due to code with syntax issues, unresolved imports, *Dockerfile* mistakes, Gunicorn misconfigurations, or insufficient resources. Under these failure scenarios, CloudFormation will attempt to deploy your ECS service update and wait for a success from ECS. ECS will start tasks, which will fail health checks and be retried repeatedly. By default, CloudFormation will allow ECS to continue in this fashion until it times out, which can take up to three hours! This is a long time to wait to find out if your deployment failed.

To avoid this, open your ECS service by navigating to the ECS console, choosing Clusters, and selecting the Trade Stock service. On the bottom half of the screen, choose the service name. Under "Deployment configuration" in the "Deployment failure detection" section, enable "Use the Amazon ECS deployment circuit breaker" and enable "Rollback on failures," as shown in Figure 5-5.

Figure 5-5. On the update service console screen, enable deployment circuit breakers

Now, if you happen to deploy a container that is unable to start ECS tasks successfully, your CDK/CloudFormation deployment will be rolled back within a few minutes, saving you frustration, lost time, and confusion. You'll be notified of this error in the CDK CLI when you deploy, so you'll know you need to research the issue and redeploy quickly. You can research task failures in the application logs, as well as in the cluster tasks, by selecting stopped tasks and then drilling in for the launch failure reason. Deployment circuit breakers are important to build into your CI/CD pipelines to reduce your mean time to detect (MTTD) and mean time to recovery (MTTR) from deployment issues. Testing in lower environments should eliminate the types of issues that are addressed by deployment circuit breakers. But since they are low-effort failsafe, you should consider enabling them in production.

Database Connection Exhaustion

Applications use *connection pooling*, caches of database connections, to improve performance by reusing active connections instead of creating a new connection for each query. It has been a common practice in web and distributed application development to cache connection pools in local memory with database libraries. Connection pooling libraries allow developers to configure a maximum number of connections. It is important to have enough reusable connections to help an application perform well, but not so many that the available database sessions on the database server are exhausted or hinder the performance of the database. In this lesson, you will demonstrate the configuration failure mode of database connection exhaustion in an elastic compute environment, and then learn how to mitigate connection exhaustion. An additional configuration risk demonstrated in this lesson is relying on default settings.

Configuring a fixed number of connections per connection pool per application server is a reliable way to configure connection pools when running a workload in a static compute environment. However, the Trade Stock service runs on ECS Fargate, so it's an elastic compute service. It will scale the number of tasks in response to increased incoming traffic, therefore growing the number of connections and connection pools. When building database connections, the Trade Stock service is configured with the default number of connections for SQLAlchemy, which is 5. Each running ECS task in the Trade Stock service will cache the default of five connections.

Let's run some traffic against the Trade Stock service to see how it performs:

```
export ORDER_ENDPOINT=$(aws ssm get-parameter --name trade_order_endpoint \
--region us-east-1 | jq -r .Parameter.Value)
for i in {1..100}; do   time curl $ORDER_ENDPOINT/db-health/; done
```

You'll notice that the first time an ECS task responds to the db-health request, it can take from 0.100 to 0.500 seconds to respond. This is the cold start of the task initializing any resources and opening connections to the database. Once the task has warmed up, responses are typically 0.050 seconds or less, and on my installation, average about 0.020 seconds, well within the 200 ms SLA defined by our brokerage business partners.

A steady load of heavy traffic will cause ECS to create new tasks, putting more demand on the database as new connection pools are created with each new task. Run the following command to issue 100 requests per second indefinitely:

```
watch -n .01 curl $ORDER_ENDPOINT/db-health/
```

Next, let's mimic some employees connecting to the database to do research. With the watch command still running 100 requests per second, open 5–10 separate admin client Session Manager terminals and connect to psql with the admin user in each of them; each will consume a DB writer instance connection. If you check the TradeStockDashboard in CloudWatch, you should see that your Stock Cluster DB Connections have risen from the default of 8, 2 per instance, to about 14.

You are looking for the count of the TradeOrderConnectionExhaustion metric to appear. To see how you are tracking this metric, reference the *trade_order_stack.py* file where a metric filter is applied over the Trade Stock API logs. You can also use the CloudWatch tailing feature to see this error in near real time:

```
logs.MetricFilter(self, "TradeOrderConnectionExhaustion",
    log_group=container.log_group,
    metric_name="OrderApiConnectionExhaustion",
    metric_namespace="TradeOrder",
    metric_value="1",
    unit=cloudwatch.Unit.COUNT,
    filter_pattern=logs.FilterPattern.string_value(
        json_field="$.exec_info", comparison="=",
        value="*remaining connection slots are reserved*"),
    dimensions={"AvailabilityZone": "$.az"}
)
```

The pattern for the metric filter matches the text remaining connection slots are reserved from the exception that is thrown once connections are exhausted:

```
psycopg2.OperationalError: connection to server at
    "stock.cluster-cce5qkaoru9j.us-east-1.rds.amazonaws.com" (10.0.2.230),
    port 5432 failed: FATAL:  remaining connection slots are reserved for
    non-replication superuser and rds_superuser connections
```

You need more traffic to exhaust connections, so you'll start a load test to simulate more user traffic on your application. To speed up the occurrence of `OrderApiConnectionExhaustion`, you can open more `psql` terminals after you start the test. Change to the *tests* subdirectory on your local terminal; you should already be in *AvailableTrade/src/trade* after you deploy the CDK. Now, run the test client for `--test 1` like this:

```
cd AvailableTrade/src/trade-stock/tests
python trade_stock_test_client.py --test 1
```

Artillery will start up traffic that can run for about 30 minutes, allowing ECS time to scale out tasks and consume more DB connections. Once you start seeing `Order ApiConnectionExhaustion` errors, you can use Ctrl + C or Cmd + C to exit. This can take some time depending on your machine, and how many `psql` sessions you opened from the admin client. Once you are seeing errors, your `TradeStockDashboard` should look similar to Figure 5-6.

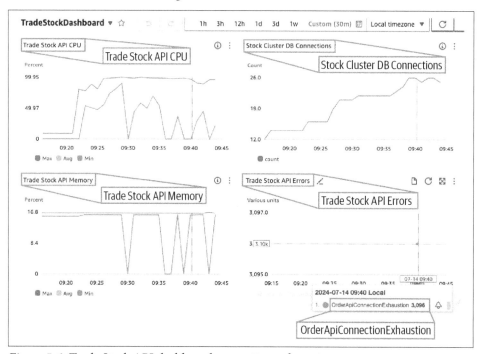

Figure 5-6. Trade Stock API dashboard connection exhaustion

If you look at the built-in RDS metrics for the `Stock` database cluster, you can see connection details by instance, as shown in Figure 5-7.

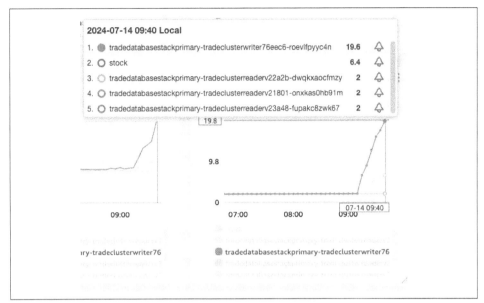

Figure 5-7. Trade Stock DB cluster connections by instance

There are multiple ways to help mitigate the DB connection exhaustion failure mode. You'll see how to implement each of them, but in your real application test them out and make sure the ones you choose are appropriate for your use case. First, use the Aurora PostgreSQL `max_connection` defaults, which use the formula LEAST({DBInstanceClassMemory/9531392},5000) allowing connections to scale with the database ACUs and memory. In your current deployment, `max_connection` were set to 28 to demonstrate connection exhaustion with minimal traffic. Open the file *AvailableTrade/src/trade-stock/trade_stock/trade_database.py* and modify the `DatabaseCluster` in `TradeOrderStack` by commenting out the line `parameter_group=parameter_group` to allow Aurora serverless to apply default connection scaling.

After commenting out the `parameter_group`, your code should look like this:

```
self.cluster = rds.DatabaseCluster(self, "TradeCluster",
    engine=rds.DatabaseClusterEngine.aurora_postgres(
        version=rds.AuroraPostgresEngineVersion.VER_16_2),
    credentials=rds.Credentials.from_generated_secret(cluster_admin),
    writer=writer,
    readers=readers,
    serverless_v2_min_capacity=0.5, serverless_v2_max_capacity=2,
    storage_type=rds.DBClusterStorageType.AURORA_IOPT1,
    storage_encrypted=False,
    vpc_subnets=ec2.SubnetSelection(subnet_type=ec2.SubnetType.PRIVATE_ISOLATED),
    vpc=vpc, default_database_name=database_name, cluster_identifier='stock',
    backup=rds.BackupProps(retention=cdk.Duration.days(15)),
    #parameter_group=parameter_group, # use default parameter group
```

```
                preferred_maintenance_window="Sun:23:45-Mon:00:15",
                cloudwatch_logs_exports=["postgresql"],
                cloudwatch_logs_retention=cdk.aws_logs.RetentionDays.TWO_WEEKS)
```

Next, take advantage of reader instances. You can see from Figure 5-7 that all traffic is directed to the writer, and it has 20 connections while other instances only have 2. Anytime you are performing a read-only operation, you can take advantage of dedicated read-only connections. The Aurora read-only endpoint load balances across reader instances; this spreads utilization across instances, preserves writer capacity for write-specific operations. Open the file *AvailableTrade/src/trade-stock/order_api/order_api.py* and replace db_engine with ro_db_engine. After the change, your code should look like this:

```
@app.route("/db-health/", methods=["GET"])
# @connection_aware
def db_health():
    with Session(ro_db_engine) as session:
        statement = select(Customer).where(Customer.first_name == "kevin")
        customer = session.scalars(statement).one()
    logger.info("Here's your customer: {}".format(customer.as_dict()), extra=d)
    return customer.as_dict()
```

In addition, you can also use the AWS RDS Proxy, or another distributed proxy. For workloads that run on serverless or container platforms that dynamically scale with utilization, it's beneficial to use a distributed connection pool. The Trade Stock containers will build connections directly to the proxy, which will manage a centralized connection pool shard across any number of tasks.

The RDS Proxy has already been created for the Trade Stock service, but it's not currently being taken advantage of. You'll need to make an update to the service code and redeploy the API to use the proxy.

In the file *AvailableTrade/src/trade-stock/order_api/order_api.py*, locate these lines within the load_db_engine and load_ro_db_engine functions:

```
def load_db_engine() -> None:
    """Load and cache read-write SQLAlchemy database connection.
        Refreshes credentials on each invocation."""
    global db_engine
    secret = json.loads(get_db_credentials_from_cache())
    host_ = secret['host']

    ...

def load_ro_db_engine() -> None:
    """Load and cache read-only SQLAlchemy database connection.
        Refreshes credentials on each invocation."""
    global ro_db_engine
    secret = json.loads(get_db_credentials_from_cache())
    host_ = secret['host'].replace("stock.cluster", "stock.cluster-ro")
```

Update the assignment of the host_ variables so that they are no longer referencing the host from the secret, but instead assign them to the appropriate rds_proxy_end point and rds_ro_proxy_endpoint values. Now redeploy the Trade Stock API with **cdk deploy TradeOrderStack** to route connections through the RDS Proxy instead of connecting directly to the database. Your updated code should look like the following before you deploy:

```
def load_db_engine() -> None:
    """Load and cache read-write SQLAlchemy database connection.
       Refreshes credentials on each invocation."""
    global db_engine
    secret = json.loads(get_db_credentials_from_cache())
    host_ = rds_proxy_endpoint

...

def load_ro_db_engine() -> None:
    """Load and cache read-only SQLAlchemy database connection.
       Refreshes credentials on each invocation."""
    global ro_db_engine
    secret = json.loads(get_db_credentials_from_cache())
    host_ = rds_ro_proxy_endpoint
```

Once you've made your changes, redeploy the Trade Stock service and your database with the command **cdk deploy TradeDatabaseStackPrimary TradeOrderStackPri mary**, and rerun the test. No matter how much load you put on the Trade Stock service, the RDS Proxy will not open more connections than the configured proxy maximum. You can see in the trade database stack that the max is 95% of the available connections configured with max_connections_percent=95 on the clus ter.add_proxy composition:

```
proxy = cluster.add_proxy("proxy",
    borrow_timeout=cdk.Duration.seconds(30),
    max_connections_percent=95,
    secrets=[order_api_secret],
    vpc=vpc
)
```

The flip side of this is if your max is too low, your available connections may not be enough. Since the RDS Proxy limits total open connections, your database won't be overloaded, but if your load is high enough, your compute could be starved, causing latency. Always measure with metrics, set alarms, and adjust your capacity to handle your demand.

Database Password Rotation Login Failures

It is no secret, pun intended, that modern applications should leverage a *secrets management* solution to control access to database credentials as a best practice. Unauthorized access to a database can lead to data exfiltration, or theft, of sensitive data. Destruction or manipulation of data can cause user-specific impairments, or even a system-wide failure. The Trade Stock API uses AWS Secrets Manager to manage database passwords for both the `clusteradmin` administrative user, who has data definition language (DDL) and data modification language (DML) privileges, and the `order_api_user`, who only has DML privileges. The `clusteradmin` manages the schema and loads reference data from the admin client, and the `order_api_user` modifies data to service customer requests from ECS.

In addition to safely storing database passwords, you should employ a password rotation strategy so that if a database password is compromised, it is automatically changed regularly. The AWS Secrets Manager supports user password rotation; in this lesson you'll learn how to apply the multiuser rotation strategy.

In addition, to avoid making a call to Secrets Manager each time the Trade Stock service needs to establish a new database connection, you'll implement the Secret Cache. This open source cache improves your service latency because retrieval is faster from a local cache, avoids unnecessary I/O, and improves availability by turning a hard dependency into a soft dependency. A hard dependency is one where your workload cannot function when it isn't available. If the AWS Secrets Manager experiences an availability issue in your region, your service won't be able to make a new database connection. Caching your secret creates a soft dependency, allowing the Trade Stock service to tolerate some unavailability of the AWS Secrets Manager.

> You can learn more about the Python Secrets Cache and how it works in the Secrets Manager documentation (*https://oreil.ly/_aLju*). You can learn more about availability with dependencies in the "Availability With Dependencies" section of the AWS white-paper "Availability and Beyond: Understanding and Improving the Resilience of Distributed Systems on AWS" (*https://oreil.ly/gAAlZ*).

Let's review password configuration strategies, exercise a few secret rotations, observe a database connection failure, and then explore how your application can best handle secret rotation. When a Trade Stock service task creates a database connection, it calls the `get_db_credentials_from_cache` function which uses lazily loaded `secrets_cache`:

```
def get_db_credentials_from_cache() -> str:
    global secrets_cache, secret_id
    try:
        if secrets_cache is None:
```

```
        boto_session = boto3.session.Session()
        secrets_client = boto_session.client("secretsmanager")
        cache_config = SecretCacheConfig(
            max_cache_size=5,
            secret_refresh_interval=300
        )
        secrets_cache = SecretCache(
            config=cache_config,
            client=secrets_client
        )
    except ClientError as e:
        raise e

    return secrets_cache.get_secret_string(secret_id=secret_id)
```

In the TradeDatabaseStack, the order_api_user_name secret is configured with a multiuser rotation strategy. Note that the administrative user for the cluster uses single user rotation, since you only access it from the admin client. Both are rotated daily:

```
cluster.add_rotation_single_user(automatically_after=cdk.Duration.days(1))
cluster.add_rotation_multi_user(order_api_user_name,
    automatically_after=cdk.Duration.days(1),
    secret=order_api_secret
)
```

A multiuser rotation strategy preserves the credentials of the currently connected database user by managing two database users, order_api_user and order_api_user_clone. Refer to Figure 5-8 where you can see that the secret trade_order_api_secret_id has two labeled versions, AWSCURRENT and AWSPREVIOUS, and those are mapped to these two users. The secrets_cache will by default always fetch the AWSCURRENT version of a secret. Your application will store a cached username with its current password.

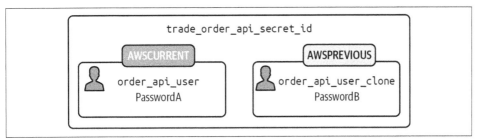

Figure 5-8. Multiuser rotation strategies rely on labeled secret versions

When the database secret is rotated, the order_api_user version label is updated to AWSPREVIOUS and retains the cached and in-use PasswordA for the order_api_user. The order_api_user_clone version becomes AWSCURRENT and its password changes, rotating `PasswordB` to `PasswordC`, as illustrated in Figure 5-9. A new secret fetch would retrieve the clone.

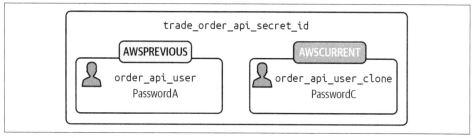

Figure 5-9. The clone user is now the AWSCURRENT secret value, with a new password

The next rotation will again swap secret version labels, this time updating the password of the `order_api_user` to `PasswordD`. It is as this point where your code can no longer rely on the cached value of `PasswordA`, and you would experience database connection failures (Figure 5-10).

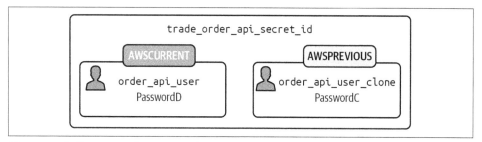

Figure 5-10. On a second rotation, the `order_api_user` again becomes AWSCURRENT, with a new password

When a database connection attempt fails, you can observe it in the OrderApi-logs as `psycopg2.OperationalError FATAL` errors from the psycopg2 Python-PostgreSQL database adapter. You'd find log entries like this:

```
ERROR:root:(psycopg2.OperationalError) connection to server at
    "stock.cluster-cce5qkaoru9j.us-east-1.rds.amazonaws.com" (10.0.2.230),
    port 5432 failed: FATAL:  password authentication failed for user
    "order_api_user_clone"
```

Let's test this out. In the CloudWatch Console, navigate to Live Tail. Choose OrderApi-logs for log groups and enter **ERROR** in all caps for the filter pattern, as shown in Figure 5-11. Choose "Apply filters" and leave the live tail running for the remainder of this lesson.

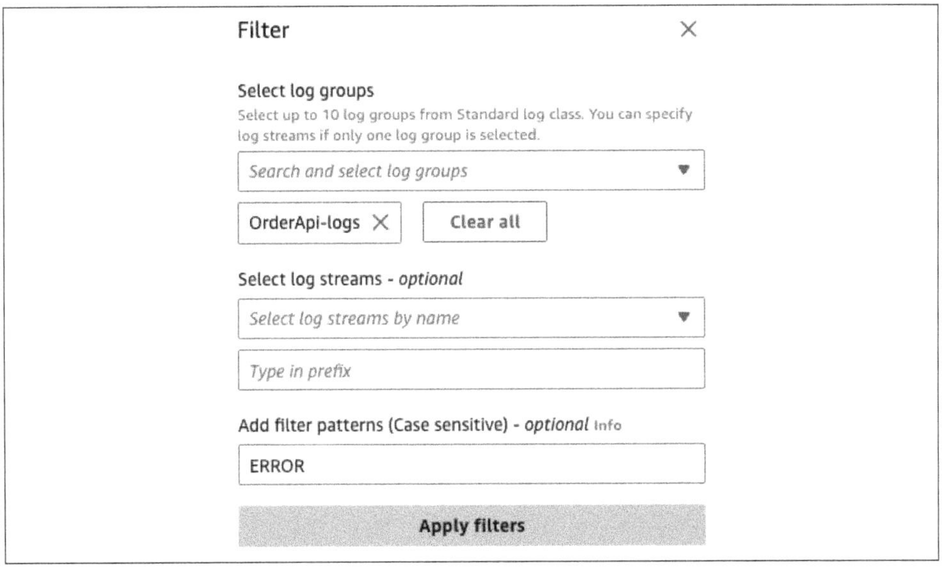

Figure 5-11. Configure and start a live tail to display any errors from the Trade Stock service

Note that you can run the following CloudWatch Logs Insights query to research historical errors in the OrderApi-logs log group:

```
fields @message
| filter @message like /ERROR/
```

With your live tail running, issue the following `watch` command against the order endpoint to check service connectivity to the database 10 times per second. You will see JSON responses containing data from a *customer* record streaming in your console. Open your admin client Session Manager terminal and run this:

```
export ORDER_ENDPOINT=$(aws ssm get-parameter --name trade_order_endpoint \
    --region us-east-1 | jq -r .Parameter.Value)
watch -n .1 curl $ORDER_ENDPOINT/db-health/
```

Now you'll rotate the `order_api_db_secret` while your `curl` command continues to issue requests to the service and process database queries. Navigate to the AWS Secrets Manager console and choose the secret named `order_api_db_secret`. Halfway down the page, select the Rotation tab, and then choose "Rotate secret immediately." You'll see a message stating that your secret has been scheduled for rotation, which only takes a few seconds (Figure 5-12).

Figure 5-12. Rotate the `order_api_db_secret` *to rotate the* `order_api_user` *database password*

You should not see any errors in your live tail. That's great; the multiuser rotation strategy worked. You've maintained availability through password rotation without impacting your running ECS tasks.

Rotate the secret again, using the same steps you just used for the first rotation. With your `curl` command still running in a loop, check your live tail. Now you will start to see `psycopg2.OperationalError` errors. The failure occurs as you predicted in your resilience analysis because your ECS task still has a cached set of credentials for the `order_api_user`. With the second rotation you rotated this password, but your code didn't refresh its cache.

While you've made the AWS Secrets Manager into a soft dependency, the Trade Stock service has a hard dependency on its database. Let's implement self-healing logic for ECS tasks that remain running for two consecutive secret rotations. Open the Trade Stock API service in the file *AvailableTrade/src/trade-stock/order_api/ order_api.py*. When a SQLAlchemy database engine connection is needed, the service calls `load_db_engine()` or `ro_load_db_engine()`. These functions subsequently call `get_db_credentials_from_cache()` which uses the `secret_cache` to fetch the AWS CURRENT value of the Trade Stock API database user's password. Then SQLAlchemy database `Engine` objects are reused across transactions to create sessions and perform database operations.

Once you rotated your secret the second time, your database connection was still using cached credentials for the `order_api_user` with `PasswordA` instead of `Pass wordD`. Your cache needs to be refreshed on connection failure to pick up `PasswordD`. A simple way to self-heal is to build retry logic into a utility function with a Python decorator. A decorator function has already been coded into the Trade Stock API, so you only need to decorate `db_health()`.

The following `connection_aware(func)` function is a Python `wrapper` function that decorates and accepts another function as an argument. A decorator is a software design pattern supported natively by Python that adds extra logic to a function without altering the existing implementation. Within the wrapper, the passed-in function is executed within a `try` clause, so if it throws an `OperationalError` indicating a possible password authentication issue, it has one chance to self-heal. This allows for refreshing changed passwords, stale database connections, or even a change in database endpoint if needed.

In the `except` block, the `load_ro_db_engine()` and `load_db_engine()` are invoked to refresh the secret for the Trade Stock API DB user, leveraging the `SecretsCache` built-in capability. Once the secret is refreshed, the database connection is also refreshed. Finally, the wrapped function is invoked again, this time with the newly created password, so the SQL operation succeeds. Note that this same pattern applies to both the read-write and read-only engines. If the second wrapped function invocation fails, something more critical than a password rotation occurred and processing stops:

```python
def connection_aware(func):
    """A decorator to refresh database connections if queries fail due to
    state credentials after rotation indicated by a
    sqlalchemy.exc.OperationalError wrapping a psycopg2.OperationalError"""

    @functools.wraps(func)
    def wrapper(*args, **kwargs):
        try:
            return func(*args, **kwargs)
        except exc.OperationalError as e:
            logging.exception("db credentials reloaded, retrying", e)
            load_db_engine()
            load_ro_db_engine()
            return func(*args, **kwargs)

    return wrapper
```

To test this out, you only need to uncomment the `@connection_aware` decorator on your */db-health/* endpoint, and then redeploy the Trade Stock API service. Once you've enabled the decorator and saved your changes so your function looks like the following code snippet, redeploy the Trade Stock service by running **cdk deploy TradeOrderService**:

```python
@app.route("/db-health/", methods=["GET"])
@connection_aware
def db_health():
    ...
```

After the deployment is complete, clear the output in your CloudWatch live tail, which should still be running. Your `curl` loop should also still be running in your Systems Manager console, producing steady traffic. If you closed out of either of these, go back and start them again with the steps described previously. With the live tail running and traffic on your service, rotate the Trade Stock API secret two times in a row. You'll see three errors in the live tail or one error per running ECS task for the Trade Stock service. Now, when database authentication errors are thrown, your service self-heals. For any running tasks, the decorator caught the exception, rebuilt the database connection, and reran your query. The end client calling your service experienced a minor increase in latency while connections refreshed, but still received a successful response.

Up until now, we've been in the AWS console, actively watching our logs. Live tails are great for development and testing exercises like you just performed, but you also need headless observability. A CloudWatch metric has been configured to observe database login failures. In the `TradeOrder` stack, you'll see the following code which creates a metric filter applied to a log group, which produces the metric `TradeOrder.OrderApiDbAuthFailure`:

```
logs.MetricFilter(self, "TradeOrderDBAuthFailure",
    log_group=container.log_group,
    metric_name="OrderApiDbAuthFailure",
    metric_namespace="TradeOrder",
    metric_value="1",
    unit=cloudwatch.Unit.COUNT,
    filter_pattern=logs.FilterPattern.string_value(
        json_field="$.exc_info", comparison="=",
            value="*password authentication failed*"),
    dimensions={"AvailabilityZone": "$.az"}
)
```

You can see the metric value in the CloudWatch console by navigating to All Metrics, selecting the `TradeOrder` namespace, "Metrics with no dimensions," and selecting `OrderApiDbAuthFailure`. It is a good idea to set up a metric alarm to notify your support team any time that a database authentication error is thrown, even though we expect our solution to self-heal. The alarm could indicate an issue with rotations happening more frequently than expected, or some other issue where passwords are not working. You'll want to alarm on repeated password failures when your service isn't able to self-heal and you need to take further actions.

Database Primary Writer Failures

Like the fault injection built into the Trade Confirms service for chaos testing, Aurora PostgreSQL also has built-in fault injection for testing. You can test the regional fault tolerance of Aurora PostgreSQL instances by issuing fault injection queries that call special Aurora PostgreSQL built-in functions. At the time of this writing, supported faults include instance crashes, replica failure, disk failure, and disk congestion. You can use these to test how your application and database cluster handle unexpected database failures.

Start up a Session Manager terminal session on your admin client and load the credentials for an admin session:

```
export ADMIN_SECRET_ID=$(aws ssm get-parameter --name trade_db_secret_id \
  --region us-east-1 | jq -r .Parameter.Value)
export ADMIN_SECRET=`aws secretsmanager get-secret-value \
  --secret-id $ADMIN_SECRET_ID --region us-east-1 | jq -r '.SecretString'`
export PGUSER="`echo $ADMIN_SECRET | jq -r '.username'`"
export PGPASSWORD="`echo $ADMIN_SECRET | jq -r '.password'`"
export PGHOST="`echo $ADMIN_SECRET | jq -r '.host'`"
export PGDATABASE="`echo $ADMIN_SECRET | jq -r '.dbname'`"
export PGPORT="`echo $ADMIN_SECRET | jq -r '.port'`"
psql -c "select version(),AURORA_VERSION();"
psql
```

Enter psql and issue the SQL query **SELECT aurora_inject_crash ('instance');** and notice that your session crashes. If you quit your client and try to connect again immediately, you will see that the endpoint is unavailable, and you cannot connect right away:

```
trades=> SELECT aurora_inject_crash ('node');
WARNING:  terminating connection because of crash of another server process
DETAIL:  The postmaster has commanded this server process to roll back the
    current transaction and exit, because another server process exited
    abnormally and possibly corrupted shared memory.
HINT:  In a moment you should be able to reconnect to the database and repeat
    your command.
SSL SYSCALL error: EOF detected
The connection to the server was lost. Attempting reset: Failed.
```

If you investigate or tail your PostgreSQL logs in the CloudWatch log group */aws/rds/cluster/stock/postgresql* during the fault injection, you'll find more insight into what happened. Additionally, you can identify log lines you might want to monitor with metric filters, for example, FATAL. Here is an excerpt from the logs that shows the error at the time of the fault-induced crash as well as when the system was back online, 23 seconds later:

```
14:10:54 UTC:10.0.0.45(43662):clusteradmin@trades:[623]:LOG:
    Simulating DB Instance node crash
14:10:54 UTC:10.0.0.45(43662):clusteradmin@trades:[623]:STATEMENT:
```

```
    select aurora_inject_crash('node');
14:10:54 UTC::@:[550]:LOG: Aurora Runtime process (PID 557)
    exited with exit code 1
14:10:54 UTC::@:[550]:LOG: terminating any other active server
14:10:54 UTC::@:[550]:FATAL: Can't handle storage runtime process crash
14:10:54 UTC::@:[550]:LOG: database system is shut down
...
14:11:17 UTC::@:[537]:LOG: database system is ready to accept connections
```

After the database is back online, you will be able to connect again. Aurora created a new instance, and did not failover to another instance. The RDS Proxy attempts to queue up requests to provide the highest possible application availability during the write availability interruption.

In the case of a real issue, you could take advantage of Aurora managed failover. Failover will promote an existing writer instance to a reader, effectively moving the writer to a healthy node. This might be useful if you are observing zonal issues, and you need to evacuate an Availability Zone, or if something is wrong with the underlying hardware. You can initiate a failover with your cluster in the AWS console, as shown in Figure 5-13, or with the CLI command:

```
aws rds failover-db-cluster --db-cluster-identifier stock --region us-east-1
```

Figure 5-13. Using the RDS console to initiate an HA failover

To learn more, review the Amazon Aurora Labs for PostgreSQL workshop (*https://oreil.ly/haYUv*), specifically the sections on high availability and durability.

You can take what you've learned so far to create your own test by using some of the watch commands we've discussed that run steady traffic on your service while you initiate a failover. You can reverse your code changes that enabled the use of the RDS Proxy. This way, you can measure the outage window when the application needs to refresh stale connections to the writer with and without the RDS Proxy in place.

In this lesson, you learned to test the Aurora PostgreSQL database automatic recovery and failover. Other AWS databases have different mechanisms for failover and recovery. If you are using another database, refer to the documentation to understand the mechanics of failover or recovery from a node or instance crash.

Dependency Intermittent Failures

Sometimes requests fail, but those failures are intermittent and don't recur consecutively for every request. Retries are a resilience design pattern that you can apply around calls to external dependencies. They help services successfully complete transactions when processing is interrupted by intermittent errors. Some examples of intermittent errors that cause failure include network blips due to packets dropped from a bad switch, timeouts on latency-sensitive transactions due to remote cold starts, or temporarily saturated resources. There are a variety of other reasons intermittent failures can happen, and regardless of the reasons, we want our systems to tolerate the failure and process the request, if possible.

The Trade Stock service is configured with a 50 millisecond timeout threshold for calls to the Trade Confirms service. If the Trade Confirms service throws an error, or takes longer than 50 milliseconds, the trade transaction will fail, return an error, and publish an increment to the OrderProcessingFailed metric.

AWS builds services with retry capabilities for the CLI, SDKs, and many under-the-hood components. To ensure optimal behavior of retries, AWS APIs also include exponential backoff, jitter, and a max retry value. An exponential backoff algorithm gradually decreases the rate of retries both to avoid overloading an impaired remote service, and to allow for recovery time between invocations. Implementing retries without jitter can result in many clients calling a service at the time of an interruption and then synchronizing spikes of retries. This results in bursts of synchronized traffic to impaired resources, which could further degrade the likelihood of a successful recovery and response. Jitter provides variation in the time delay between retries. This helps spread out requests across clients to avoid patterns of spiking retries to improve the chance of successful calls.

You can read more about retries with exponential backoff and jitter in the AWS Well-Architected best practice "REL05-BP03 Control and Limit Retry Calls" (*https://oreil.ly/wwl89*), and Mark Brooker's "Exponential Backoff And Jitter" AWS blog post (*https://oreil.ly/K8sHQ*). Mark explains the pattern with illustrations for clarity.

To resilience test an intermittent failure, a parameter-controlled fault is built into the Trade Confirms API. Remember that the Trade Confirms API is a mock or a third-party service you would consider as a black box. Coding a fault into production code is not advised, but is convenient in a mock scenario. The parameter `trade_con firms_glitch_factor` allows you to toggle the fault "ON" and "OFF". While processing incoming requests, an error is thrown any time the request count is divisible by three with no remainder using the modulo operator, as follows. In other words, every third request will fail:

```
if get_exchange_glitch_factor(count) == "ON" and count % 3 == 0:
    logger.error("glitch_factor is: {}".format(glitch_factor), extra=d)
    raise RuntimeError("Unexpected glitch, please try again...")
```

The Trade Confirms service will only refresh chaos parameters every 10 requests per ECS task. To quickly test this, it's best to run requests in a continuous loop, forcing a refresh. The Trade Confirms service was deployed with the simulated network glitch fault turned off; turn it on to observe the behavior. Run the following commands to both turn on glitching and send continuous traffic:

```
aws ssm put-parameter --name "trade_confirms_glitch_factor" \
--type "String" --value "ON" --overwrite --region "us-east-1"

bash
cd ~
export ORDER_ENDPOINT=$(aws ssm get-parameter --name trade_order_endpoint \
  --region us-east-1 | jq -r .Parameter.Value)

cat <<'EOF' > trade.sh
curl \
--request POST \
--header "Content-Type: application/json" \
--data '{"request_id": "'$(uuidgen)'", "customer_id": "4", "ticker": "IPAY",
 "transaction_type": "buy", "current_price": 40.06,
 "share_count": '$RANDOM'}' \
$ORDER_ENDPOINT/trade/
EOF

chmod u+x trade.sh
watch -d -n 1 ./trade.sh
```

You'll see a response with your confirmed trade data. You can also query PostgreSQL to see your results with **psql -c "select * from activity;"**. Be sure you have loaded database credentials before trying to run a query. If you see records in the `trades.activity` table, Trade Stock order requests are being serviced successfully, and based on `activity.status`, you can tell if they are being "filled" or "rejected".

Take a look at the CloudWatch metrics under All → TradeOrder → AvailabilityZone as this command continues to run. You'll see metrics for `TradeOrderRequested`, `TradeOrderFilled`, and `TradeOrderRejected`. This provides the business metric for trade orders you can use as service-level indicators to ensure you are meeting your SLA, as shown in Figure 5-14.

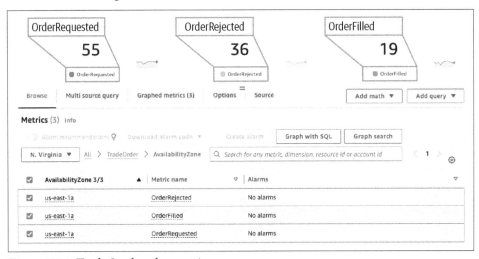

Figure 5-14. Trade Stock order metrics

You will see some rejects by design; these are because the randomly generated `share_count` value will sometimes result in a total purchase price exceeding the customer's currently available balance. The balance is also randomly generated between $5,000 and $1,000,000 on each trade order request:

```
balance = float(random.randrange(5000, 1000000))
```

Rejects do not constitute an SLA breach; rejecting a trade is valid. If the total `TradeOrderRequested` for an Availability Zone is higher than the sum of the `Trade OrderFilled` and `TradeOrderRejected`, then there is likely an issue. Or if 100% of `TradeOrderRequested` are `TradeOrderRejected`, you might trigger an SLA breaching alarm. The important concept is to think about your business case, track your SLAs with metrics, and alarm on outliers or anomalies.

As you watch the Trade Stock order output, the first 30 or so requests will have succeeded without issue. You have three tasks running load balanced traffic. Each of them needs to process 10 requests before refreshing the cached glitch value, and once the glitch is "ON", you'll start to see errors.

Now you are ready to configure retries into the Trade Stock service and redeploy it. Once again, open the file *src/trade-stock/order_api/order_api.py* where you'll make your changes. You'll use an open source library to avoid having to write a custom implementation. The `retry` library (*https://pypi.org/project/retry*) offers a simple implementation that supports both exponential backoff and jitter.

Find the following line within the `trade` flask handler function where `execute_trade` is called off the Trade Stock service. You can leave the `@circuit` decorator from the prior lesson in place on the `execute_trade` function. The retry and circuit breaker patterns work together for an optimal solution that retries to recover from gray failures but opens a circuit for persistent failures:

```
result = execute_trade(activity.as_dict())
```

Once you've located this line, replace it with the following `retry_call` function:

```
result = retry_call(execute_trade, fargs=[activity_record.as_dict()],
    fkwargs={"info": "ip"}, tries=3, backoff=0.2, jitter=0.5
)
```

Now save your file and redeploy the Trade Stock service with the following command:

```
cdk deploy TradeOrderService
```

If the `watch curl` command is still running after your code updates are deployed, you'll notice that trade orders stop failing once the new code is deployed. The retry is working! At this point, you can choose to leave the glitch on as your service handles it, or turn it off. You can use the following command to turn intermittent glitching off:

```
aws ssm put-parameter --name "trade_confirms_glitch_factor" \
--type "String" --value "OFF" --overwrite --region "us-east-1"
```

Detecting and Handling Availability Zone Issues

In Chapter 1, you learned that the AWS Availability Zones (AZs) within an AWS Region create fault isolation boundaries. You leverage AZs to increase your availability when you deploy your resources across two or more AZs. If one or more AWS services are impaired in a single AZ, the remaining AZs can continue to serve your application. Some AWS services handle AZ impairments by automatically evacuating the zone; while in other scenarios, the choices you make allow you to make zonal shift decisions.

To understand when to perform a zonal shift, you need to understand the zonal health of your workload. You may have noticed by now that all the metrics in this chapter include an AZ dimension. You'll use this dimension to understand zonal health.

Availability Zone impairments can have several root causes, including configuration issues, AWS service or network issues, or physical issues like power outages or damage to data centers. Regardless of the cause, if the expected service level of an Availability Zone signals workload degradation through your metrics, you are at risk of breaching your SLA. The technique to deal with a zonal impairment is called a zonal shift, where you temporarily exclude processing work in an impaired AZ.

Now, you'll use the AWS Fault Injection Service (FIS) to impair a single AZ and observe. Remember that Availability Zones are fault isolation boundaries, so an issue in one AZ within a region does not affect other AZs or network connectivity within the region. See Figure 5-15 for a visual explanation of an AWS Region.

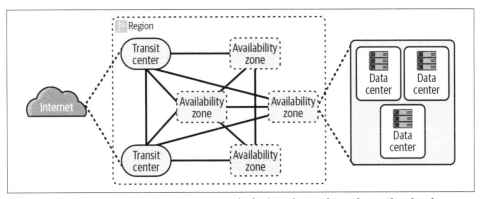

Figure 5-15. AWS Availability Zones provide fault isolation boundaries for cloud workloads

You will build your first resilience experiment in the AWS FIS console. You'll be simulating a network interruption impacting a single subnet of the Trade Stock VPC. Navigate to the FIS Console, choose "Experiment templates," and choose "Create experiment template." If you are prompted to select your current account, or multiple accounts, select your current account. Specify the following:

- For Name and Description, use the value "Trade Stock VPC subnet network disruption."
- Add an action named "TradeStock_subnet_network_disruption."
- For action type, select NETWORK and aws:network:disrupt-connectivity.
- Accept the default Target Subnets-Target-1, set the Duration to 5 minutes, and select availability-zone for the scope.

Once you've created your target, click on your resource and choose one of your TradeVpcStackPrimary subnets, but be sure not to select the same subnet that your admin client runs in. Otherwise, you won't be able to generate traffic during the disruption.

- In the Logs section, choose "Send to CloudWatch Logs"; you'll need to create a CloudWatch log group, something like TradeStockFIS, and provide the ARN.
- In the Service access section, choose "Create a new role for the experiment template."
- Choose "Create experiment template."

Your completed experiment template should look similar to Figure 5-16.

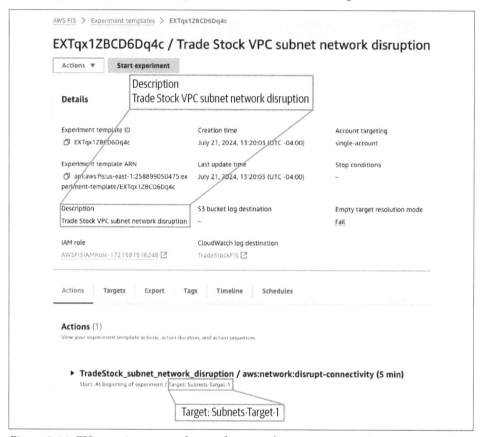

Figure 5-16. FIS experiment template to disrupt subnet connectivity impacting a single AZ

Now start generating Trade Stock traffic by opening your admin client Session Manager and running this script:

```bash
cd ~
export ORDER_ENDPOINT=$(aws ssm get-parameter --name trade_order_endpoint \
  --region us-east-1 | jq -r .Parameter.Value)
```

```
cat <<'EOF' > trade.sh
curl \
--request POST \
--header "Content-Type: application/json" \
--data '{"request_id": "'$(uuidgen)'", "customer_id": "4", "ticker": "IPAY",
 "transaction_type": "buy", "current_price": 40.06,
 "share_count": '$RANDOM'}' \
$ORDER_ENDPOINT/trade/
EOF

chmod u+x trade.sh
watch -d -n 1 ./trade.sh
```

Once you have traffic flowing, you will start your experiment. Choose "Start experiment" and complete the prompts. If your CloudWatch live tail on your OrderApi-Logs filtered on "ERROR", you'll see exceptions indicating that your Trade Stock service cannot access the Trade Confirms service before timing out:

```
ReadTimeoutError: HTTPConnectionPool(host=
    'internal-tradec-confi-xdv0vpjc6zaz-1232154034.us-east-1.elb.amazonaws.com',
    port=80): Read timed out.
```

Problems processing trades can be observed by monitoring the Trade Stock metrics TradeOrderAborted, TradeOrderRequested, TradeOrderFilled, and TradeOrder Rejected on the AZ dimension. Using anomaly or threshold alarms on zonal metrics enables you to alert on metrics indicating zonal errors, or a drop-off in zonal activity. In the case of this experiment, you'll see zonal activity drop-off. When the experiment ends, activity returns to normal in the impaired AZ.

To mitigate this network impairment, perform a zonal shift. To support zonal shift, your load balancer is required to have cross-zone load balancing turned off. For an ALB like we are using in the Trade Stock service, this setting is controlled by the attribute load_balancing.cross_zone.enabled on the target group. See the def use_service function in the custom PrivateAlbExtension ECS service extension, in the file *src/trade-stock/trade_utils/private_lb_extension.py*. The following code snippet shows the code to configure the target group and disable cross-zone load balancing:

```
def use_service(
        self, service: typing.Union[ecs.Ec2Service, ecs.FargateService]
) -> None:

    target_group = self.alb_listener.add_targets(
        self._parent_service.id,
        deregistration_delay=Duration.seconds(10),
        port=80,
        targets=[service]
    )
    target_group.set_attribute("load_balancing.cross_zone.enabled", "false")
```

In addition, find the `cross_zone_enabled` parameter on the ALB and NLB defined in the prehook function, and set them both to `False`, `cross_zone_enabled=False`. Redeploy the Trade Stock service and Trade Confirms with the command **cdk deploy TradeConfirmsStackPrimary TradeOrderStackPrimary**. Then, with your traffic still flowing to the service, restart the network disruption experiment. With the experiment running, perform a zonal shift; be sure to set the `--away-from` flag to the AZ that matches the subnet you selected for network disruption:

```
export ORDER_ALB_ARN=$(aws elbv2 describe-load-balancers --region us-east-1 \
    --query 'LoadBalancers[?contains(LoadBalancerName,`Order`)].LoadBalancerArn' \
    --output text)

aws arc-zonal-shift start-zonal-shift --away-from us-east-1b --expires-in 20m \
    --resource-identifier $ORDER_ALB_ARN
```

The ALB will not send traffic to the AZ `us-east-1b` for the next 20 minutes. It's a good idea to create scripted AWS Systems Manager Automations for your run books (*https://oreil.ly/OFwCa*). For this type of recovery activity, your operations team will be most effective with automated and tested procedures. You can use FIS experiments like the one you created in this lesson for game-day scenarios with your team, allowing them to experiment and build effective recovery procedures.

 The techniques you learned in this chapter to detect and shift away from zonal impairments provide you a way to deal with zonal failures that can manifest themselves as gray failures. Gray failures are failures where different entities, in this case, your Trade Stock tasks in different AZs, observe a failure differently. Read more in the AWS whitepaper "Advanced Multi-AZ Resilience Patterns" (*https://oreil.ly/zaESt*) to effectively build multi-AZ observability and alerting mechanisms for gray failures.

Finally, notice that the zonal shift was set to 20 minutes. You'll need to monitor the impairment. Zonal shifts can be for longer periods of time or extended as needed. Once you can confirm that a zonal impairment has ended, you can resume normal activity in that AZ by cancelling your zonal shift or letting it expire.

Dependency Outages

You just worked through two types of impairments that could be mitigated. For intermittent errors, you found retries can improve success, and for zonal impairment, a zonal shift avoided zonal failures. Sometimes failures are linked to a dependency, which is a single point of failure (SPOF). The Trade Confirms API is a SPOF, and it's a hard dependency for the Trade Stock service. When Trade Confirms are impaired, Trade Stock orders cannot be serviced.

One way to deal with a service that repeatedly fails when called is to implement a circuit breaker. Circuit breakers allow you to temporarily halt traffic to dependencies when the dependency is failing or overloaded. You will need to carefully consider whether this pattern is a good fit on a case-by-case basis.

In this lesson, you'll work through a scenario where the Trade Confirms service has a documented error type indicating system maintenance. When in maintenance mode, all requests will be rejected with a `ConfirmsMaintenanceError`. For this error, the team decided that a circuit breaker is appropriate. There are a few benefits we can think about. First, by avoiding traffic to the Trade Confirms system, capacity is reserved, potentially shortening the maintenance window. Second, the Trade Stock service can quickly mark orders as aborted, save processing resources, and quickly provide feedback to customers.

Let's test the circuit breaker, which is already built into the Trade Order service. Start by sending continuous traffic:

```bash
bash
cd ~
export ORDER_ENDPOINT=$(aws ssm get-parameter --name trade_order_endpoint \
  --region us-east-1 | jq -r .Parameter.Value)

cat <<'EOF' > trade.sh
curl \
--request POST \
--header "Content-Type: application/json" \
--data '{"request_id": "'$(uuidgen)'", "customer_id": "4", "ticker": "IPAY",
 "transaction_type": "buy", "current_price": 40.06,
 "share_count": '$RANDOM'}' \
$ORDER_ENDPOINT/trade/
EOF

chmod u+x trade.sh
watch -d -n 1 ./trade.sh
```

Next, you will inject a fault into the Trade Confirms service to observe what happens during a failure. The Trade Confirms service has parameters wired into the mock service logic that allow you to inject failures. You can see the `circuit` decorator in the Trade Stock service, and throughout the body of the `execute_trade` function, you'll see how the code handles open and closed states of the `circuit_state`, defined as `CircuitBreakerMonitor.get('execute_trade').state`. See the file *src/trade-stock/order_api/order_api.py* to review this in depth:

```
@circuit(failure_threshold=15, expected_exception=RuntimeError,
    recovery_timeout=60)
def execute_trade(activity: dict) -> Response:
```

When the solution was deployed, the trade_confirms_exchange_status parameter was set to "AVAILABLE". However, if you update the parameter and set the trade_con firms_exchange_status to "IMPAIRED" or anything other than "AVAILABLE", the Trade Confirms service will throw a ConfirmsMaintenanceError. With your order requests still running, issue the following command in a new Session Manager terminal, your local CLI, or manually make your update at the AWS Systems Manager console:

```
aws ssm put-parameter --name "trade_confirms_exchange_status" \
--type "String" --value "IMPAIRED" --overwrite --region "us-east-1"
```

You'll start seeing the aborted status on your Trade Stock requests, as attempts to confirm the trade throw exceptions. In CloudWatch, you'll also see a new metric, TradeOrder > AvailabilityZone > TradeOrderAborted value being published to track the errors. Notice that this metric not only tells you that an order failed to process, but which zone it failed in. The service captures issues with TradeOrderAbor ted metrics, and as discussed in the last lesson, you can create zonal alarms on this metric.

So how does the circuit breaker work in the Trade Stock API? When an electrical circuit is closed, current flows through it. When a circuit is open, that flow is turned off. In distributed software, circuit breakers are a design pattern used to increase resilience. They enable your service to avoid making requests to an external service that is impaired and repeatedly does not return successful responses.

At the code level, a circuit breaker is a construct that monitors the function responsible for calling a dependent service. It counts consecutive failures as it monitors the outcome of each invocation. If the number of errors thrown surpasses the configured failure count threshold, the circuit will open, short-circuiting further invocations. The following figures illustrate the lifecycle of a circuit breaker. Start with the default behavior of a closed circuit; all traffic flows from the Trade Stock service to the Trade Confirms service, as shown in Figure 5-17.

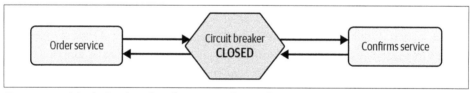

Figure 5-17. Trade Stock orders flow to Trade Confirms when the circuit is closed

If calls from the Trade Stock service to the Trade Confirms service fail repeatedly and breach the circuit breaker threshold configured to 15 failures, the circuit will fail open and short-circuit all calls to the Trade Confirms service, as shown in Figure 5-18.

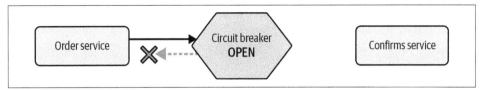

Figure 5-18. Trade orders are aborted because Trade Confirms will not be issued when the circuit is open

When a circuit is open, circuit breaker implementations should include logic to operate in a half-open state, predictably testing the external dependency connection. If retry tests fail, the circuit remains open, as shown in Figure 5-19.

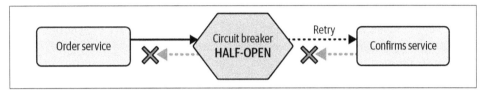

Figure 5-19. Circuit breaker behavior when the circuit is half-open and periodically tested

Once a retry test succeeds, as shown in Figure 5-20, the circuit closes and traffic flows normally. The circuit progresses back to closed status, as shown in Figure 5-17.

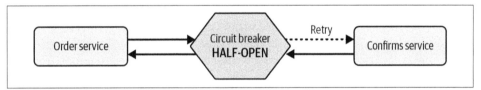

Figure 5-20. Circuit breaker behavior when the circuit is half-open and a retry succeeds

 You can learn more about the circuit breakers by reading Martin Fowler's explanation of the design pattern (*https://oreil.ly/42YYy*) and in the AWS prescriptive guidance for cloud design patterns for the circuit breaker (*https://oreil.ly/0qUcK*). This will help you assess when it's a good fit to apply this design pattern.

In closing, run the following command to end the Trade Confirms impairment, and you'll see trade orders begin successfully processing again:

```
aws ssm put-parameter --name "trade_confirms_exchange_status" \
--type "String" --value "AVAILABLE" --overwrite --region "us-east-1"
```

If you plan to work through each chapter in Part II, you can leave this stack installed until you have worked through Chapters 2–7. But be aware that if you stop working through the lessons and leave your infrastructure running, you will be charged for it.

Cleaning Up

To avoid accruing AWS costs, you can remove all resources created in this chapter with the CLI command **cdk destroy --all**. Everything will be destroyed as your database is configured in CDK to "DeletionPolicy": "Snapshot", which will delete the database but save a snapshot. You can use this snapshot to restore the database if you need it; otherwise, you can also delete the snapshots manually.

If your VPC fails to delete, check for resources added by other means than the CDK stack. For example, Amazon GuardDuty adds a guardduty-data VPC endpoint and security group, which you'll need to delete manually.

Chapter 6 relies on this microservice. If you plan to work through all of Part II, "Reliable Trading Portal", you can leave this stack installed until you have worked through the lessons from Chapters 2 through 7.

Summary

In this chapter, you explored resiliency for a stock Trade Stock service. This service has a low-latency SLA and applies techniques to achieve high availability in a single region. You designed your architecture with ECS, an Aurora PostgreSQL cluster, and an external service. You built in observability and resilience for your database to deal with connection exhaustion, zonal instance failure, and password rotations. You also learned how the RDS Proxy can help manage connection pools in dynamic compute environments.

At the ECS service level, you learned how to trigger rollbacks for bad deployments, retry for intermittent error, and how to observe zonal impairments. You learned how to evacuate an impaired AZ, a technique that takes advantage of AWS AZ fault isolation boundaries. Finally, you learned techniques to deal with hard failures from your external dependencies. This enabled you to improve your customer experience and avoid overloading an already impaired system.

In the next chapter, you'll explore resiliency concepts for disaster recovery of the trading portal. You'll have the opportunity to wire the frontend up to the Account Open and Trade Stock services. Once the solution is integrated, you'll inject faults that replicate regional outages both from code/configuration issues and AWS impairments. You'll then explore and work through configurations that allow the trading portal and services to failover to a secondary region where they can continue to process incoming customer requests.

Integrated AvailableTrade Frontend with APIs

Up to this point, you've been learning and implementing resilient patterns for individual microservice components. You've successfully deployed the AvailableTrade single-page application, the Account Open serverless API, and the containerized Trade Stock APIs. Your retail stock trading application only becomes useful when these components are integrated. In this chapter, you'll integrate the UI with the backend services to prepare for recovery orchestration in Chapter 7 and learn more resilience patterns along the way.

In this chapter, you will accomplish the following:

- Integrate your microservices with the UI
- Automate endpoint configuration
- Integrate API calls
- Configure rational client timeouts
- Deal gracefully with API unavailability
- Monitor real user experience
- Observe and track JavaScript errors
- Trace user actions to backend processing

Technical Requirements

The functional requirement of this chapter is to integrate the AvailableTrade UI with the Trade Stock and the Trade Confirms microservices using the JavaScript

Fetch API. In addition to integration, as with prior chapters, you'll make informed design decisions to ensure a reliable user experience. You'll also apply nonfunctional instrumentation to capture usage and performance data to help engineers reliably operate the AvailableTrade system. Figure 6-1 shows an overview of the data flow from the brokerage customer's browser as they load your website and take actions that send JSON messages to your APIs, which process and store that data in their respective databases.

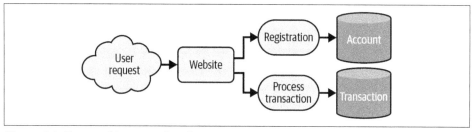

Figure 6-1. Frontend integrated with services

In addition to being able to interoperate with backend APIs, the UI should be instrumented to support the resilience goals required to meet user experience and service-level expectations. You'll need ways to deal with APIs that are unavailable or are underperforming, and to detect and address client-side JavaScript code issues.

 This chapter is focused on resilience patterns. It will demonstrate examples of integration to unauthenticated public API endpoints to simplify working through examples; however, user management, authentication, and authorization are critical in your production solution. You can use Amazon Cognito or other frameworks to manage your requirements for managing identities, authenticating, and authorizing API access.

Architecture Overview

In Chapter 3, you focused on deploying a website and ensuring that your website remained available under load and when the primary regional S3 bucket hosting your website was impaired. You also deployed a synthetic canary to monitor and ensure the website was reachable; otherwise, you would be alerted. The focus was on website infrastructure like the CloudFront content delivery network (CDN) to improve availability with origin redundancy, reduce latency with caching at AWS points of presence, and rate limit bad actor IP addresses with AWS Web Application Firewall (AWS WAF).

Now, you'll dive deep into the JavaScript and HTML configuration for your single-page application (SPA). The application is built with the popular Vue.js framework with the Vee-Validate and Pinia components. You'll apply simple form validation to protect your APIs from invalid inputs, and use intelligent components to configure resilient behaviors. Bootstrap CSS is used to apply layout and styling while keeping your HTML and custom CSS styles minimal.

Figure 6-2 shows an overview of the website architecture and a high-level view of the AWS services running your APIs. You're already familiar with Amazon CloudWatch for observability, instrumenting metrics, and alarms. Now you'll add CloudWatch Real User Monitoring (RUM) for the ability to observe client-side user behavior and add to existing CloudWatch X-Ray tracing.

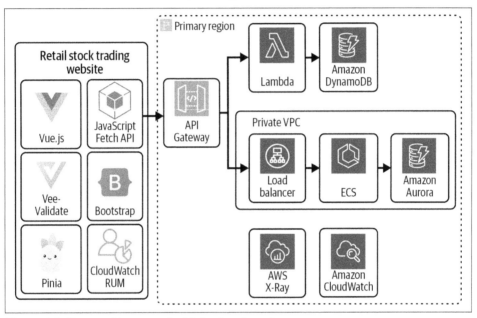

Figure 6-2. Frontend integrated with backend services

Recall that the Trade Stock microservice runs in a private isolated VPC. You'll deploy a regional Amazon API Gateway REST API to expose a public endpoint. You'll use AWS VPC PrivateLink to route requests to a private AWS Network Load Balancer (NLB) sitting in front of the existing Trade Order service AWS Application Load Balancer (ALB). This is required to make your AvailableTrade application publicly available to your customers.

In the next section, you will explore the structure of the Vue.js application. It is helpful to understand HTML, CSS, JavaScript, and reactive SPA development.

Deploying the AWS CDK Application

You do not have to deploy a new CDK application for this chapter. Instead, you'll work with the existing CDK applications from Chapters 3, 4, and 5. If you have not already installed them or have deleted them, you'll need to install all three of them now. Refer to and complete the sections "Deploying the AWS CDK Application" on page 55, "Deploying the AWS CDK Application" on page 93, and "Deploying the AWS CDK Application" on page 125. Implementing all resilience lesson improvements provided in the lessons in Chapters 3, 4, and 5 is not required to complete this chapter, but it is encouraged. Minimally, complete the steps in "Amazon Route 53" on page 60, "Sunny Day Scenario" on page 96, and "Prepare the Database" on page 128.

Once you have deployed your frontend website, new Account Open API, and Trade Stock API, you are ready to work on integration resilience. Each of the following lessons assumes you are already in the main working directory, the root directory of the Git project *AvailableTrade*. To get started in this chapter, getting familiar with the website and technologies used to build it will be helpful. Change into the website directory and start the website locally after installing npm dependencies, if you don't already have it running:

```
cd AvailableTrade/src/frontend/website
npm install
npm run dev
```

With the Vite development server running, open your browser to the locally running AvailableTrade web application in your web browser at the address *http://localhost:5173*. If everything works, you'll see your AvailableTrade portal, as shown in Figure 6-3. If you had issues, use your browser development console. As you work through this chapter, your browser development console will be useful in understanding application performance and behavior.

Figure 6-3. AvailableTrade running locally

Now we'll quickly run through the structure of the Vue.js application so that you understand it before you make modifications in the following lessons. Vue.js was selected because it is a simple framework for reactive JavaScript, and its single file components make it easy to work with JavaScript, HTML, and CSS for each component in one file. There are four main pages in the application. Account Open and Trade Stock will be integrated to backend APIs. Insights is a placeholder for market data and news insights which you'll explore in Part III, "Discovering Trading Opportunities". Utilities will be used for observing JavaScript errors with CloudWatch RUM.

Let's dig into the code. Start by opening your IDE and navigating to the main website directory, *src/account_open/website*. There are three files in the main *website* directory to be aware of:

Index.html
> This file is the single page of your SPA and is loaded by your browser when you navigate to the website root. *Index.html* loads the global JavaScript and CSS files that are required for Vue.js to run, and provides top-level HTML structure.

Package.json
> This file contains metadata for npm. It's where you define dependencies and runnable scripts you use to package your site, or run it locally with Vite.

Vite.config.js
> This file is where you can set options for the Vite development tool. Vite provides both a development server and build tool for creating a distributable version of your website.

The Vue.js code for the website can be found under *src/frontend/website/src*. The *src/frontend/website/src/main.js* file is the entry point for the Vue application. The root *index.html* file loads this JavaScript file. When *main.js* loads the Vue.js App, it loads the *src/frontend/website/src/App.vue* file. Then the Vue.js router is loaded from *src/frontend/website/src/router/index.js* to configure the SPA navigation across views. The *App.vue* file is the top-level *template* for the Vue.js application; it formats HTML for navigation links with <RouterLink> tags to provide navigation to different Vue.js views. These views are in the *src/frontend/website/src/views* folder. There is a corresponding view for each application page; the AvailableTrade icon points to the Home view.

Lastly, note that each of the *.vue* files have a common structure: HTML code between <template> tags, and JavaScript code between <script> tags. Take a look at the contents of *src/frontend/website/src/views/HomeView.vue* to see an example of a *.vue* file where JavaScript is loaded in a setup script, Vue.js directives enrich HTML tags with special JavaScript expression attributes in templates like <p v-else>, and page

variables can be accessed inline with double handle bars like {{ customer.first
Name }} for text interpolation:

```
<template>
  <main>
    <div class="row">
      <div class="col-md-3"></div>
      <div class="col-md-6">
        <p>Welcome the AvailableTrade Electronic Trading Application</p>
        <p v-if="customer.isRegistered">You are current registered as:
            {{ customer.firstName }}</p>
        <p v-else>To get started, open a new account</p>
      </div>
    </div>
  </main>
</template>

<script setup>
import {useCustomerStore} from "@/stores/customer.js";

const customer = useCustomerStore();
</script>
```

From here on, you'll do most of your code changes in Vue.js *.vue and JavaScript *.js
files. Let's get started.

Automating AvailableTrade Endpoint Configuration

Applications that integrate with APIs require configuring environment-specific endpoint HTTP addresses. Until now, you've been managing service endpoints with the
CDK by storing them in AWS Systems Manager Parameter Store parameters. This
is a useful technique for enabling the automation of environment configuration for
AWS infrastructure. Each application instance creates self-managed SDLC-specific
variables as you deploy CDK applications to SDLC environments. AWS-hosted components look these up at runtime from the SSM Parameter Store.

You'll also leverage the use of these SSM parameters to configure API endpoints
for the AvailableTrade website automatically. Vite exposes environment variables
on a special import.meta.env object so that you can access environment variables
in your JavaScript code. You'll take advantage of Vite packaging with environment-
specific configuration files to always load the correct environment-specific endpoint
addresses. Vite supports global, development, production, and custom config files.
This approach is easier to maintain and more reliable than manually configured
endpoint values.

In this lesson, you take advantage of Vite built-in support for the *.env.development* file
for your locally running website, and *.env.production* for the version of the website
you deploy to S3 and CloudFront. A Python script is provided to generate these

files for you. In your IDE, open the file *src/frontend/website/configure_website_envi-ronment.py*. Note that this file requires AWS credentials and uses the AWS Python boto3 library to pull SSM parameters and CloudFormation output values. It writes these out into Vite configuration files that Vite loads when the code is run locally or packaged for distribution.

 The takeaway for misconfigured API endpoints is that you should understand the negative consequences of misconfigurations that cross SDLC environment boundaries, like a production service pointing to a test endpoint. Crossing your test and your production configuration can have severe consequences for users, especially when the impacts are financial, and test data does not represent the actual money or activities of a user. Using SSM parameters with automation ensures accurate and reliable environment config-uration for CI/CD pipelines to avoid misconfigurations.

In your IDE, open and review the file *src/frontend/website/package.json*. Recall that this is the file npm uses to manage dependencies and expose utility scripts for local development and application packaging. Your CI/CD pipelines should be configured to run similar npm scripts as build steps when they package, archive, and deploy application versions.

Locate the scripts section of the *package.json* file, which looks like this:

```
"scripts": {
  "dev": "vite",
  "build": "vite build",
  "preview": "vite preview"
},
```

You will add the line "configure": "python configure_website_environ ments.py", above the "dev": "vite", line. Remember the trailing comma. Now your *package.json* file should look like this:

```
"scripts": {
  "configure": "python configure_website_environments.py",
  "dev": "vite",
  "build": "vite build",
  "preview": "vite preview"
},
```

With *package.json* updated and saved, you can access and run the new script with npm. You need your AWS credentials configured to run this script, so as with each chapter, you should have already loaded your Python virtual environment with source .venv/bin/activate and run source env.sh. If you have not, do it now. See Chapter 2 for a refresher if you need to.

In a terminal, move into the *website* directory and run **npm run configure** by following these steps:

```
cd AvailableTrade/src/frontend/website
npm run configure

> portal-integrated-ui@0.0.0 configure
> python configure_website_environments.py
```

After running this script, you should see two new files appear: *src/frontend/website/.env.development* and *src/frontend/website/.env.development*. Vite will automatically load *.env.development* if you still have your web server running locally. Open *.env.development* in your IDE and inspect the contents:

```
VITE_NEW_ACCOUNT_ENDPOINT= \
    https://XXX.execute-api.us-east-1.amazonaws.com/prod/
VITE_TRADE_STOCK_ENDPOINT= \
    internal-Trade0-Order-XXX.us-east-1.elb.amazonaws.com
```

The AWS regional endpoints for the Account Open API and the Trade Stock API are configured. In your Vue.js application, these will now be accessible like `import.meta.env.VITE_NEW_ACCOUNT_ENDPOINT`. Vite requires these variables to be prefixed with `VITE_`. You've successfully provided reliable and automated environment-specific configuration of endpoints for your website.

Integrating AvailableTrade Microservices

This lesson will demonstrate the JavaScript Fetch API combined use of Pinia stores to manage state. This is a required step for integrating AvailableTrade with its APIs, and sets the stage for the following lessons.

You'll focus on setting up a new account opening request. A web form has already been created, and if you want to review the HTML and JavaScript code, look at *src/frontend/website/src/views/AccountOpenView.vue*. The Account Open view contains a web form that uses `vee-validate` to provide user input validation, JavaScript code to convert form data into the required JSON schema to post a new Account Open API request, and establishes a contextual customer state to make other views aware of a newly created customer and account.

It should not be surprising that the integration's first line of defense for resilience is user input validation. Try submitting the form without entering data into any form fields, and you'll see the validation in effect, as shown in Figure 6-4.

The validation provided is straightforward and only enforces that fields are required, using the Yup library to define your validation schema. For example, `first_name: yup.string().required()` requires the First Name. A real-life solution would provide a more robust form and more complex validation. The `vee-validate` built-in `handleSubmit` function handler ensures that validations pass, according to the validation schema, before it will allow the `processAccount` function to run and submit a request to the Account Open API:

```
const openAccount = handleSubmit(values => {
    processAccount()
})
```

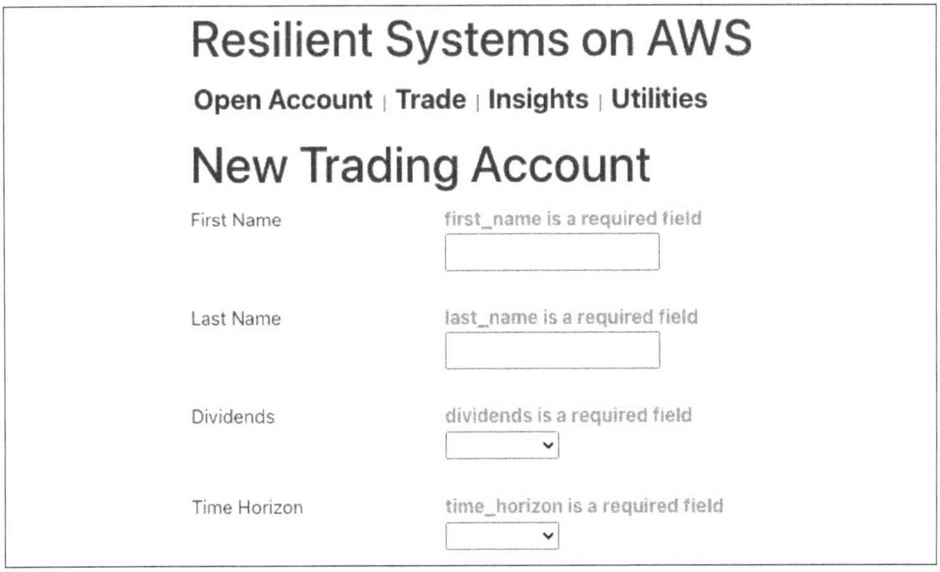

Figure 6-4. New account form validation

If you fill out all the required values, the form will be submitted and create a new record in your `brokerage_accounts` DynamoDB table. Once the account is created, the call to `customer.refresh(values)` updates the customer store with account and customer data, and `customer.confirmRegistration()` makes other pages aware that customer and account data is available for use. See the response handling block of JavaScript code:

```
if (json.ok) {
    console.log("refreshing customer and confirming registration");
    let result = await json.json()
    console.log(result);
    customer.refresh(values);
    customer.confirmRegistration();
    submit_failure.value = ''
}
```

If you're following along in your local environment, you'll notice that the page no longer shows the form; instead, you see a welcome message because registration is confirmed. UI validation is in addition to the existing JSON schema validation built into the Amazon API Gateway, and any additional validation in the Account Open Lambda function.

Most of the lessons in this chapter can be completed using your local Vite development server. Of course, the real test is when your application is deployed to AWS, and your resilient patterns uphold resilience for your customers. To deploy the changes for each lesson, you'll need to package your changes, then deploy them to S3. You can package your code from the Vue.js *src/frontend/website* directory, and then deploy them with the AWS CDK from the *src/frontend* directory. The following sequence of commands provides steps to deploy updated website code to AWS:

```
cd AvailableTrade/src/frontend/website
npm run configure n
npm run build
cd ..
cdk deploy --all --require-approval never
```

You should sequence the `configure` and `build` steps in the build and deploy stages of your CI/CD pipeline. Be sure your builds run both steps in sequence before deploying changes to an AWS environment. Once deployed, you can automate integration tests along with resilience tests.

Configuring Client Timeouts

When a user interface sends a request to a backend API, some impairments can cause a request to appear unresponsive for amounts of time that violate your SLA. The best practice for resilience in handling this scenario is to set client timeouts. Timeouts allow the system to notify the user that a request took too long to process, and timeouts release resources that are otherwise consumed waiting for a response that takes too long.

Setting a timeout seems simple enough, but the complexity lies in deciding what timeout value to set. It's important to handle timeouts gracefully and coordinate them all the way through your system's call stack. Choosing the correct value requires ensuring timeouts don't conflict with each other or complicate retries if you are using them. When timeouts are set too low, they can cause transactions to fail artificially. When timeouts are set too high, wait times cause latency SLA breaches and unnecessarily tie up compute resources, potentially leading to failures in multiple system components. If you want to learn more, look up the industry terms for these side effects: "retry storms" and "cascading failures."

Unresponsive actions can confuse users causing them to attempt to resubmit requests, refresh pages, or re-enter form data. You must balance client experience while ensuring you don't exit processes that are still running and will succeed. To help address timeouts in the AvailableTrade application, you already have timeouts, retries, and idempotency implemented in the API layer. Your web forms need to set and manage unique request IDs to protect you from duplicate submissions when you retry after a failure caused by a timeout. At the UI tier, you'll let the user decide when to retry rather than building in automated retries to avoid making users wait for more than three seconds without informing them if their trade succeeded or failed.

 Learn more about best practices for client timeouts from the Well-Architected best practice "REL05-BP05 Set Client Timeouts" (*https://oreil.ly/lccRK*). Be aware of timeout and retry default behavior for your selected libraries so you can explicitly configure the behavior you expect.

In the Trade view, you'll review the `AbortSignal`, which is applied to the JavaScript `fetch` operation to enable timeouts for trading stocks. Before jumping into that code, you'll need to perform analysis of the timeouts through your call stack. Recall that the Stock Trade API dependencies include an API Gateway, an NLB and ALB, an ECS task for the Trade Stock service, and an ECS task for the Trade Confirms services. See Figure 6-5 for a visual of these interactions, and callouts for timing information about each interaction.

Working backward, we start with the PostgreSQL write operations and review these configurations. In the file *AvailableTrade/src/trade-stock/order_api/order_api.py*, you will recall that you managed connections to the database for write operations in the function `load_db_engine()`. Take another look at that code and notice the `connect_args` parameter which passes in the configuration {`"options": "-c state ment_timeout=100"`}. This informs the `Psycopg` database client to abort any operation that runs more than 100 milliseconds:

```
def load_db_engine() -> None:
    """Load and cache read-write SQLAlchemy database connection
    Refreshes credentials on each invocation."""
    global db_engine
    secret = json.loads(get_db_credentials_from_cache())
    host_ = secret['host']  # rds_ro_proxy_endpoint
    db_conn_string = f'''postgresql://{secret['username']}:
        {secret['password']}@{host_}:{secret['port']}/
        {secret['dbname']}?sslmode=require'''
    db_engine = create_engine(db_conn_string, pool_size=25,
        connect_args={"options": "-c statement_timeout=100"})
```

Next, observe in Figure 6-5 that the ECS service for trades has a retry for three calls over a 300 ms timeout call to Trade Confirms. You can revisit "Dependency Outages" on page 158 to deep dive into this configuration.

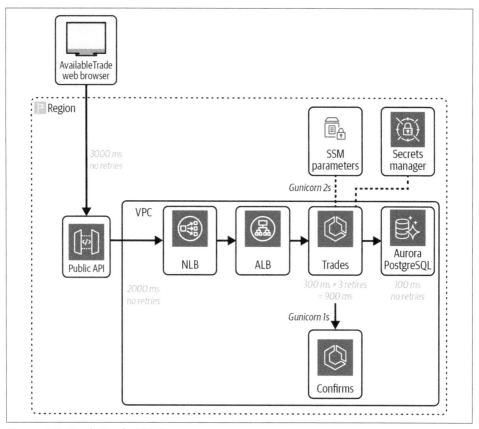

Figure 6-5. Trade Stock API timeouts

The key for client timeouts is knowing that the sequence of three calls can take up to 900 milliseconds to complete if all three retries are executed. Database calls can take at most 100 ms, and you make a few of them. The Gunicorn WSGI server for Trade Confirms kills processes after one second and for trade orders after two seconds. And, before we get to your client timeout, you also have a 2,000 millisecond timeout set at the API Gateway. Each successive timeout allows for downstream processing to complete before abandoning processing. This way, the downstream can adhere to an SLA, and either successfully complete or abort processing with a useful response message back to the client. The client should only execute the timeouts when the client has a relative level of confidence that the downstream has become unresponsive; then it's time to give up.

Now, aware of your comprehensive configuration, you are ready to review the configuration of your JavaScript `fetch` code in the file *src/frontend/website/src/views/TradeStockView*:

```
async function postTrade(data = {}, options = {}) {
  const request_json = {...} // code collapsed for brevity

  return fetch(import.meta.env.VITE_TRADE_STOCK_ENDPOINT + "trade/", {
    signal: AbortSignal.timeout(3000),
    method: "PUT",
    mode: "cors",
    cache: "no-cache",
    headers: {'Content-Type': 'application/json'},
    body: JSON.stringify(request_json)
  });
}
```

The `AbortSignal` has a method `timeout()` that takes an integer argument in milliseconds. You may be aware that `fetch` also supports an older approach for timeouts using the `AbortController`, which takes more lines of code; for completeness you can see an example of this style used in the Account Open view. Now, inspect the `processTrade` function to see how error handling and logging are applied for an aborted `fetch`.

> You can learn more about the `AbortSignal` and `AbortController` classes in the MDN web docs (*https://oreil.ly/2um1F*).

A failure can occur at any component layer of a system. In "Database Primary Writer Failures" on page 149, you learned about Aurora fault injection queries. Here, you can test a SQL query timeout by using the fault injection query technique again. This time, inject disk congestion to slow down response times:

```
SELECT aurora_inject_disk_congestion(100, 15, true, 20, 30, 40)
```

You can also introduce integration or network latency within the API call stack using the AWS Fault Injection Service, or with the custom chaos parameters you created in Chapter 5. Make sure you test your application timeout strategy carefully. If you have built in retries, test those for timeouts. Make sure you understand default timeouts and retries, ensure you've adjusted them when you can, or accounted for them when you can't.

In closing, you've already learned how to review CloudWatch Logs and metric filters. Ensure you are measuring latency and errors at each connection point in Figure 6-5, or correspondingly in your workload, so that you will be aware of issues early and can address them before they become bigger problems and start impacting your application availability. You can use the metrics you create to build comprehensive dashboards and composite alarms. If you were to create a separate alarm on each metric, when things go wrong, you might end up with alarm fatigue. It's a best practice to combine alarms into a summarized, single health indicator with composite alarms (*https://oreil.ly/9FVjM*).

Gracefully Degrading Features

Handling failures gracefully improves your ability to build or maintain customer trust in your application through times when it would otherwise be lost because your system has not been prepared to deal with impairments. Graceful degradation is a technique for being statically stable, or maintaining static state and continuing normal operation during dependency unavailability or during dependency failures. Offering a partial customer experience may not be ideal, but is better than no customer experience. Failures will inevitably occur at some point; the ways that you anticipate, plan, and handle failures allow your customers to continue using available functionality. Not all systems are able to isolate the impact of a failure; doing so is a way to differentiate your application.

In Chapter 4, you were introduced to the concept of the Account Open service as the control plane, and the Trade Stock service as the data plane. You'd commonly see additional services in a stock trading platform, like ticker feeds, news insights, and profile management. These are all candidates to degrade gracefully; trading stocks and moving money are the core system functions that users need from AvailableTrade.

In this lesson, you'll explore an example of how to gracefully degrade your user interface when faced with an impaired single point of failure.

 Learn more about how to reason about graceful degradation of systems from the AWS Well-Architected Reliability Pillar best practice "REL05-BP01 Implement Graceful Degradation to Transform Applicable Hard Dependencies into Soft Dependencies" (*https://oreil.ly/U3hgN*).

Customers typically don't open accounts on a regular and recurring basis, but will need or want to repeatedly make trades on accounts once they are open. Opening a new account is highly important to our business, but trading is critical to generating revenue. In addition, customers lose money when they can't trade. And when stock prices fluctuate, it can result in customer service requests that require AvailableTrade to fill the price gap to make customers whole. So, similar to the separation of concerns between your control and data plane at the API level, you'll ensure a separation of the control and data plane in the UI design as well.

Because the Account Open API is asynchronous and simply passes requests off to SNS, simple API availability is a straightforward single point of failure to reason about. Either the API is available and can receive a message, or it cannot. So, you'll check whether the API is online; it's that simple for this lesson. Remember that these examples are oversimplified on purpose, so they are easy to work with. For more complex real-world APIs and UI components, you may need to think about other scenarios, like out-of-SLA latency, the validity of response data, and more.

If your application will act on a failure, it first needs to observe it. AvailableTrade will use a heartbeat to monitor the availability of the Account Open API. There isn't a one-size-fits-all approach to building web components that observe API health. In AvailableTrade, a Pinia store is the mechanism you'll use for monitoring the Account Open service. To keep the example simple, the JavaScript Fetch API will make an HTTP OPTIONS request to determine the availability of the Account Open API. The fetch call is made within a JavaScript setInterval global function, making it easy to consistently repeat this request at a set interval. You'll configure your heartbeat monitor in a Pinia store called useDegradingStore that exposes a Boolean flag indicating API health based on the responses of your heartbeat check. The Boolean flag is the key to conditional behavior in your UI code that can gracefully hide system features.

Before implementing graceful degradation, first consider error handling and observe how an API failure manifests in account opening without graceful degradation. Open the file *src/frontend/website/env.development* and alter the URL of the variable VITE_NEW_ACCOUNT_ENDPOINT. You can change the stage name from */prod/* to */pro/* at the end of the line, for example. Now fill out the New Account form and submit it. You'll need to have your browser development tools panel open to see the network failure. The UI doesn't provide any useful message to the user, but fails hard. This was observed in the Chrome browser, but all modern browsers have developer tools. You can view yours and see a network failure on the timeline similar to Figure 6-6.

Figure 6-6. New Account preflight dependency failure

This is a poor and confusing experience. To the end user, the form just seems stuck. The user might just keep clicking Create Account, call or chat with Support, or altogether leave AvailableTrade frustrated and confused, off to trade with a competitor. Now add a user-facing notification. The failure from the cross-origin request sharing (CORS) 403 error from API Gateway is no longer silent. Find the following line around line 25 in the `<template>` section of the Account Open View *src/frontend/website/src/views/HomeView.vue*, and uncomment it:

```
<!--<span class="error">{{ submit_failure }}</span>-->
```

Now your HTML can interpolate and display a `submit_failure` message:

```
<span class="error">{{ submit_failure }}</span>
```

If you try to submit the form by clicking Create Account, you'll see a more informative message, as shown in Figure 6-7.

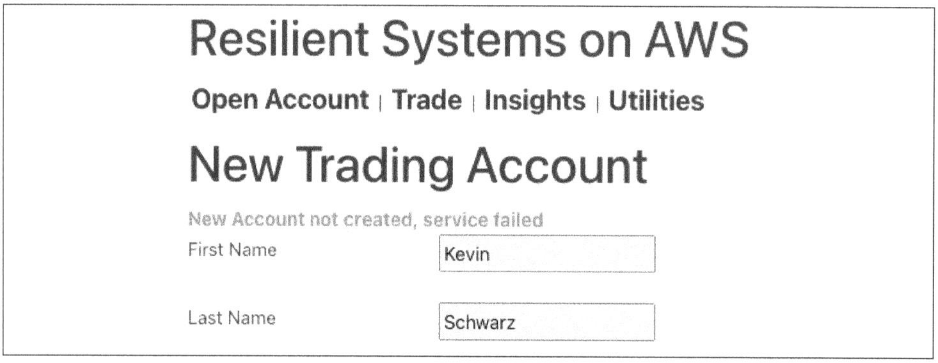

Resilient Systems on AWS

Open Account | **Trade** | **Insights** | **Utilities**

New Trading Account

New Account not created, service failed

First Name

Kevin

Last Name

Schwarz

Figure 6-7. Create account submit failure messaging

This message is a slightly better experience that you'll keep in place in case future errors do occur that aren't handled by `useDegradingStore`. When errors are persistent, you can provide improvement over simply displaying a failure message by gracefully degrading the user experience. When the service is not available, inform the customer up front and disable the form. This avoids the customer performing data entry work with no return in value, which is frustrating and degrades trust. Instead, when your API is down, you'll hide the form and display an informational message about the issue and what to do next. This lesson will focus on the UI code to gracefully degrade the user experience. The technique used for detecting a failure is artificial, so if you implement this pattern, think about how you can best indicate failures to your UI.

Now, if you'd like to explore the code that will monitor your endpoint, review the file *src/frontend/website/src/stores/degrade.vue*. You'll notice in the `actions` section that to use this component, a view will need to call the `monitorAccountOpenAvailability` action. This function uses the built-in JavaScript `setInterval` function configured to run the call `accountOpenHeartbeat` every 5 seconds (5,000 ms). Again, keep in mind that this heartbeat is a simplified example, in your real-world examples you will have to handle both transient and persistent failures. You might even drive your degradation with a feature toggle.

```
actions: {
monitorAccountOpenAvailability() {
  setInterval(this.accountOpenHeartbeat, 5000)
  // set availability immediately to activate, then monitor the heartbeat
  this.account_open_available = this.accountOpenHeartbeat().ok
},
```

Because opening a new account is constrained to a single Vue.js view, you only need to initialize this store to monitor the Open Account page in your application. To start the monitor before a user navigates to the Open Account page, you'll also configure it on the home page. Open the Home view file *src/frontend/website/src/views/Home-View.vue* in your IDE, find these two lines that are commented out, and uncomment them:

```
//const degradeStore = useDegradingStore();
//degradeStore.monitorAccountOpenAvailability();
```

Make sure to save your changes; once done, they should look like this:

```
const degradeStore = useDegradingStore();
degradeStore.monitorAccountOpenAvailability();
```

Now the account open availability monitoring starts as soon as a customer loads the home page. You can verify this by checking the network tab of your browser's development tools on the AvailableTrade home page, as shown in Figure 6-8.

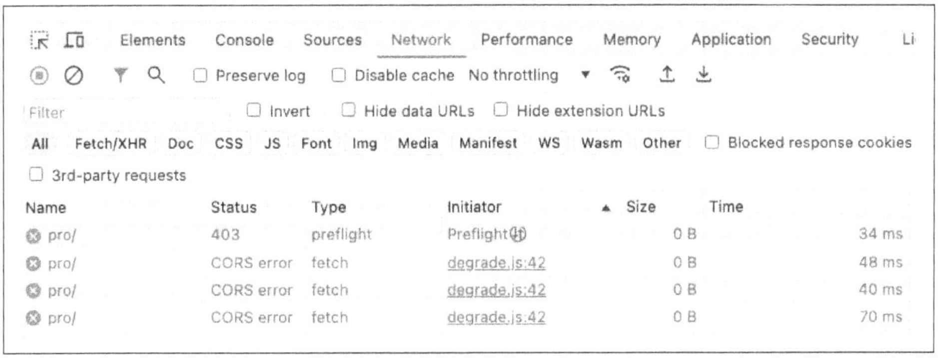

Figure 6-8. New account service home page network monitor

With account open heartbeat monitoring enabled on the AvailableTrade home page, let's also enable the monitor on the Open Account page. Open *src/frontend/web-site/src/views/AccountOpenView.vue* in your IDE. Now, within the `<script setup>` section, find the following lines:

```
import {useDegradingStore} from "@/stores/degrade.js";

//const degradeStore = useDegradingStore();
//degradeStore.monitorAccountOpenAvailability();
```

You can see that like in the Home view, `useDegradingStore` has already been imported but has not been enabled to start monitoring. Uncomment the lines that initialize the `degradeStore`, and enable monitoring so that your code now looks like this:

```
import {useDegradingStore} from "@/stores/degrade.js";

const degradeStore = useDegradingStore();
degradeStore.monitorAccountOpenAvailability();
```

Navigate to the Open Account view if you are not already there, and you should see graceful degradation in action. It hides the form, explains that opening new accounts is not currently working, and lets the customer know that the other features of the portal are still available. Finally, the customer is informed that a fallback option is available. They can open an account by phone by calling (555) GET-WISE. While not ideal, this is a better customer experience and will retain more trust than a broken or unresponsive application page. Your AvailableTrade portal is more reliable, even with an API that is unavailable. Figure 6-9 shows how the UI appears when the API is impaired.

Figure 6-9. New account service unavailable

Your takeaway from this lesson is that designing, building, and testing for graceful degradation for impairments to single points of failure in your application improves customer experiences. When you can quickly detect problems and proactively disable functions that do not impair core features, you can use that information to gracefully handle the problem without impacting or degrading other core features. By continuing to service core requests when ancillary services are not available, you will be able to gracefully degrade and avoid cascading failures and provide a partial experience.

And ideally, if your Open Account page was not working, the AvailableTrade team would detect the issue with CloudWatch metric alarms. They should then have the service restored soon. However, sometimes users experience issues that are not obvious from monitoring backend components alone. Let's find out how to observe and react to frontend issues. You can now revert the change in *.env.development* or rerun npm run configure in your *website* directory to see your Open Account form come back online with correct endpoint configuration.

Real User Monitoring

With real user monitoring (RUM), you can make important resilience decisions, including whether to automatically roll back a deployment, turn off an A/B feature, or be alerted that you need to investigate an error. In Chapter 3, you learned to use synthetic canaries to proactively understand user experience and identify potential issues. Synthetics allow you to test APIs and user interfaces. RUM frameworks help you observe telemetry from your user interface. RUM works in tandem with synthetics to help you resolve user interface problems faster than when RUM is not used. Without a RUM solution in place, you would only know about a problem in your user interface once a user reported the issue. Wikipedia defines real user monitoring (*https://oreil.ly/BaJ3e*) as passive monitoring that records user interactions with a website, including capturing errors. RUM captures the performance of actual users regardless of device, browser, network, or geographic location.

You can select your RUM solution from several available products; in this lesson you'll implement Amazon CloudWatch RUM. By capturing transparent telemetry, then using it to analyze real-time user interactions and experiences, CloudWatch RUM offers valuable insights into application performance, usability, and reliability. Amazon CloudWatch RUM is integrated with the CloudWatch Service Map and X-Ray, and the transparent data transmission is nonblocking. The asynchronous events do not create any perceptible impact on application load times.

 Learn more about CloudWatch RUM in the CloudWatch User Guide section for RUM (*https://oreil.ly/6Cpew*), part of CloudWatch Application Signals.

You've already seen a configuration-based failure mode in the last section where a misconfigured URL for the Account Open API caused JavaScript errors and an unresponsive HTML form. With RUM, you'll be able to track and alarm on client-side errors. There are two steps to implementing RUM. First, you need to create your CloudWatch RUM application in the cloud, and then you'll need to install the monitoring JavaScript into AvailableTrade. You'll start with creating the AWS infrastructure.

The RUM client requires authorization to send data to AWS. The default option is the Amazon Cognito identity pool, which we'll use in this implementation. However, you could also configure an existing Cognito identity pool with your RUM application, so keep this in mind when you configure RUM in your production implementation.

A RUM CDK stack is provided with the frontend chapter, but it hasn't been configured into the CDK application. Let's integrate and deploy the stack. In your IDE, open the file *src/frontend/app.py*. At the top of the file, you'll need to add the import statement from `stacks.front_end_rum_stack` import `FrontEndRumStack` underneath the existing `import` statements. After the CanaryStacks instantiations, you'll add the `FrontEndRumStack` stack. Your *app.py* file now should look like this:

```python
#!/usr/bin/env python3
import os
import aws_cdk as cdk
from stacks.front_end_canary_stack import FrontEndCanaryStack
from stacks.front_end_website_stack import FrontEndWebsiteStack
from stacks.front_end_secondary_bucket_stack import FrontEndSecondaryBucketStack
from stacks.front_end_rum_stack import FrontEndRumStack

account = os.getenv('AWS_ACCOUNT_ID')
primary_region = os.getenv('AWS_PRIMARY_REGION')
secondary_region = os.getenv('AWS_SECONDARY_REGION')
website_domain_name = os.getenv('AWS_DOMAIN_NAME')
primary_environment = cdk.Environment(account=account,
    region=primary_region)
secondary_environment = cdk.Environment(account=account,
    region=secondary_region)

app = cdk.App()

FrontEndSecondaryBucketStack(app, "FrontEnd-BucketStack-Secondary",
    env=secondary_environment)
FrontEndWebsiteStack(app, "FrontEnd-WebsiteStack",
    env=primary_environment,
    domain_name=website_domain_name, secondary_region=secondary_region)
FrontEndCanaryStack(app, "FrontEnd-CanaryStack-Primary",
    env=primary_environment,
    endpoint_url=website_domain_name)
FrontEndCanaryStack(app, "FrontEnd-CanaryStack-Secondary",
    env=secondary_environment,
    endpoint_url=website_domain_name)
FrontEndRumStack(app, "FrontEnd-RumStack",
    env=primary_environment,
    endpoint_url=website_domain_name)

app.synth()
```

Reviewing the `FrontEndRumStack` code, you'll see it creates a regional Amazon Cognito identity pool with `allow_unauthenticated_identities` set to `True`. This allows unauthenticated users to assume an identity mapped to a `FederatedPrincipal`, a role with a policy allowing your RUM application to record and monitor user events with the action `rum:PutRumEvents`.

CloudWatch RUM is implemented by creating an *app monitor* and then including a provided JavaScript snippet into your application. The app monitor provides information about the performance, errors, sessions, user journeys, and more, and is bound to a domain. If performance is enabled, RUM will use Web Vitals (*https://web.dev/articles/vitals*) measure loading, interactivity, and visual stability data to help you optimize your site performance.

Since you are currently working with `localhost` and a single deployed environment, you need at least two application monitors. For each environment in your SDLC, you'll create a separate app monitor to demarcate collected data. RUM will only accept requests that match the originating domain of the request.

Deploy this stack with the CDK command **cdk deploy --all** from your *src/frontend* directory. Once installed, you are ready to enable RUM in your application. The RUM stack emits the local and configured domain application IDs into the CloudFormation output. The Python configuration program that writes Vite variables for endpoints is also coded to pick up Cognito application IDs and write them into the correct environment configuration files. In a terminal, change into the *_src/frontend/website* directory and run **npm run configure**. Now, if you check the *.env.development* and *.env.production* files, you will see they have the application IDs for the respective RUM application monitors.

You are ready to enable monitoring in the AvailableTrade views. You'll need to update each view you want to monitor. In each of the five views in the application, you will find the monitor `import` statements and code that runs the monitor, as well as the code that captures Vue.js error events. This code is in each view, but is currently commented out:

```
//const monitorStore = useUserMonitorStore();
//onErrorCaptured((error) => { monitorStore.recordError(error) });
```

In each view file, uncomment these two lines:

```
const monitorStore = useUserMonitorStore();
onErrorCaptured((error) => {monitorStore.recordError(error) });
```

> Modern web and mobile application frameworks provide hooks that allow you to capture error events with your RUM implementation. You can learn more about the `onErrorCaptured` lifecycle hook for Vue.js in the public documentation (*https://oreil.ly/Qm8Vb*).

With your local Vite web server running, you should start seeing requests in the network tab of the developer tools in your browser as you browse around in your local AvailableTrade. You will also see the events flowing into the RUM console (Figure 6-10).

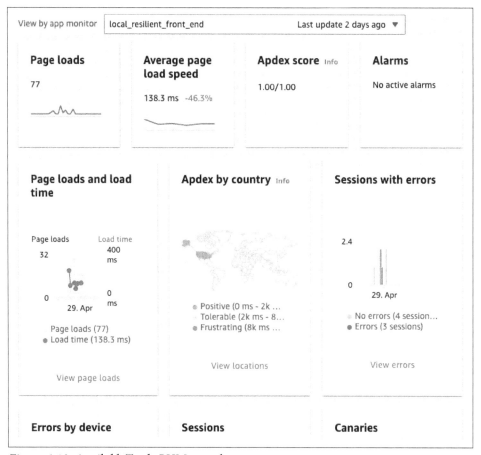

Figure 6-10. AvailableTrade RUM console

Now you have insights into traffic on your site. From a resilience lens, focus on the errors. You can use RUM to monitor errors, including device type, browser type, and details about the JavaScript error like the `pageId`, `userId`, `sessionId`, and full details of the JavaScript stack trace. You can configure custom metrics, but for this example, you'll use the AWS vended RUM metric `JsErrorCount`.

Open the file *src/frontend/stacks/front_end_rum_stack.py* in your IDE and look at the end of the file, where you'll see two metric alarms defined. The first is for the local RUM application monitor, and the second is for prod. To create metrics alarms, you can reference the metric simply by specifying the vended `metric_name` and `name space` attributes. By specifying the application monitor name in the `dimensions_map`, we can differentiate the environment and customize the settings appropriately. Here is the configuration for the local application monitor:

```
local_js_error_metric = cloudwatch.Metric(
    metric_name="JsErrorCount",
    namespace="AWS/RUM",
    dimensions_map={"application_name": local.name})
cloudwatch.Alarm(self, "LocalRumJavascriptErrorsAlarm",
    metric=local_js_error_metric,
    threshold=5,
    evaluation_periods=3,
    datapoints_to_alarm=1)
```

When you drill into CloudWatch to the `jsErrorCount` metric, you'll see both alarms configured. You can see them by looking at Alarms in the console, or with this AWS CLI query:

```
aws cloudwatch describe-alarms --alarm-name-prefix FrontEnd-RumStack
```

You just learned how to build an alarm on user interface telemetry. You've added observability you can use to make resilience decisions about your user interface.

X-Ray for End-to-End Tracing

AWS X-Ray with CloudWatch is an active tracing solution to make it easier for you to observe and debug applications. *Tracing* provides an end-to-end full picture of your application component interactions, including a segment timeline to measure latency, resource metadata, error details, and integrated logs. In Chapter 4 you enabled X-Ray for the new Account Open API, and in Chapter 5 you enabled X-Ray for the Trade Stock API. You'll end this chapter by exploring X-Ray starting at the RUM client, all the way through the call stack. You'll find errors faster, and you can set up latency metrics.

 You can learn more about how tracing provides a full picture of your application performance in the AWS Well-Architected Resilience best practice "REL06-BP07 Monitor End-To-End Tracing of Requests Through Your System" (*https://oreil.ly/rBvxI*).

Open your CloudWatch console in the us-east-1 region, and from the lefthand navigation browse to Cloudwatch → Traces. Most of the requests you'll see by default are from your canaries. The traces capture a sampling of all activity for your AvailableTrade application components, so you can filter them. Submit a few new Account Open forms to create traces, and then you can filter down to this request type. In the "X-Ray Traces query refiners" section (hidden in Figure 6-11), enter or build the following query:

```
(http.url = "https://elu3bc2iih.execute-api.us-east-1.amazonaws.com/prod/") AND
(http.method = "PUT")
```

Note that you will need to use your own API Gateway endpoint. You can build this using the query builder by picking the correct http.url, and the http.method of PUT, which is the Account Open request. Click the "Run query" button, and your query results should look similar to Figure 6-11.

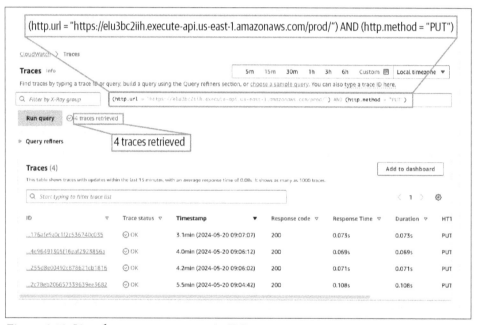

Figure 6-11. List of account open traces in X-Ray

If you click on one of the trace IDs, you'll be able to see a trace map that gives you a visual view of the AWS service resources that process your request. Your trace map should look similar to Figure 6-12.

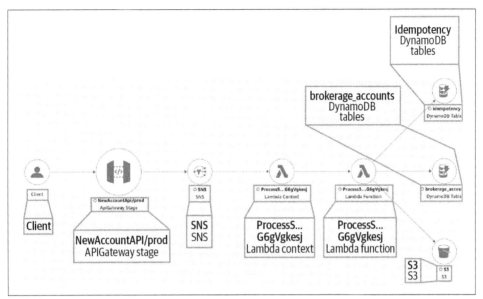

Figure 6-12. X-Ray trace map for Account Open

Scrolling down past the trace map, you'll see a segment timeline. There are actually two linked traces. The first covers API Gateway proxying your client request to the SNS topic for new Account Open. The second, the linked trace, details the Lambda that processes your request from the SQS queue. Note that SQS is not visible in this trace. Expand the second trace and review the timings for each step. You can see that ListObjectsV2 consumes over 50% of the call in Figure 6-13. When you need to understand request processing to improve performance, X-Ray makes it easy to determine where bottlenecks are.

Finally, X-Ray includes the log statements for a trace, making it easy to correlate logs with the steps of your request processing without having to jump between different CloudWatch log groups and streams. Scroll past the segment timeline and you'll see the Logs section. Click on different segments to filter to the logs. In Figure 6-14 you can see the Lambda logs for new Account Open.

You just touched the tip of the iceberg for X-Ray tracing and quickly learned that it is a powerful tool for understanding both the aggregate and individual request level behavior of your application. Tracing is an important observability tool for reducing the time it takes to understand and resolve issues. You will benefit from active tracing both during development and after you have deployed your application into production.

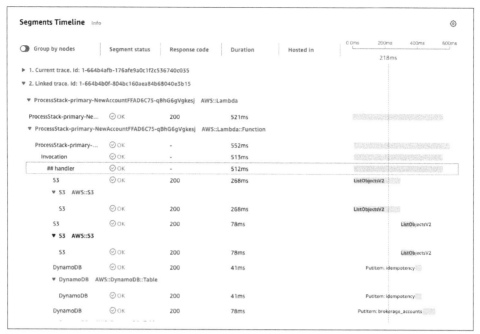

Figure 6-13. X-Ray segments view for Account Open

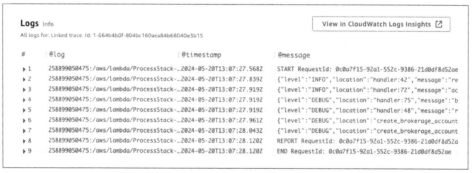

Figure 6-14. X-Ray view of Account Open logs

Cleaning Up

If you plan to work through Chapter 7, you'll want to leave the stacks from Chapters 3 through 6 installed. Chapter 7 depends on the CDK applications from these chapters. But be aware that if you stop working through the lessons and leave your infrastructure running, you will be charged for the running resources.

To remove AWS resources used in this chapter, refer to the "Cleaning Up" sections for Chapters 3 through 6. Follow the instructions to delete each of the CDK applications and the resources they leave behind, including logs, S3 buckets, and databases.

Summary

In this chapter, you learned how to build resilience in a frontend that is integrated with backend APIs. These resilience techniques include automated environment configuration, client timeouts, graceful degradation, and real user monitoring. In the next chapter, you will consider how to respond when the highly available features you've added are not enough to mitigate a failure.

There are failure modes that could impact the usability of your primary region, and you may consider multi-region failover as a mitigation strategy for these types of events. In these cases, you need to enact AWS regional failover strategies. In Chapter 7, you'll learn how to detect and determine when it is time to failover, as well as how to build a rehearsed and reliable automatic failover solution.

When Recovery Is Required

You have now reached the point where you have built out your reliable Available-Trade application. You have integrated your frontend and backend, and have been configuring these components to be resilient. As previously discussed, there will be failure modes where you will want to recover your applications. Your mitigations to certain failure modes may require you to use fault boundaries to provide a bounded recovery time.

Testing your recovery process is not just a task—it's a responsibility. It forms the backbone of your application's resilience. This process, comprising people, processes, and technology, must be thoroughly tested to instill a deep sense of commitment to its effectiveness during critical situations.

The primary purpose of these tests is to validate that all recovery mechanisms function as intended during an actual disruption. Regularly conducting recovery tests can identify potential weaknesses and gaps in your recovery plans, allowing for proactive improvements before actual incidents occur. This proactive approach minimizes the risk of prolonged downtime and data loss, which can have significant financial, operational, and reputational repercussions.

Recovery process testing is more than just familiarizing the team with the procedures and tools. It's about giving you a sense of control and confidence. This familiarity ensures that the response is swift and efficient when an actual incident occurs, reducing the impact on business operations. Regular testing also allows refining and optimizing recovery processes, incorporating lessons learned from each exercise. Ultimately, the consistent validation and enhancement of recovery processes build confidence not only in the organization's ability to maintain continuity and resilience in the face of unexpected challenges, but also confidence that the recovery plan works, so if it's required to execute, there won't be any hesitation.

This chapter focuses on technology-driven recovery. While we acknowledge the criticality of people and processes, our primary aim is to guide you through the technological aspects of recovery and how you orchestrate it. There are several ways to orchestrate a failover and recovery. The first step is to review your current process. You want to identify areas that can be automated, understand the sequence of events and dependencies, and, if there are any manual steps, ensure that these are documented clearly and concisely to avoid any human errors.

The recovery process should be designed to be flexible and empower you to choose the best method suited to your team's capabilities and preferences. Whether you write your own scripts or use AWS Systems Manager (SSM) documents, AWS Lambda, open source, or third-party options, the choice is yours. This trust in your expertise is crucial for the success of the recovery process.

This chapter uses AWS Systems Manager Automation, creating SSM documents to define the steps involved in failover and recovery processes. SSM documents are chosen because they allow the orchestration to be broken down into individual steps, making it easier to observe and understand the failover and recovery procedures. In real-world scenarios, these SSM documents can be the foundation for creating a comprehensive runbook that outlines all the steps for a failover. Recovery tasks can be created using either AWS Systems Manager or AWS Step Functions, depending on the tools your team is most familiar and comfortable with. The goal is to leverage the tools that best suit your team's expertise and preferences, and to minimize dependencies and make the recovery as simple as possible.

For the sake of this exercise, we will assume that our primary region is impaired and that we will want to failover and recover to our secondary region. It's important to note that we will run the failover and recovery from our secondary region since we assume our primary region is impaired.

Architecture Overview

The simplified full-stack architecture for the AvailableTrade application is shown in Figure 7-1.

Throughout this chapter, we'll explore the orchestration process in greater depth, breaking it down into individual steps to clarify understanding. We'll explore each step in detail, allowing you to grasp the intricacies of the failover and recovery procedures.

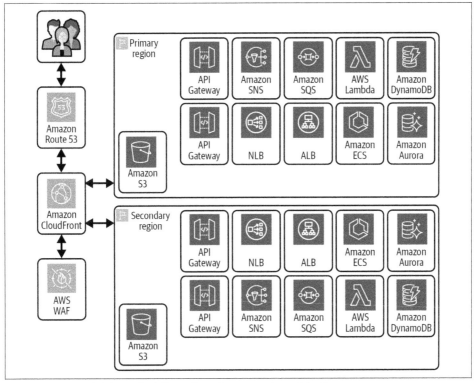

Figure 7-1. AvailableTrade full-stack architecture (simplified)

Deploying the AWS CDK Application

Before starting the hands-on lessons, you must have an Amazon Route 53 fully qualified domain name (FQDN) to continue. If you don't have a domain but want to obtain one, revisit Chapter 2. If you don't have a domain name and wish to avoid getting one, you can read through this chapter without doing the hands-on exercises.

To deploy these components, activate your Python virtual environment and set environment variables for the CDK solution. Be sure to review the *env.sh* file for the primary and secondary regions you've selected, confirm that you have the required permissions, and use the correct AWS account.

If you've already been working with a domain name, you can skip to the next section; otherwise, update the AWS_DOMAIN_NAME value in your *env.sh* file with your newly created domain name.

You will need to redeploy the frontend stacks in order to create Amazon Route 53 hosted zone and routing record:

```
cd AvailableTrade
source env.sh
cd AvailableTrade/src/frontend
cdk deploy --all --require-approval never
```

Deploy the AWS CDK Trade Stock Stack in Secondary Region

First, you'll need to deploy the Trade Stock API in the secondary region:

```
cd resiliency-engineering-on-aws
source .venv/bin/activate
source env.sh
cd resiliency-engineering-on-aws/src/trade_stock
cdk deploy TradeStockApiGatewayStackPrimary --require-approval never
cdk deploy TradeVpcStackSecondary --require-approval never
cdk deploy TradeDatabaseStackSecondary --require-approval never
cdk deploy TradeConfirmsStackSecondary --require-approval never
cdk deploy TradeOrderStackSecondary --require-approval never
cdk deploy TradeStockApiGatewayStackSecondary --require-approval never
```

Deploying the AWS CDK Orchestration Stack

Deploy your orchestration stack, providing the resources needed for this chapter:

```
cd AvailableTrade
source env.sh
cd AvailableTrade/src/recovery
cdk deploy Orchestration-Secondary-Stack Orchestration-Primary-Stack \
  --require-approval never
```

To ensure proper deployment, wait for the `Orchestration-Secondary-Stack` and `Orchestration-Primary-Stack` to finish creating their resources. Once complete, you can safely deploy the `Orchestration-Route53-Secondary-Stack` and `Orchestration-Route53-Primary-Stack` using the following commands:

```
cdk deploy Orchestration-Route53-Secondary-Stack \
  Orchestration-Route53-Primary-Stack --require-approval never
```

The first time you deploy the application, the deployment will run for several minutes as resources are created. Upon executing the **cdk deploy** command, a series of interconnected resources were orchestrated across your two AWS Regions to create automated failover capabilities.

In your primary AWS Region:

Amazon API Gateway custom domain names
  Two custom domain names, prefixed with `api-account` and `api-trade`, were established for your Amazon API Gateway endpoints. These domain names

enhance the user-friendliness and branding of the APIs and allow you to use Route 53 routing for failover.

Domain name association
The newly created custom domain names were linked to their respective Amazon API Gateway resources, ensuring that incoming requests are routed correctly.

In your secondary AWS Region:

AWS Certificate creation
A security certificate was generated to enable HTTPS encryption for the custom domain names. A security certificate protects data transmitted between clients and the APIs.

Amazon API custom domain names (secondary)
Mirroring the primary region, custom domain names for `api-account` and `api-trade` were also created in the secondary region.

Domain name association (secondary)
The secondary custom domains were associated with their corresponding Amazon API Gateway resources, preparing for failover scenarios.

Amazon CloudWatch custom metric and alarm
A metric was established within Amazon CloudWatch to monitor a custom metric created to control failover. An alarm was configured to trigger when this metric exceeds a defined threshold, indicating a failover is required.

Amazon Route 53 health check and failover record set
An Amazon Route 53 health check was created and linked to the Amazon CloudWatch alarm. A failover record set was also configured, with the primary record pointing to the primary region's Amazon API Gateway and the secondary record pointing to the secondary region's Amazon API Gateway. This setup ensures that traffic is automatically redirected to the secondary region if the health check fails in the primary region.

AWS SSM automation documents
A set of SSM documents was created to automate the failover process (Figure 7-2). These SSM documents will execute a series of steps in the event of a failure, including:

1. Amazon Aurora Global Database switchover: initiate the switchover process for the Amazon Aurora global database to the secondary region.

2. Signal AWS Lambda failover: upload a *failover.txt* file to an Amazon S3 bucket. This file signals the stack's AWS Lambda functions to switch operations to the secondary region.

3. Trigger Amazon CloudWatch alarm: update the custom metric to trigger the alarm, initiating the Amazon Route 53 failover.

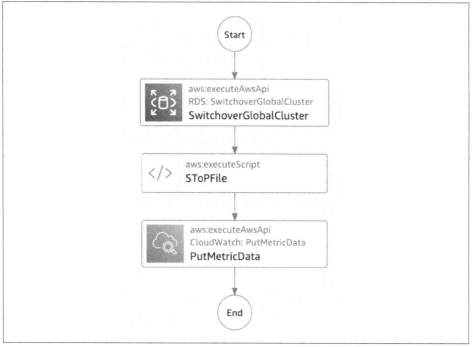

Figure 7-2. GUI representation of the SSM documents included in the automation

At the core of any failover strategy lies the orchestration component. You should build this to act as the conductor, coordinating the various actions to ensure a graceful failover. These actions should include people, processes, and technology, and can be a combination of manual and automated actions. Its primary responsibilities can include:

Monitoring
    The orchestration service continuously monitors primary region health. Monitoring is typically done through a combination of health checks, metric thresholds, synthetic canaries, and other indicators of system health.

Decision making
    Upon detecting an impairment or degradation in the primary region, the critical decision is made to initiate the failover process. A person usually makes this decision based on predefined criteria and thresholds, ensuring that failover occurs only when necessary.

Triggering

Once the decision to failover is made, the orchestration service triggers the execution of the AWS SSM documents. These documents contain step-by-step instructions for performing the failover process.

Coordination

The orchestration service oversees the execution of the SSM documents, ensuring that each step is completed successfully and in the correct order. It acts as a central point of control, coordinating the actions of various components involved in the failover.

Integrating Backend API to Frontend

Now that you've created custom domains for your backend APIs, you'll need to redeploy your frontend application to use the updated endpoints. To do this, follow the directions in this section.

To configure the frontend, run the following command, providing two parameters:

First parameter

Use Y (or y) to indicate that you're using custom domain endpoints.

Second parameter

Insert your full custom domain name (e.g., *api.yourcompany.com*).

```
cd AvailableTrade/src/frontend/website
npm run configure y <replace with your domain name>
npm run build
```

This command will generate configuration files (*.env.development* and *.env.production*) with the correct endpoint URLs for your frontend to use:

```
VITE_NEW_ACCOUNT_ENDPOINT=https://api-account.<your domain name>
VITE_TRADE_STOCK_ENDPOINT=https://api-trade.<your domain name>
```

To redeploy your frontend with the updated configuration, run the following commands:

```
cd AvailableTrade/src/frontend
cdk deploy --all --require-approval never
```

Validating the Region

Before you begin, let's verify that your AvailableTrade application is running in your primary region. Run the following command, replacing *<your-domain-name>*, and you will see an Availability Zone in your primary region being returned:

```
curl https://api-trade.<your-domain-name>/resilient/region-az

us-east-1b <== Response from curl
```

Database Failover and Switchover

First let's focus on the database stack shown in Figure 7-3.

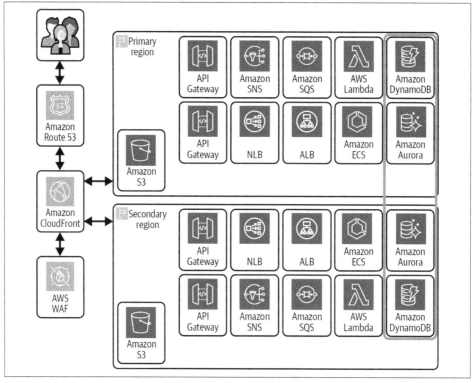

Figure 7-3. The database stack in the AvailableTrade architecture

Amazon Aurora Global Database is a powerful feature within the Amazon Aurora relational database service. It's designed to address the needs of globally distributed applications, providing high availability, disaster recovery, and low-latency reads across multiple AWS Regions.

An Amazon Aurora Global Database consists of a primary Amazon Aurora Database cluster in a designated primary region and up to 15 read-only secondary clusters in different regions. Write operations are performed exclusively on the primary cluster. Amazon Aurora Global Database leverages storage-based replication, where changes made to the storage layer of the primary cluster are asynchronously replicated to the secondary clusters. This design differs from traditional database replication, which typically occurs at the database engine level.

Replication between the primary and secondary clusters is remarkably fast, often achieving subsecond latency. This enables low-latency reads from the secondary clusters, allowing applications to serve users from geographically closer regions.

In the event of a region-wide service impairment or performance degradation in the primary region, one of the secondary regions can be promoted to take over as the new primary. This failover process is designed to be rapid, ensuring minimal downtime. You can customize the instance types and storage options for both the primary and secondary clusters, allowing you to optimize for cost and performance based on your specific requirements.

Key benefits include:

High availability
By replicating data across multiple regions, Amazon Aurora Global Database provides a high level of availability, minimizing the impact of regional outages.

Disaster recovery
The ability to quickly promote a secondary region to a primary ensures rapid recovery from region-wide service impairments.

Low-latency reads
Fast replication enables applications to serve read requests from the closest region, reducing end-user latency.

Global scalability
You can quickly scale read capacity by adding or removing secondary clusters as needed.

Amazon Aurora Global Database is ideal for applications with users spread across the globe, requiring low-latency access to data from different regions. It also provides a solution for disaster recovery, ensuring business continuity in the face of regional service impairments. Amazon Aurora Global Database also ensures high availability for critical applications that cannot tolerate downtime.

Promoting a secondary region to a new primary when initiating a failover is essential because, in a global cluster, this promotion ensures that the application can continue to perform read and write operations without interruption when the primary region becomes unavailable. This promotion is crucial for maintaining data consistency and operational continuity during a failover, minimizing downtime and mitigating the impact of regional service impairments.

There are two methods to promote an Aurora Global Database: failover and switchover.

Failover

In the Amazon Aurora Global Database context, *failover* is the process of promoting a secondary region to take over as the new primary region (writer) when the current primary region cluster experiences an unexpected outage or failure. This promotion can be done automatically or manually. Failover is commonly used in disaster recovery situations where the primary region cluster faces an unplanned disruption, such as a regional impairment or critical infrastructure failure. By failing over to a secondary region, the database remains available and writable, minimizing downtime and ensuring application continuity during unforeseen events. It's important to note that there is a risk of data loss during a failover scenario. Be aware of this potential issue and ensure you have a well-defined data reconciliation process in place to handle such situations when a failover is necessary.

Aurora Global Database failover comes in two forms: managed and manual. Managed failovers, the preferred option for disaster recovery, seamlessly transition your primary cluster to a chosen secondary region while preserving your database's replication topology. The selected secondary cluster promotes a read-only node to full writer status, assuming the primary cluster's role with minimal downtime. However, data not replicated to the chosen secondary cluster before the failover will be lost.

Conversely, manual failovers are used when managed failovers aren't possible, such as when primary and secondary regions have incompatible engine versions. Manual failovers disrupt the cluster topology, requiring you to manually reconfigure the Aurora Global Database topology.

When the recovery point objective (RPO) is greater than zero, it implies that some data loss is tolerable in a disaster recovery scenario. Several reconciliation methods are used to address potential data inconsistencies and ensure data integrity after recovery:

Checksum comparisons
> This method involves comparing checksums (e.g., MD5, SHA-256) of data blocks or files before and after replication. Discrepancies in checksums indicate data corruption or loss during replication, triggering the need for further investigation and potential retransmission of the affected data.

Journaling and log shipping
> Database systems often maintain transaction logs (journals) to record changes. Log shipping involves replicating these logs to the secondary site, allowing for replaying transactions and bringing the secondary data store up to a consistent state. The RPO in this case is limited by the frequency of log shipping.

Delta replication
> Instead of replicating the entire dataset, only the changes (deltas) made since the last synchronization are transferred. This reduces the amount of data transferred,

potentially improving recovery time. The RPO depends on the frequency of delta synchronization.

Timestamp comparisons

Each data item or transaction is tagged with a timestamp. During recovery, the system compares timestamps of the primary and secondary data stores. Data with newer timestamps on the secondary site is discarded, while data with older timestamps on the primary site is retransmitted. Replication lag metrics and monitoring, if available, can be used for comparison.

Application-level reconciliation

Some applications have built-in mechanisms for data reconciliation, such as conflict resolution for collaborative documents or version control systems for code. These mechanisms are leveraged to identify and resolve inconsistencies in application-specific data.

Manual verification

In certain scenarios, manual verification of data consistency may be required, especially for critical applications or where automated methods are not feasible. This involves human intervention to compare data between primary and secondary systems and manually correct any discrepancies.

Choosing the most appropriate reconciliation method depends on several factors, including:

RPO

The acceptable amount of data loss influences the choice of method. For example, log shipping might be suitable for low RPOs, while delta replication might be more appropriate for higher RPOs.

Data type

The nature of the data being replicated (structured, unstructured, etc.) can dictate the appropriate method.

Application requirements

The specific needs and capabilities of the application may necessitate specific reconciliation techniques.

Cost and complexity

Some methods are more complex and resource intensive to implement than others, affecting the overall cost and effort of maintaining data consistency.

In practice, a combination of these reconciliation methods is often used to achieve the desired level of data consistency and meet the defined RPO objectives in a disaster recovery strategy.

Switchover

In Amazon Aurora Global Database, *switchover* is a planned process involving intentionally switching the primary region role to a secondary one. This operation is usually performed for maintenance or when a regional impairment affects another component in your architecture, but you must failover the entire stack. Unlike failover, switchover is a controlled and coordinated activity designed to ensure data integrity. There is no data loss during a switchover scenario because your primary database remains intact. The process starts by stopping writes to the primary cluster and waiting for data replication from the primary to the secondary cluster to catch up. Once the replication is complete, the secondary cluster is promoted to become the new writer.

While failover is an emergency response to unexpected outages, switchover is a proactive, planned activity for maintenance or controlled failover. Understanding these differences helps ensure appropriate measures are taken to maintain the high availability and resilience of your Aurora Global Database deployments.

In this exercise, we will demonstrate a switchover scenario.

Navigate to the SSM documents dashboard in your secondary region and click on the "Owned by Me" tab. You will see a document that starts with *Orchestration-Secondary-Stack-AvailableTradeFailoverAutomation*. If you view the document content, you can see the first step of the document is executing the SwitchoverGlobalCluster AWS API call, as shown in the code snippet:

```
{
    "inputs": {
      "TargetDbClusterIdentifier": "arn:aws:rds:us-west-2:xxxx:cluster:stock",
      "Service": "rds",
      "Api": "SwitchoverGlobalCluster",
      "GlobalClusterIdentifier": "global-trade-cluster"
},
      "name": "SwitchoverGlobalCluster",
      "action": "aws:executeAwsApi",
      "nextStep": "SToPFile"
},
```

Click "Execute automation," then click Execute. Navigate back to the Amazon RDS Databases dashboard, and you'll notice that the stock-global cluster's status has changed to "Switching over," as illustrated in Figure 7-4. This indicates that the switchover process is in progress.

You're also leveraging Amazon DynamoDB global tables in your architecture. This powerful feature extends the capabilities of Amazon DynamoDB, a fully managed NoSQL database service, by enabling seamless replication of your tables across multiple AWS Regions. Global tables provides fast, local read and write performance for globally distributed applications.

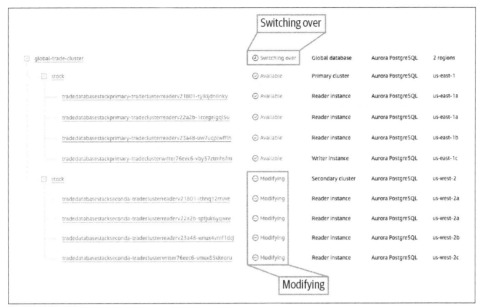

global-trade-cluster	⊙ Switching over	Global database	Aurora PostgreSQL	2 regions
stock	⊘ Available	Primary cluster	Aurora PostgreSQL	us-east-1
tradedatabasestackprimary-tradeclusterreaderv21801-tylkljdn8nky	⊘ Available	Reader instance	Aurora PostgreSQL	us-east-1a
tradedatabasestackprimary-tradeclusterreaderv22a2b-1ccegeigql5u	⊘ Available	Reader instance	Aurora PostgreSQL	us-east-1a
tradedatabasestackprimary-tradeclusterreaderv23a48-uw7uqpiwffih	⊘ Available	Reader instance	Aurora PostgreSQL	us-east-1b
tradedatabasestackprimary-tradeclusterwriter76eec6-vby57ztmhsfm	⊘ Available	Writer instance	Aurora PostgreSQL	us-east-1c
stock	⊙ Modifying	Secondary cluster	Aurora PostgreSQL	us-west-2
tradedatabasestacksecondа-tradeclusterreaderv21801-ithnq12rruve	⊙ Modifying	Reader instance	Aurora PostgreSQL	us-west-2a
tradedatabasestacksecondа-tradeclusterreaderv22a2b-spfjuk6yqwre	⊙ Modifying	Reader instance	Aurora PostgreSQL	us-west-2a
tradedatabasestacksecondа-tradeclusterreaderv23a48-wnux4vmf1dcj	⊙ Modifying	Reader instance	Aurora PostgreSQL	us-west-2b
tradedatabasestacksecondа-tradeclusterwriter76eec6-smux85kkeoru	⊙ Modifying	Reader instance	Aurora PostgreSQL	us-west-2c

Figure 7-4. Amazon Aurora RDS switchover in progress

An Amazon DynamoDB global table consists of one or more replica tables, each residing in a different AWS Region. You designate one table as the primary table, and all others are secondary replicas. Amazon DynamoDB automatically replicates data between the primary and secondary tables. Changes made to the primary table are propagated asynchronously to all replicas, ensuring that all tables eventually have consistent copies of the data. Since writes can happen concurrently in different regions, conflicts might arise. Amazon DynamoDB global tables offer two conflict resolution strategies:

Last writer wins (LWW)
  The most recent write operation, regardless of the region, is considered the winner.

Custom conflict resolution
  You can write your own conflict resolution logic using AWS Lambda functions.

Applications can read and write data from the Amazon DynamoDB table in the region that is closest to them. This reduces latency and improves the user experience. If a region experiences a service impairment, Amazon DynamoDB can automatically promote a secondary table to become the new primary table, ensuring continuous availability of your application.

Key benefits include:

Low-latency access
Users can access data from the nearest region, reducing latency and improving application performance.

High availability
Data is replicated across multiple regions, providing resilience against regional outages.

Disaster recovery
Automatic failover ensures that your application can continue operating even if a region becomes unavailable.

Global scalability
You can easily add or remove replica tables to scale your application globally.

Amazon DynamoDB global tables are ideal for globally distributed applications with users spread across the globe, requiring low-latency access to data from different regions. It is also suitable for applications that need to keep data synchronized across multiple regions in near real time. For high-traffic websites and mobile applications, Amazon DynamoDB global tables provide the scalability and resilience needed to handle large volumes of traffic from users around the world.

If you are considering using DynamoDB global tables, be sure to carefully evaluate your application's requirements and choose the conflict resolution strategy that best suits your needs.

Scaling Compute

Next let's focus on the compute stack shown in Figure 7-5.

Your compute layer uses AWS Fargate for Amazon Elastic Container Service (Amazon ECS) and AWS Lambda, which offer significant benefits for managing compute resources, particularly during failover situations.

AWS Fargate for Amazon ECS is a serverless compute engine for containers. It allows you to run containers without having to manage the underlying infrastructure, like servers or clusters of Amazon EC2 instances. With AWS Fargate for Amazon ECS, you define the resources your containers need (CPU, memory, etc.), and AWS handles the rest, including scaling, patching, and securing the infrastructure.

One key advantage of using AWS Fargate for Amazon ECS is its ability to scale automatically based on demand. Automatically scaling means AWS Fargate for Amazon ECS can automatically launch new containers to handle the increased load when traffic is directed to the secondary region during a failover. Auto-scaling eliminates the need for you to manually scale up the infrastructure in the secondary region before or during a failover event.

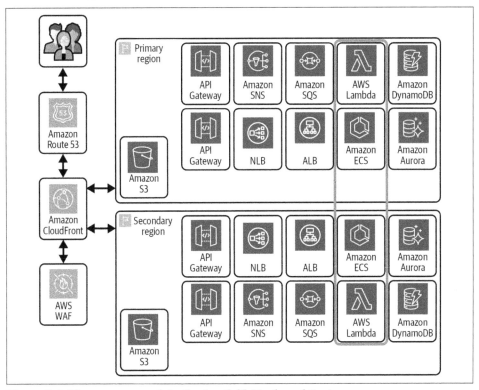

Figure 7-5. The compute stack in the AvailableTrade architecture

Here's how it works in the context of a failover:

1. Primary region service impairment: if the primary region experiences a service impairment or performance degradation, after a failover decision has been made, your application's traffic will be redirected to the secondary region.

2. Increased load: the secondary region will experience an immediate increase in traffic due to the failover.

3. Fargate auto scaling: AWS Fargate for Amazon ECS will detect this increased load and automatically launch additional containers in the secondary region to handle the traffic.

4. Seamless transition: the failover process is transparent to your users, who will continue to access your application uninterrupted.

AWS Lambda is a serverless computing service that can run code without provisioning or managing servers. It executes your code only when needed and scales automatically, from a few requests per day to thousands per second. You pay only for the computing time you consume, and there is no charge when your code is not running.

One of AWS Lambda's core features is its inherent scalability. AWS Lambda functions are designed to scale automatically based on the incoming workload. Automatically scaling means that when traffic is directed to the secondary region during a failover, AWS Lambda can seamlessly handle the increased load by spinning up new instances of your functions as needed.

Here's how it works in the context of a failover:

1. Primary region service impairment: if the primary region experiences a service impairment or performance degradation, after a failover decision has been made, your application's traffic will be redirected to the secondary region.

2. Increased load: AWS Lambda in the secondary region will experience an immediate increase in invocations due to the failover.

3. AWS Lambda auto-scaling: AWS Lambda automatically scales up by creating new instances of your functions to handle the increased traffic. This scaling happens rapidly, often within milliseconds, ensuring that your application can handle the load seamlessly.

4. Seamless transition: the failover process is transparent to your users, who will continue to access your application without interruption.

Keep in mind that while each of these services offers automatic scaling, it's not instantaneous. Under extreme load, it's possible to exceed your application's capacity before scaling mechanisms can fully respond. This can lead to temporary overload and potentially impact service availability during a failover. To ensure a seamless failover experience, it's crucial to thoroughly test your system under realistic load conditions.

Testing will help you identify any bottlenecks or limitations in your configurations and allow you to optimize your scaling settings accordingly. Depending on your application's traffic patterns and scaling behavior, you should consider proactively scaling out your Amazon ECS cluster in the secondary region before initiating a failover. For AWS Lambda, you can scale out proactively using the provisioned concurrency feature. This feature allows you to set a minimum number of execution environments that are always ready to respond to requests, eliminating the cold start latency. Setting provisioned concurrency ensures sufficient resources are available to handle the sudden influx of traffic and maintain optimal performance during the transition.

By taking these precautions and conducting thorough load testing, you can confidently rely on auto-scaling capabilities to handle failovers gracefully, minimizing any potential disruptions to your application's availability and performance.

Routing at the Lambda Layer

In the lesson "STOP: Business Continuity Regional Switchover" on page 115, you were able to test the pattern by uploading the *failover.txt* file to an Amazon S3 bucket. In the AWS Lambda function code, when processing each message in a batch, the presence of the file is checked to determine whether it is currently running in your primary or secondary region.

Since you are in recovery mode, you will want to incorporate this step into your orchestration layer. The *failover.txt* file needs to be uploaded to your Amazon S3 bucket. Navigate back to the SSM documents dashboard and view the document content. Here you can see the next step of the document is executing the `executeScript` command, as shown in the code snippet:

```
{
    "inputs": {
      "InputPayload": {
        "bucket_name": "failover-bucket-us-west-2-xxxx"
      },
      "Script": "import boto3\n\n
          # Create the text file\n
          with open(\"failover.txt\", \"w\") as f:\n
          f.write(\"This is a test file for failover.\")\n\n
          # Upload the file to the S3 bucket\n
          s3 = boto3.client('s3')\n
          bucket_name = event['InputPayload']['bucket_name'] \n
          file_name = \"failover.txt\"\n
          s3.upload_file(file_name, bucket_name, file_name)\n\n
          print(f\"File '{file_name}' uploaded to bucket '{bucket_name}'.\")",
      "Runtime": "python3.10",
      "Handler": "uploadFile"
  },
    "name": "SToPFile",
    "action": "aws:executeScript",
    "nextStep": "PutMetricData"
}
```

Check the status of your document. Once the `SToPFile` step has finished executing, navigate to the Amazon S3 buckets dashboard and into your *failover-bucket-*. You will see the *failover.txt* file, as illustrated in Figure 7-6. Having the file in the Amazon S3 bucket indicates that the AWS Lambda function is currently processing in the secondary region.

Figure 7-6. Amazon S3 failover bucket

DNS Failover

And finally, now that our secondary region is ready to accept requests, let's focus on the routing layer, as shown in Figure 7-7.

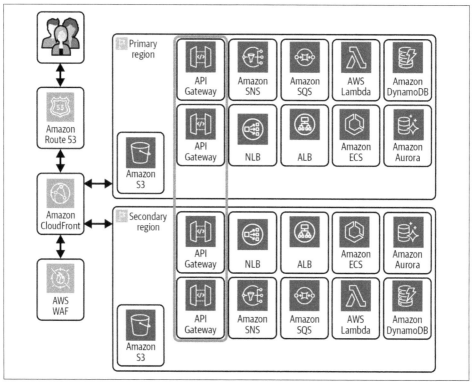

Figure 7-7. The frontend stack in the AvailableTrade architecture

When using Amazon Route 53 for DNS, you can utilize health checks in combination with Amazon CloudWatch alarm metrics to manage routing. This method is effective for manually transferring workloads to another region, combining the DNS management capabilities of Amazon Route 53 with the comprehensive monitoring features of Amazon CloudWatch to respond proactively and efficiently to service disruptions.

Amazon Route 53 offers health check functionality to monitor the availability and performance of your endpoints, such as web servers, databases, or API resources. These health checks can be configured to toggle traffic, allowing you to switch from your primary site to your secondary site as part of your recovery plan.

Failover records in Amazon Route 53 ensure high application availability and resiliency by routing traffic to alternate resources when primary resources become unavailable. When configured, Amazon Route 53 continuously monitors the health of the specified primary resources using health checks. Amazon Route 53 automatically redirects traffic to the secondary resources if these health checks detect an issue. This failover routing policy ensures minimal end-user disruption by seamlessly shifting the workload to healthy endpoints. Our application is configured to use health checks and Amazon Route 53 DNS failover records to control when failover occurs manually.

Amazon Route 53 offers three distinct types of health checks, each serving a unique purpose in ensuring the optimal performance and reliability of your applications and services:

Endpoint health checks
These versatile checks monitor the health of specific endpoints, such as web servers, application load balancers, or custom APIs. By periodically sending requests to the designated endpoint, Amazon Route 53 verifies its availability and responsiveness. If an endpoint fails the check, indicating potential downtime or unavailability, Amazon Route 53 can automatically reroute traffic to a healthy endpoint, ensuring uninterrupted service for your users. This is especially valuable for highly available architectures with multiple endpoints, as it allows for seamless failover and minimizes the impact of service disruptions.

Calculated health checks
Acting as the orchestrators of your health check ecosystem, calculated health checks aggregate the results of multiple endpoint health checks. They provide a holistic view of your system's health by evaluating the combined status of individual components. You can define complex logic to trigger specific actions based on the overall health. For instance, you might configure a calculated health check to trigger a failover only if a majority of your endpoints fail, or initiate different levels of alerts depending on the severity of the health degradation. This level of granularity enables sophisticated traffic management and resilience strategies.

Amazon CloudWatch alarm health checks

Integrating directly with Amazon CloudWatch, these health checks monitor the status of Amazon CloudWatch alarms, which are triggered based on various metrics. This provides a broader perspective on the health of your application or infrastructure, as it takes into account performance and resource utilization in addition to simple availability checks. When an Amazon CloudWatch alarm is triggered, indicating a potential issue, Amazon Route 53 can adjust traffic routing to minimize the impact of the problem. This proactive approach allows you to maintain service levels even when performance degrades, enhancing the overall user experience.

You are utilizing an Amazon CloudWatch alarm monitoring a custom metric as the failover criteria. You are gaining precise control over determining resource health and triggering failovers in Amazon Route 53. Unlike standard endpoint health checks, custom metrics offer the flexibility to define specific conditions tailored to your application's unique health indicators. This allows you to proactively trigger a failover by simply sending metric data that breaches the alarm's threshold, providing you with more control and adaptability in managing failover scenarios.

As part of the CDK deployment in this chapter, you have already deployed Amazon Route 53 failover records and an associated health check to monitor the critical Amazon API Gateway endpoints in the primary region. Figure 7-8 is a representation of the Amazon Route 53 failover record set that was created during deployment.

Navigate to the Amazon Route 53 health check dashboard to inquire about this health check. You should see a health check named `AvailableTradeFailoverHealth Check`, as shown in Figure 7-9.

This health check has been associated with the DNS failover record that is routing for the Amazon API Gateway requests. Navigate to the Amazon Route 53 hosted zones dashboard to observe this association. There will be two DNS failover records per Amazon API Gateway endpoint: `api-account.your-domain-name.com` and `api-trade.your-domain.name.com`. The primary record will be routed to the Amazon API Gateway in your primary region, and the secondary will be routed to the Amazon API Gateway in your secondary region. Review the record details to verify the health check ID corresponds to your health check.

Additionally, the associated Amazon CloudWatch alarm and custom metric have been created for you in your secondary region. The Amazon CloudWatch alarm is also associated with the Amazon Route 53 health check. It's important to monitor your primary region's workload from your secondary region to ensure comprehensive visibility and proactive management of your system's health.

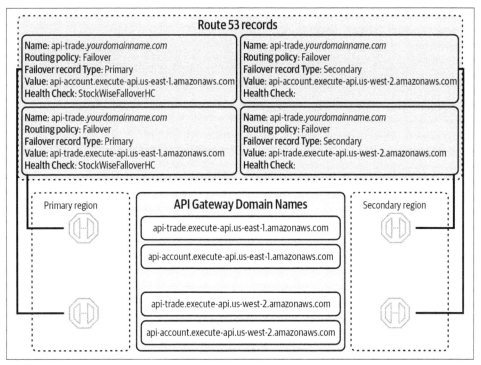

Figure 7-8. Amazon Route 53 failover record set

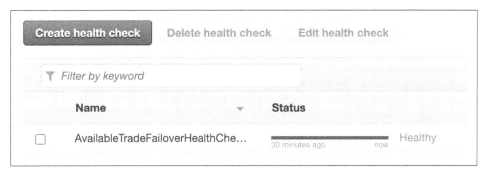

Figure 7-9. Amazon Route 53 health checks

Monitoring allows you to detect and respond to issues in the primary region more swiftly, even if the primary region's monitoring capabilities are compromised. Cross-region monitoring enhances reliability and resilience by independently verifying the primary region's status. It ensures that failover mechanisms are triggered accurately and promptly, minimizing downtime and maintaining seamless service availability for end users. Additionally, it helps validate the readiness of the secondary region to take over, ensuring a smooth transition during failover events.

Navigate to your secondary region's Amazon CloudWatch alarms dashboard and choose the `AvailableTradeFailoverAlarm` alarm. The alarm should be in an "Insufficient data" state, as shown in Figure 7-10. This status is because the metric still needs to get data points. The Amazon CloudWatch alarm will trigger when the `AvailableTradeFailoverMetric` metric has a data point value greater than 2 within 1 minute.

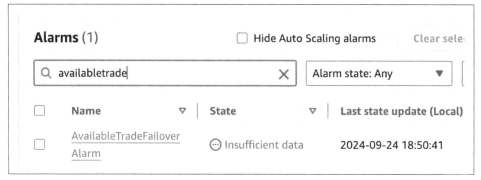

Figure 7-10. Amazon CloudWatch alarm metric

Navigate back to the SSM documents dashboard and view the document content. You can see that the next step of the document is executing the `PutMetricData` AWS API call, as shown in the code snippet:

```
{
  "inputs": {
    "Service": "cloudwatch",
    "Api": "PutMetricData",
    "Namespace": "AvailableTrade",
    "MetricData": [
      {
        "MetricName": "AvailableTradeFailoverMetric",
        "Value": 3
      }
    ]
  },
  "name": "PutMetricData",
  "action": "aws:executeAwsApi",
  "isEnd": true
}
```

Check the run status of your document. Once the `PutMetricData` step is finished executing, navigate back to the Amazon CloudWatch alarms dashboard, and you'll see that the `AvailableTradeFailoverAlarm` alarm status has changed to "In alarm," as shown in Figure 7-11. This status change indicates that the alarm has been triggered.

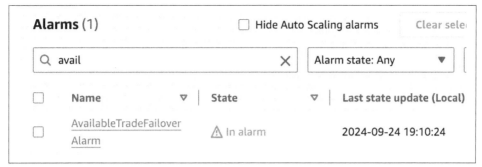

Figure 7-11. Amazon CloudWatch alarming

 It will take about a minute for the `AvailableTradeFailoverAlarm` to show an "In Alarm" status.

You can examine the alarm's details and the associated metric by clicking the provided link. The alarm is configured to trigger when the `AvailableTradeFailoverMetric` value exceeds 2, as illustrated in Figure 7-12. While 2 is an arbitrary threshold in this example, the core principle is to establish a metric with a predefined threshold, allowing you to deliberately trigger the alarm by sending a metric value that breaches this threshold. This threshold serves as a critical trigger point for the Route 53 health check, which monitors the metric data.

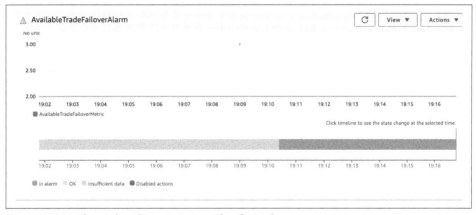

Figure 7-12. Alarm details in Amazon CloudWatch

Navigating back to the Amazon Route 53 health check dashboard, you'll see the `AvailableTradeFailoverHealthCheck` health check is Unhealthy, as shown in Figure 7-13. This status is because the health check is associated with `AvailableTrade FailoverAlarm`.

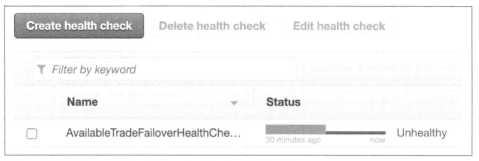

Figure 7-13. Amazon Route 53 unhealthy health checks

Controlling failover empowers your team to assess the situation and make informed decisions, providing control over the failover process. Your organization or team must establish clear criteria for initiating a failover. The decision to failover should be based on your business requirements and the application's recovery objectives. Failover decisions can vary from organization to organization and even application to application.

Importance of Backups

In this chapter, we demonstrated how to orchestrate failovers for Amazon Aurora (using replication and promotion) and Amazon DynamoDB (leveraging replication alone). As best practices dictate, automated backups for Aurora and point-in-time recovery for DynamoDB were enabled to further enhance data protection. Our hypothetical failure scenario assumed no data loss or corruption. However, it's important to highlight that a robust data protection strategy encompasses more than just failover mechanisms and should include a multifaceted approach incorporating backups, replication, and other disaster recovery measures.

Backups are essential for ensuring business continuity and data resilience. A well-defined data management strategy outlines what data needs to be backed up and the frequency of those backups. This strategy should align with your RPO, which defines the maximum tolerable data loss in a recovery scenario.

Many industries are subject to regulations that require regular data backups and the ability to restore data within specific time frames. Adhering to these requirements helps protect organizations from legal and financial risks. Furthermore, the prevalence of cyber threats, such as ransomware, makes regular, secure backups essential. These backups provide a critical safeguard, allowing businesses to recover their data in the event of a cyberattack, thereby minimizing downtime and potential financial losses.

Human error, such as accidental deletions or modifications, is another common cause of data loss. Routine backups act as a safety net, enabling the restoration of data to its previous state and reducing the impact of such errors on business operations.

A consistent backup schedule is key to ensuring the most recent and critical data is always protected. Frequent backups minimize the risk of significant data loss and maintain up-to-date recovery points. In the event of a disaster, a recent backup can be restored, minimizing downtime and ensuring business continuity.

To further enhance data protection, storing backups offsite or across multiple regions is recommended. This practice safeguards data against localized disruptions or failures. If one location becomes unavailable, data can be retrieved from another, ensuring business operations can continue. It's important to note that data restoration from backups can differ from replication-based recovery and may impact recovery time objectives (RTO). Regular testing of backup and restoration procedures is therefore vital to guarantee data availability, functionality, and reliability within acceptable time frames.

AWS Backup significantly aids data recovery by offering a robust and centralized solution for backing up your AWS resources. It simplifies the creation, scheduling, and management of backups across multiple services, ensuring that your data is protected and readily available for recovery in the event of data loss, corruption, or accidental deletion.

AWS Backup simplifies data protection by offering a centralized interface for managing backups across various AWS services, including EC2 instances, EBS volumes, RDS databases, DynamoDB tables, EFS filesystems, and Storage Gateway volumes. This unified approach streamlines backup processes and ensures consistent backup policies across your AWS resources.

Automated backups can be scheduled at your preferred frequency (hourly, daily, weekly, monthly, or yearly), keeping your data current and minimizing the risk of human error. AWS Backup also supports copying backups to different regions or accounts for enhanced resilience and disaster recovery.

The service's point-in-time recovery feature enables you to restore data to a specific point in time before an incident, mitigating data loss. Additionally, you can configure AWS Backup to automatically transition older backups to lower-cost storage tiers like Amazon S3 Glacier, optimizing storage costs while retaining backups for long-term archival or compliance purposes.

Avoiding Configuration Drift

Configuration drift, the divergence of AWS service configurations in a multi-region deployment from their intended state due to unplanned changes or inconsistencies, can severely undermine the success of your failover strategy.

When AWS infrastructure and services are not identically configured across primary and secondary regions, your application's behavior during a failover can become unpredictable. This inconsistency can manifest as unexpected errors, performance bottlenecks, or even complete application failure. Additionally, configuration drift can directly impede the failover process itself. For instance, if a security group in the secondary region isn't configured to allow necessary traffic, the failover may be unsuccessful.

In the event of a failover, manually identifying and rectifying configuration discrepancies would drastically increase the recovery time, prolonging downtime and causing significant disruptions for your users. Furthermore, configuration drift can inadvertently introduce security vulnerabilities in the secondary region that were not present in the primary region. As an example, if an Amazon S3 bucket in the secondary region lacks the same encryption settings as the primary bucket, sensitive data could be exposed.

To guarantee the seamless operation of your applications and services across multiple regions, it's imperative to establish and maintain consistent configurations for your AWS resources. This minimizes the risk of unexpected behavior or failures during failovers or regional disruptions. Additionally, proactively monitoring and managing service quotas is essential to prevent application downtime or throttling.

Here are several strategies you can employ to achieve configuration consistency and manage service quotas:

Infrastructure as code (IaC)
Use IaC tools like AWS CloudFormation or Terraform to define your infrastructure as code. This allows you to version control your configurations, easily replicate them across regions, and automatically provision resources with identical settings.

AWS Config
Leverage AWS Config to track and assess the configuration settings of your AWS resources. It provides a detailed inventory of your resources and their configurations, alerting you to any deviations from desired baselines.

AWS CloudFormation StackSets
Employ StackSets to deploy and manage stacks across multiple accounts and regions, ensuring consistent configurations for shared infrastructure components.

AWS Service Quotas
> Monitor service quotas for each AWS service in all regions your application uses. You can set Amazon CloudWatch alarms to notify you when usage approaches quota limits.

Automated quota increases
> Use the AWS Service Quotas API to programmatically request quota increases when usage approaches predefined thresholds. This helps prevent service disruptions due to quota limitations.

Automated testing
> Implement automated tests that verify the configuration of your AWS services in all regions. This will help you identify and fix any configuration drift before it causes problems.

Regular audits
> Conduct periodic audits of your AWS resource configurations and service quotas across regions. This helps identify and rectify any inconsistencies or limitations that may have arisen due to manual changes or drift.

Change management processes
> Establish rigorous change management processes to ensure that any changes to AWS resource configurations are carefully planned, reviewed, and tested before being deployed across regions.

By incorporating these strategies, you can proactively manage configuration drift, prevent service disruptions due to quota limitations, and maintain a resilient and reliable multi-region AWS environment.

Failover Verification

Let's verify that our AvailableTrade application is now running in your secondary region. Run the following command, replacing *<your-domain-name>*, and you will see an Availability Zone in your secondary region being returned:

```
curl https://api-trade.<your-domain-name>/resilient/region-az

us-west-1b <== Response from curl
```

Your application's stacks have failed over as part of the series of AWS Systems Manager documents run as part of your orchestration. You may choose to failover components or services in your application versus an entire stack in your own applications.

Cleaning Up

The cleanup process is even more straightforward since you have used the AWS Cloud Development Kit (CDK) throughout this chapter. CDK provides a convenient command to destroy all the stacks and resources your CDK application creates. To clean up your environment and avoid unnecessary charges, run the following commands:

```
cd AvailableTrade/src/frontend
cdk destroy --all
```

This will initiate the destruction process for all the stacks defined in your CDK application. When prompted, type **y** to confirm the deletion.

CDK will then begin destroying all the stacks and their associated resources. This process may take some time, depending on the number and complexity of the resources within the stacks. You can monitor the terminal output destruction progress. Once the destruction process is complete, CDK will display a success message indicating that all the stacks have been successfully destroyed. At this point, all the resources created by your CDK application will be removed, and you will no longer incur charges for those resources. With the **cdk destroy --all** command, you can easily clean up your environment and avoid unnecessary costs. It's a best practice to run this command when you no longer need the resources created by your CDK application, ensuring that your AWS account remains tidy and cost-effective.

Summary

In this chapter, you gained a deeper understanding of orchestrating a failover in AWS, recognizing that the specific AWS services used in your applications determine the required implementation details. While the decision to initiate a failover is typically a human one, the subsequent failover and recovery steps in a production environment are usually automated through a runbook, as demonstrated in this chapter.

Critically, you learned that people and processes are as integral to a successful recovery as the technology itself. To ensure confidence in your recovery strategy, it's imperative to conduct thorough testing that simulates real-world failure scenarios, evaluating the effectiveness of your people, processes, and technology under pressure.

Looking ahead, Part III will guide you through building a new architecture focused on streaming and batch services, expanding your understanding of resilient system design in AWS.

Discovering Trading Opportunities

As a trader or financial analyst, your objective is to identify profitable opportunities by buying low and selling high. But how do you determine what price points are considered low or high? The answer lies in leveraging technical analysis and fundamental research to make informed trading decisions.

In this part of the book, you'll embark on a journey to build a market analysis solution that empowers you to discover trading opportunities by harnessing the power of real-time market data, news insights, and resilient streaming architectures. You'll learn how to engineer systems that consume high volumes of data and transform it into actionable insights with low latency, giving you a competitive edge in the fast-paced world of stock trading.

Imagine having the ability to ingest real-time stock prices, enrich them with proprietary information, and identify buy and sell signals using custom APIs and scalable microservices. You'll explore techniques to consume market data feeds, such as OHLCV (Open, High, Low, Close, Volume) data points, and apply technical analysis to uncover patterns and trends.

But technical analysis alone is not enough. Fundamental research plays a crucial role in shaping market opinions and influencing price movements. You'll learn how to systematically leverage news reports from trusted sources like *The Wall Street Journal* and Bloomberg. By collecting, curating, and cleaning news articles, you'll build a pipeline that indexes them into NoSQL databases, enabling you to quickly retrieve relevant information and gain valuable insights.

To make your market analysis solution even more powerful, you'll integrate natural language interfaces that combine technical and fundamental insights from proprietary databases and custom APIs. This will enable you to ask questions, explore signals, and find the needle in the haystack, as if you had your own personal research analyst at your fingertips.

However, building a resilient and highly available market analysis solution is not without its challenges. You'll need to design your system to withstand common hardware failures and even infrequent large-scale events (LSEs) to ensure that your trading decisions are based on up-to-date and accessible information.

In this part of the book, you'll learn how to tackle these challenges head-on. You'll gain the skills and knowledge to build a mission-critical market analysis solution while balancing cost and performance. Here's a glimpse of what you'll accomplish:

Chapter 8, "Real-Time Market Data Analytics"
  In this chapter, you'll discover how to create market signals using technical analysis with industry-standard services like Apache Kafka. You'll learn to reliably stage, process, and distribute massive volumes of structured data, enabling you to make timely trading decisions based on real-time market movements.

Chapter 9, "Building Reliable News Feed Ingestion and Search APIs"
  Fundamental research is key to understanding the underlying drivers of price fluctuations. In this chapter, you'll explore techniques to collect, curate, and clean news articles from third-party sources. You'll build an ingestion pipeline that indexes these articles into Amazon OpenSearch and related NoSQL databases, empowering you to quickly retrieve relevant news and gain valuable insights.

Chapter 10, "Building Resilient Multi-Region Architectures"
  Building a resilient market analysis solution requires careful consideration of disaster recovery strategies. In this chapter, you'll learn how to design cross-regional architectures for real-time market data and news ingestion services. You'll explore best practices and techniques to ensure high availability and fault tolerance, even in the face of regional outages or large-scale events.

Here, you'll find sample code and AWS CDK (Cloud Development Kit) templates in the book's GitHub repository. These resources will enable you to quickly provision and modify the necessary constructs on AWS, accelerating your learning journey.

Get ready to embark on an exciting adventure that will transform your approach to discovering trading opportunities. By the end of Part III, you'll have the skills and knowledge to build a powerful market analysis solution that leverages real-time data, news insights, and resilient streaming architectures. You'll be equipped to make data-driven trading decisions with confidence, giving you a competitive edge in the dynamic world of stock trading. Let's dive into the world of building resilient and scalable market analysis solutions.

## CHAPTER 8

Real-Time Market Data Analytics

Edward Calahan invented the ticker tape in 1867, using telegraph lines to transmit updates about stock market activity. The name refers to the rhythmic sound of the machine printing a continuous stream of information. Within a few years, other inventors built upon this protocol, evolving it into the scrolling stock price updates we see on news channels today.

Streaming information has fundamentally transformed the stock industry, enabling market participants to make time-sensitive decisions from virtually anywhere. Businesses have matured their data consumption practices, transforming raw data into actionable insights that fuel their processes with ever-increasing volumes at microsecond latencies.

While the underlying technology has shifted from telegraph to electronic circuits, the core process remains and has been replicated across industries. Today, data publishers organize these streams into distinct topics, optimizing the delivery of relevant information to their consumers. For example, individuals interested solely in stock updates can subscribe to a dedicated topic, avoiding irrelevant noise.

The sequential update pattern from a durable list has broad applicability for microservice synchronization. Imagine two services managing recent stock pricing information and client stock portfolios. Modern architectures avoid sharing databases between microservices for scalability and performance reasons, creating the need for discrete systems to maintain a consistent view of the broader workload's state. Using event streams simplifies these data synchronization scenarios within cloud architectures.

In this chapter, you'll learn how to approach resilient streaming architectures using open source technologies like Apache Kafka, a popular messaging solution. You'll explore best practices for implementing fault-tolerant producers and consumers, and implement downstream analytics over the stock market data.

By the end of this chapter, you'll know how to:

- Design and implement a robust data ingestion layer using Amazon Managed Streaming for Apache Kafka (MSK)
- Build fault-tolerant producers and consumers with AWS Lambda
- Enrich market data through stream processing and API integration
- Store processed data using Amazon Data Firehose and query it with Amazon Athena
- Monitor and optimize the performance and reliability of your streaming pipeline

Technical Requirements

In this section, you'll deploy the streaming architecture into your AWS account using the AWS Cloud Development Kit (AWS CDK), a toolset for rapidly deploying cloud resources in a repeatable manner. Chapter 2 provides detailed instructions for installing, configuring, and troubleshooting the AWS CDK. To deploy this chapter's example:

1. Clone this book's GitHub repository to your local machine.
2. Navigate a command terminal into the *ch08-real-time_stocks* folder.
3. Run the command `cdk deploy`.
4. Grab some coffee and return in 30 minutes.

After the deployment, the following reference architecture will be available for experimentation. There are four core components to this solution (Figure 8-1):

Data ingestion
These components receive incoming stock price updates and route them to internal subscribers.

Data consumers
These components subscribe to the event topics and perform business processes.

Data enrichment
These components support transforming the raw data into business insights.

Data analytics
These components collect business insights for data-driven decisions.

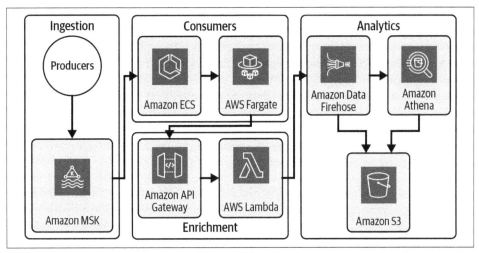

Figure 8-1. Technology reference architecture showing the integration of various AWS services for real-time market data analytics

This chapter introduces key technologies and their roles in building a real-time market data analytics pipeline on AWS (Table 8-1).

Table 8-1. AWS streaming architecture

Technology	Role in the streaming architecture
Amazon MSK	Fully managed service for deploying and managing Apache Kafka clusters, providing a scalable and durable streaming platform for ingesting real-time market data
Amazon API Gateway	Fully managed service for creating, publishing, and securing APIs, enabling data enrichment by integrating with external services or microservices
Amazon Data Firehose	Fully managed service for reliably capturing and delivering streaming data to destinations like Amazon S3, enabling durable storage of processed market data
Amazon Athena	Serverless query service for running SQL queries directly on data stored in Amazon S3, enabling ad hoc analysis and querying of processed market data
AWS Fargate	Serverless compute engine for running containers, used to run stream processing containers in the architecture

Combining AWS-managed services and open source streaming technologies creates a robust foundation for building a reliable and scalable real-time market data analytics pipeline. This architecture empowers you to focus on developing the core business logic and data processing workflows. At the same time, AWS handles the underlying infrastructure complexities. You can build a resilient and cost-effective solution tailored to your organization's unique requirements using features like automatic scaling, high availability, and seamless integration.

Designing a Reliable Data Ingestion Layer

Building a reliable front door for the application is critical in mitigating risks associated with sudden spikes in data volume or market volatility. Scenarios like the 2008 Great Recession and the 2020 COVID-19 pandemic experienced droves of panic selling, leading to rapid stock price changes and increased market data throughput. Similar challenges exist across industries, such as ecommerce sites struggling to handle peak orders during Black Friday and Cyber Monday. In these situations, a poorly designed data ingestion layer can result in data loss, inconsistent application state, and missed business opportunities.

In this section, you'll examine an industry-standard solution to message routing, the data ingestion layer, and essential design decisions to ensure it is resilient within the cloud. See Figure 8-2 for an overview of AWS services for data ingestion.

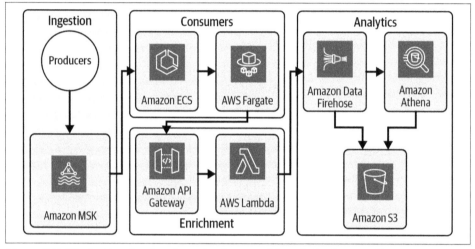

Figure 8-2. Illustrating the data ingestion layer and its role in the overall streaming architecture

When designing a resilient data ingestion layer, you'll want to consider common failure modes and apply suitable resiliency patterns. By addressing these potential issues up front, you can prevent service disruptions, data inconsistencies, and enhance the overall resilience of your streaming architecture. Implementing the right resiliency patterns will help mitigate the impact of failures and maintain your desired levels of availability, consistency, and performance (Table 8-2).

Table 8-2. Common data ingestion failure modes and resiliency patterns to mitigate them

Failure mode	Resiliency pattern
Poison pill messages	Robust error handling, message validation, dead-letter queues
Downstream dependency failures	Timeouts, retries, circuit breaker, fallback, caching
Stale or inconsistent state	Versioning, conditional updates, optimistic concurrency control
Consumer failures or restarts	Consumer group rebalancing, checkpoint management, exception handling
Scalability limitations	Horizontal scaling, dynamic scaling based on consumer lag, partition management

These business challenges and potential failure modes directly influence the technical architectures and design decisions required to build a resilient data ingestion layer. Architects must carefully consider factors such as high availability, fault tolerance, scalability, and security when designing the ingestion layer. Implementing the appropriate resiliency patterns and leveraging the right technologies can help mitigate the risks associated with these challenges and ensure the reliable and consistent delivery of real-time market data.

Role of Apache Kafka in Data Ingestion

1. When your organization depends on real-time data streams, such as for financial market analytics, you need a robust event management system to ensure reliable data ingestion and maintain a consistent application state. The system must handle the entire lifecycle of your data streams: partitioning high-volume data across multiple nodes, replicating data for fault tolerance, and expiring stale data to keep things running smoothly while optimizing cost.

Building all these capabilities from scratch would take significant time and resources. That's why most organizations use open source streaming technologies that provide these features out of the box, along with development support, extensive ecosystems, and cloud portability.

To mitigate situations where data streams are disrupted or inconsistent, you'll want a sophisticated event management database system. It should be able to handle the complete lifecycle of your data streams while providing high availability and fault tolerance. That way, you can focus on deriving insights from your data without worrying about the underlying plumbing.

 When selecting a streaming technology like Apache Kafka, consider your organization's service-level objectives (SLOs) for data ingestion, such as expected throughput, latency requirements, and durability guarantees. Kafka's partitioning, replication, and fault tolerance capabilities allow you to design a data ingestion layer that meets your SLOs, ensuring reliable and consistent data delivery with minimal data loss or staleness.

Table 8-3 presents a subset of the most common streaming solutions. While they each have their strengths, this chapter dives into Apache Kafka, the market leader. Don't worry if you're using one of the other technologies, though; the framework and decision processes we'll cover later in the chapter are broadly applicable. You'll be able to apply the concepts to your streaming platform of choice.

Table 8-3. Resilient streaming data options

Streaming technology	Scalability	Fault tolerance	Use cases
Apache Kafka	High	High (with replication)	High-throughput, distributed streaming platform for real-time data pipelines and streaming analytics
Amazon Kinesis Data Streams	High	High (with sharding)	Real-time data processing and analytics for high-velocity data streams
Apache Pulsar	High	High (with geo-replication)	Low-latency, distributed pub-sub messaging with multitenancy and persistent storage
AmazonMQ	Moderate	Moderate (with clustering)	Reliable messaging and event-driven architectures with support for various protocols

Within a Kafka cluster are multiple broker nodes that manage the publisher-subscriber model (Figure 8-3). Multiple topics on the cluster can represent the different occurring update streams. When a publisher sends an update to the topic, it persists to a primary node and replicates to any secondary instances. After confirming the event's durability meets your SLOs, the cluster returns an acknowledgment to the publisher.

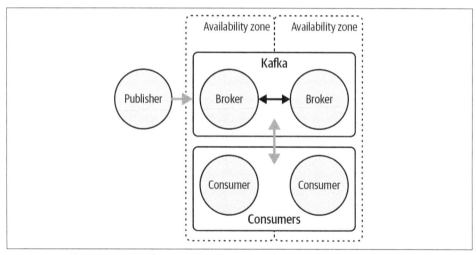

Figure 8-3. Illustrating the decoupled nature of Kafka producers and consumers

The cluster uses a quorum controller to manage metadata about the roles of the different nodes. This controller maintains a consistent view of the cluster state and ensures fault tolerance through a quorum-based consensus algorithm. A quorum is a majority of nodes that must agree on the current state of the cluster before any updates can be applied. This approach helps prevent data inconsistencies and ensures that the cluster can remain operational even if some nodes fail or become unavailable. Using a quorum controller, Apache Kafka ensures that critical metadata, such as partition assignments and broker roles, remains consistent across the cluster, enabling reliable and fault-tolerant data ingestion.

 Apache Kafka's quorum-based consensus algorithm and fault tolerance capabilities enable the deployment of multi-AZ or multi-region clusters, ensuring high availability and automatic failover in case of zone or regional outages.

Apache Kafka's design principles and features make it popular for building reliable and scalable data ingestion layers. Amazon MSK simplifies the deployment and management of Apache Kafka clusters, allowing organizations to focus on building their streaming applications without infrastructure provisioning and maintenance complexities. By leveraging Amazon MSK and Apache Kafka's capabilities, such as partitioning, replication, and fault tolerance, you can establish a robust foundation for your real-time market data analytics pipeline. This foundation ensures high availability, scalability, and consistent data delivery, enabling your application to handle high-velocity data streams from multiple sources while minimizing operational overhead and maximizing resiliency.

Designing the Kafka Topic Structure

Designing an effective Kafka topic structure is key to optimizing the performance, scalability, and maintainability of your data ingestion layer. In this section, you'll learn about the key considerations and best practices for structuring Kafka topics in the context of a real-time market data analytics application.

To get started, let's understand the various data sources and their characteristics. In a market data analytics scenario, you may receive data from multiple stock exchanges, data providers, and other sources. Each source may provide different data types, such as stock prices, trading volumes, order book updates, or news feeds. By separating these data types into distinct Kafka topics, you can improve processing efficiency and enable parallelism and scalability.

Next, you'll dive into the concepts of partitioning and replication in Kafka and how they contribute to fault tolerance and scalability. Kafka allows you to distribute data across partitions and replicate partitions across brokers, enabling parallel processing and ensuring data availability even during broker failures.

To help you visualize this, think of Kafka topics and partitions like a pizza cut into slices. Each slice (partition) can be consumed independently by different consumers, allowing for concurrent processing. Replication is similar to making multiple copies of each slice and distributing them across different pizzerias (brokers). If one pizzeria goes down, the others can still serve the slices, providing fault tolerance.

When determining the number of partitions and replication factors for your Kafka topics, it's important to consider your SLOs for data availability, scalability, and fault tolerance. By increasing the partition count, you can improve parallelism and throughput. Similarly, higher replication factors enhance data durability and availability in case of broker failures.

Here's a code snippet that shows you how to provision an Amazon MSK cluster using the AWS CDK. It also creates a topic with 6 partitions and 3 replicas (18 total units):

```
def create_ingestion_layer(self):
    ...
    kafka_cluster = msk.Cluster(
        self, "KafkaCluster",
        cluster_name="RealTimeMarketData", ❶
        kafka_version=msk.KafkaVersion.V2_8_1,
        vpc=self.get_or_create_vpc(),
        ...
    )

    stock_trades_topic = kafka_cluster.add_topic(
        topic_name="stock-pri", ❷
        partition_count=6,
        replication_factor=3,
    )
```

❶ Specify the cluster name for Amazon MSK.

❷ Create a Kafka topic for stock trades.

When planning for data retention, you'll need to consider several factors that have significant implications for your approach to data management. Data retention policies define how long data should be retained in each Kafka topic based on factors such as regulatory compliance requirements, data archiving needs, and storage cost considerations. As a resiliency architect, you'll need to carefully balance these factors to ensure that valuable data is retained for the necessary duration while optimizing storage costs and performance.

Amazon MSK provides a tiered storage feature that allows for the automatic movement of older data to lower-cost storage tiers. This feature enables cost-effective long-term data retention without sacrificing performance for recent data. It's important to understand the trade-offs between different retention strategies and their impact on data durability, availability, and recovery capabilities in case of failures or data loss scenarios.

Securing the Kafka Cluster

Securing your data ingestion layer is especially important when dealing with sensitive financial information. Amazon MSK provides several out-of-the-box security features to help protect your Kafka cluster and data.

First, authentication controls are a critical aspect of security in a Kafka cluster. Amazon MSK supports multiple authentication mechanisms, including AWS Identity and Access Management (IAM), Salted Challenge Response Authentication Mechanism (SCRAM or SASL/SCRAM), and mutual TLS (mTLS). By configuring appropriate authentication mechanisms, you can ensure that only authorized clients can produce or consume data from your Kafka topics, helping prevent unauthorized access and protecting sensitive data from being compromised.

Often the unauthorized occurs due to negligence and erroneous manual processes. For example, you might incorrectly deploy a producer to the test environment and begin sending data into the production cluster. You can mitigate these situations through data security controls (Table 8-4).

Table 8-4. Data ingestion authentication options

Authentication option	Description	When to use
AWS Identity and Access Management (IAM)	Authenticate clients using AWS IAM roles and policies	When you want to leverage existing AWS IAM infrastructure and integrate with other AWS services
SASL/SCRAM	Industry-standard authentication mechanism using usernames and passwords	When you require granular access control and authentication for individual clients or applications
Mutual TLS (mTLS)	Authentication based on client and server certificates	When you need to enforce strict encryption and authentication requirements for secure communication

Second, encryption is another essential security measure. Amazon MSK offers data encryption at rest and in transit, ensuring that data stored on disk is encrypted using AES-256 encryption, and securing communication between clients and brokers using Transport Layer Security (TLS) protocols:

```
def create_secure_cluster(self):
    ...
    kafka_cluster = msk.Cluster(
        ...
```

```
        encryption_in_transit=msk.EncryptionInTransit(
            instance_roles=[self.get_or_create_instance_role()],
        ),
        client_authentication=msk.ClientAuthentication(  ❶
            sasl=msk.SaslScram(scram_secret_key_arn=
                self.get_or_create_secret("kafka-scram-secret").secret_arn  ❷
            )
        )
    )

def get_or_create_secret(self, secret_name):
    secret = secretsmanager.Secret.from_secret_name(
        self, secret_name, secret_name=secret_name)

    if not secret:
        secret = secretsmanager.Secret(…)
    return secret
```

❶ Enable client authentication for the Kafka cluster.

❷ Specify the SASL/SCRAM secret key ARN.

Using the built-in security features of Amazon MSK, you can establish a robust security posture for your data ingestion layer, safeguarding your market data from potential breaches and ensuring compliance with industry regulations and security best practices.

Implementing Reliable Consumers

In the previous section, you learned how to configure a high-availability Kafka cluster and message topics to receive real-time market data. Now, let's focus on consumers, the critical components responsible for consuming and processing these data streams (Figure 8-4). Consumers enable downstream business processes, analytics, and decision making. Implementing reliable and fault-tolerant consumers is essential to ensure the consistent and timely processing of market data, preventing data loss or inconsistent application state that could lead to missed trading opportunities or suboptimal decisions.

You can implement topic consumers using different computing services like Amazon Elastic Container (or Kubernetes) Service, AWS Lambda, and Amazon Elastic Compute Cloud (EC2). Each technology comes with its own trade-offs and benefits (Table 8-5). For example, Lambda functions are automatically invoked as new messages arrive, while container-based consumers must implement a message pump using the Kafka SDK. However, container-based services also provide more control, which can be beneficial for specific use cases.

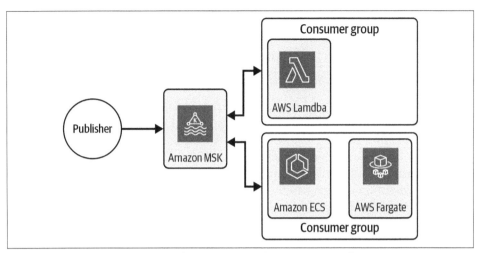

Figure 8-4. Illustrating the role of consumers in the streaming architecture

Table 8-5. Compute options for message consumption

Compute service	Resiliency	Scalability	Control and flexibility	Operational overhead
AWS Lambda	Managed execution environment, automatic scaling, limited state management	Automatic scaling based on workload	Limited control over runtime environment, execution duration limits	Minimal operational overhead
Amazon EC2	Manual failover and recovery, complete control over runtime environment, stateful processing	Manual scaling based on workload	Complete control over runtime environment, custom runtime requirements	High operational overhead for provisioning, scaling, and failover
AWS Fargate (Amazon ECS)	Managed compute, automatic scaling, stateful processing	Automatic scaling based on workload	Moderate control over runtime environment, integration with other AWS services	Moderate operational overhead for managing ECS clusters and services
Amazon Elastic Kubernetes Service (EKS)	Managed Kubernetes control plane, automatic scaling, stateful processing	Automatic scaling based on workload	High control over runtime environment, Kubernetes ecosystem integration	Moderate operational overhead for managing Kubernetes clusters and deployments

Let's start by implementing a reliable consumer using AWS Lambda. Lambda's event-driven architecture provides most of the plumbing for retrieving batches of events from the Kafka topic and transforming them with custom code. The following snippet illustrates how to deploy the stock_prices_consumer. You can review its complete implementation within the chapter's repository:

```
def create_lambda_consumer(self):
    stock_prices_consumer = lambda_.Function(
```

```
        self, "StockPricesConsumer",
        ...
        environment={
            "KAFKA_TOPIC": "stock-prices",
        },
    )
```

There are many scenarios where containerized consumers are better suited than Lambda, as they offer more control for long-running operations. In "Technical Requirements" on page 222, you deployed a second consumer within AWS Fargate, a serverless compute engine for running containers. Fargate provides a managed compute environment with automatic scaling, making it suitable for running stateful workloads while offloading operational tasks like provisioning and scaling infrastructure. The following CDK code snippet illustrates the deployment for the Fargate task definition and service:

```
def create_fargate_consumer() method
    stock_prices_task_definition = ecs.FargateTaskDefinition(
        self, "StockPricesTaskDefinition",
        memory_limit_mib=1024,
        cpu=512,
    )

    stock_prices_task_definition.add_container(
        "StockPricesContainer",
        image=ecs.ContainerImage.from_asset("path/to/container/code"),
        logging=ecs.AwsLogDriver(
            ...
        ),
        environment={
            "KAFKA_BOOTSTRAP_SERVERS": kafka_cluster.bootstrap_servers,
            "KAFKA_CONSUMER_GROUP": "stock-prices-consumer-group",
            "KAFKA_TOPIC": "stock-prices",
        },
    )

    stock_prices_service = ecs.FargateService(
        self, "StockPricesService",
        cluster= self.get_or_create_ecs_cluster(),
        task_definition=stock_prices_task_definition,
        desired_count=2,
    )
```

Ensuring Fault Tolerance and Scalability

To ensure fault tolerance and scalability, which are core aspects of designing reliable consumer applications, let's consider a scenario where a consumer instance within a consumer group fails or becomes unresponsive. This can impact the processing of messages from the assigned partitions, potentially leading to data loss or inconsistent application state.

To mitigate this risk, it's recommended to configure multiple consumer instances within a consumer group. By having parallel instances, you can distribute the workload and ensure that if one instance fails, the remaining instances can continue processing messages from the assigned partitions.

Kafka's consumer group rebalancing mechanism plays a vital role in enabling fault tolerance and scalability. When a new consumer instance joins the group or an existing instance leaves (due to failure or intentional shutdown), Kafka triggers a rebalance operation. During this rebalance, the partitions are reassigned evenly among the active consumer instances, ensuring a balanced workload distribution.

For example, let's say your `trade-processors` consumer group has three instances, and the `stock-trades` topic has six partitions. Initially, each instance might be assigned two partitions. If a new consumer instance joins the group, Kafka will rebalance the partitions, reassigning them evenly across the four instances. Conversely, if an instance fails, the remaining instances will automatically take over the partitions previously assigned to the failed instance.

This automatic rebalancing ensures that message processing continues without interruption, even in the face of consumer failures or changes in the number of consumer instances. By leveraging this mechanism and configuring multiple instances within a consumer group, you can achieve fault tolerance and horizontal scalability for your consumer applications.

Scalability is another important aspect of building resilient consumer applications, as it enables your system to handle increasing workloads and maintain consistent performance. In the context of Kafka consumers, scalability is often achieved by dynamically adjusting the number of consumer instances based on metrics like consumer lag or processing rate. The following CDK snippet demonstrates how to configure automatic scaling for an AWS Fargate service based on the consumer lag metric for the `order-book-consumer-group`:

```
def scaling_fargate_consumer(self):
    ...
    scaling = order_book_service.auto_scale_task_count(max_capacity=10)  ❶
    scaling.scale_on_metric(
        "ScaleOnConsumerLag",
        metric=cloudwatch.Metric(
            namespace="AWS/Kafka",
            metric_name="ConsumerLag",  ❷
            dimensions={
                "Cluster Name": kafka_cluster.cluster_name,
                "Consumer": "order-book-consumer-group"
            },
            period=cdk.Duration.minutes(1)
        ),
        scaling_steps=[  ❸
            cloudwatch_actions.ScalingInstruction(
```

```
                        change=+1,
                        lower=100,
                        upper=300,
                        min_adjustment_magnitude=1,
                    ),
                    cloudwatch_actions.ScalingInstruction(
                        change=-1,
                        lower=0,
                        upper=100,
                        min_adjustment_magnitude=1,
                    ),
                ]
            )
```

❶ Set the maximum capacity for the ECS service task count.

❷ Define the `ConsumerLag` metric for the `order-book-consumer-group`.

❸ Configure scaling steps based on the `ConsumerLag` metric.

To handle consumer failures gracefully and ensure reliable message processing, it's important to implement robust exception handling and diagnostic logging in your consumer code. When an exception occurs during message processing, catching, and handling, it can help prevent data loss or inconsistent application state.

In your exception handling logic, make sure to log detailed error information, including the exception type, message, and relevant context data (e.g., the message payload, partition, or offset). This information will be invaluable for troubleshooting and root cause analysis, enabling you to efficiently identify and address the underlying issues.

Based on the nature of the exception and the specific use case, you can then decide on an appropriate error-handling strategy. Here are a few possible strategies:

- Retry the failed message processing with exponential backoff to allow for temporary failures or downstream dependencies to recover.

- Skip the message and continue with the next batch, potentially logging the skipped message for manual intervention or reprocessing later.

- Route the failed message to a dead-letter queue (DLQ) or error topic for manual inspection and remediation.

- Implement fallback or degraded functionality if the failure is noncritical, and the application can continue processing with partial data or functionality.

By implementing comprehensive exception handling and diagnostic logging, you can develop more resilient consumer applications. These applications can gracefully handle failures, minimize data loss, and maintain a consistent application state, even in the face of unexpected errors or issues with downstream dependencies.

Consumer Groups and Record Processing

Kafka organizes consumers into consumer groups, allowing multiple consumer instances to collaborate and share the workload of processing messages from a topic. When you create a consumer group, Kafka assigns each consumer instance a subset of the topic's partitions. Keep in mind that the number of consumer instances in a group cannot exceed the total number of partitions in the topic. This restriction ensures that each partition is assigned to only one consumer instance within a group, preventing duplicate processing of messages.

Consumer groups and partition assignments are fundamental concepts in Kafka that enable parallelism, fault tolerance, and consistent state management. By distributing partitions among multiple consumer instances, you can achieve concurrent processing of messages, improving overall throughput and performance. If a consumer instance fails, Kafka automatically reassigns its partitions to the remaining available consumers within the group, ensuring uninterrupted message processing.

In the case of the `trade-processors` group, Kafka will assign each consumer instance a subset of the partitions from the `stock-trades` topic. For example, if the topic has six partitions and you have three consumer instances, each instance will be responsible for processing two partitions. This distribution of partitions allows for parallel processing of messages, improving your application's overall throughput and performance.

Another important aspect of consumer group management is committing offsets. By committing the offsets of successfully processed events, consumers can resume processing from the last committed offset in case of failures or restarts. This ensures that events are not missed or duplicated during recovery, maintaining a consistent application state.

Your specific implementation retrieving messages from the stream differs between Lambda functions and containerized consumer applications. The Lambda service handles most of the Kafka SDK operations through its Event Source functionality. For instance, the partition offsets automatically update if your function handler returns success. The following snippet demonstrates how to integrate into these behaviors. Containerized services use the Kafka consumer client to manage these details.

```
import json
import base64

def lambda_handler(event, context):
    records = event["records"]  ❶

    for record in records:
        payload = base64.b64decode(record["data"]).decode("utf-8")  ❷
        print(f"Received payload: {payload}")
```

```
        do_stuff(payload)

    return {
        "statusCode": 200,
        "body": json.dumps("Message batch processed")
    }
```

❶ Extract the records from the event object.

❷ Decode the base64-encoded data and extract the payload.

You can implement the message pump for containerized processes using the Kafka SDK. The following snippet demonstrates a generic implementation for your reference:

```
import asyncio
from kafka import KafkaConsumer

kafka_config = {
    'bootstrap_servers': ['kafka_broker_host:9092'], ❶
    'group_id': 'my-consumer-group',
    'auto_offset_reset': 'earliest'
}

consumer = KafkaConsumer(
    topic_name= 'my-topic'
    **kafka_config
)

checkpoint_interval = 60

async def read_and_checkpoint():
    last_checkpoint = time.time()

    while True:
        try:
            messages = await asyncio.wait_for(
                consumer.getmany(timeout_ms=1000), timeout=1.0) ❷

            if not messages:
                if time.time() - last_checkpoint >= checkpoint_interval: ❸
                    await consumer.commit()
                    last_checkpoint = time.time()
                    print("Progress checkpointed.")
                await asyncio.sleep(1)
                continue

            for message in messages.values(): ❹
                for record in message:
                    message_value = json.loads(record.value.decode('utf-8'))
                    print(f"Received message: {message_value}")
        except asyncio.TimeoutError:
```

```
        continue
    except KeyboardInterrupt:
        print("Shutting down...")
        await consumer.stop()
        break

await consumer.commit()
print("Final progress checkpointed.")

if __name__ == "__main__":
    asyncio.run(read_and_checkpoint())
```

❶ Specify the bootstrap endpoint and consumer group name for initializing the client.

❷ Request a batch of messages and wait up to one second.

❸ Periodically checkpoint the progress of reading the assigned partition.

❹ Iterate through the events returned.

With an understanding of message retrieval and load distribution under your belt, it's time to explore common failure scenarios you may encounter during this process.

Handling Invalid Messages

When consuming messages from Kafka, you may come across incorrectly formatted or invalid messages, often referred to as "poison pills." These messages can cause your consumer to crash or behave unexpectedly if not handled properly. For instance, suppose you receive a stock price update that's missing required fields. In such cases, you'll need to decide how to proceed by implementing robust error handling and message validation logic in your consumer code.

Here are a few steps you can take to gracefully handle these scenarios:

1. Parse and validate the message format. Before processing a message, validate its structure and data types against the expected schema. Consider using schema validation libraries or custom validation logic to ensure the message adheres to the defined format.

2. Handle exceptions gracefully. Wrap the message processing logic in try-except blocks to catch any exceptions that may occur. Make sure to log the error details and the problematic message for further investigation.

3. Decide on message disposition. Based on the nature of the invalid message, determine whether to discard it, route it to a dead-letter queue for manual intervention, or apply custom error-handling logic. This approach allows you to

isolate the impact of poison pill messages and prevent them from disrupting the entire consumer application.

The following code snippet demonstrates how to implement these steps using the jsonschema module to validate the message payload. This example ensures that the stock price update includes a stock symbol (e.g., AMZN for Amazon), current price, total share volume traded, and a timestamp:

```python
import json
import base64
import jsonschema    ❶

STOCK_TRADE_SCHEMA = {
    "type": "object",
    "properties": {
        "symbol": {"type": "string"},
        "price": {"type": "number"},
        "volume": {"type": "integer"},
        "timestamp": {"type": "string", "format": "date-time"}
    },
    "required": ["symbol", "price", "volume", "timestamp"]
}

def lambda_handler(event, context):
    ...
    for record in records:
        ...
        if is_invalid_payload(payload):    ❷
            handle_invalid_payload(payload)    ❸
        else:
            do_stuff(payload)
    ...

def is_invalid_payload(payload):
    try:
        payload_data = json.loads(payload)
        jsonschema.validate(
            instance=payload_data, schema=STOCK_TRADE_SCHEMA)    ❹

    except (json.JSONDecodeError, jsonschema.exceptions.ValidationError):
        return True
    return False
```

❶ Import the jsonschema library for schema validation.

❷ Call the is_invalid_payload function to validate the payload.

❸ Call the handle_invalid_payload function if the payload is invalid.

❹ Validate the payload against the defined schema using jsonschema.

By leveraging the `jsonschema` module, you can define the expected schema for the message payload and validate incoming messages against it. If a message doesn't conform to the schema, an exception is raised, allowing you to handle it gracefully. In this example, invalid messages are logged and routed to a dead-letter queue for further analysis, while valid messages are processed normally.

Incorporating schema validation and error-handling techniques like this helps you build resilience into your consumer code, enabling it to handle unexpected or malformed messages without crashing or compromising the integrity of your application.

Dealing with Downstream Dependencies

When working with real-world scenarios, it's important to consider that your consumer applications often rely on external services or APIs to enrich or process the consumed data further. For example, in your market data analytics application, the consumer might need to fetch additional stock information or news sentiment data from third-party APIs to enhance the trade data before performing downstream analytics or decision making.

These downstream dependencies introduce potential failure modes that can impact the reliability and performance of your consumer applications. Increased latency from these dependencies can lead to delays in processing messages, resulting in backlogs and inconsistent application states. Moreover, failures or outages in the downstream services can completely block message processing, causing data loss or missed opportunities.

To build resilient consumers that can handle such scenarios, consider implementing the following patterns and techniques:

Timeouts and retries
> Set appropriate timeouts for API calls to downstream services. If a request exceeds the timeout threshold, treat it as a failure and implement retry mechanisms with exponential backoff. This approach gradually increases the wait time between retries, giving the downstream service a chance to recover.

Circuit breaker
> Implement a circuit breaker pattern to handle cascading failures. If the downstream service consistently fails or exceeds error thresholds, the circuit breaker can trip and temporarily block further requests to the service. This prevents the consumer from continuously making failed requests and allows it to gracefully degrade functionality or use fallback mechanisms. See Chapter 3 for more information.

Fallback and caching

Provide fallback options or use caching mechanisms to handle scenarios where the downstream service is unavailable or slow to respond. For instance, if the API call to fetch additional stock information fails, the consumer can use a cached version of the data or provide default values to allow processing to continue.

Asynchronous and nonblocking processing

Design your consumer to process messages asynchronously and avoid blocking on I/O operations. Utilize asynchronous programming techniques, such as async/await or reactive libraries, to handle downstream service interactions without blocking the main message processing loop. This allows the consumer to continue processing messages while waiting for the downstream service to respond.

For more information on implementing patterns like timeouts, retries, circuit breakers, and fallback mechanisms, check out Part II of this book. The lessons from those chapters can be broadly applied here to build resilient consumers that can handle failures and latency in downstream dependencies.

Integrating Consumers and APIs

Enriching data streams with contextual information from external sources is often essential in modern data-driven applications. In your market data analytics application, for instance, the Kafka consumers might need to integrate with third-party APIs or microservices to fetch additional data, such as company fundamentals, news sentiment, or historical price trends. This enrichment process enables downstream analytics, decision making, and business processes to operate on a more comprehensive and valuable dataset.

However, incorporating data from external sources introduces new challenges, including handling failures, latency, and scalability concerns. To address these challenges and enable reliable and efficient data enrichment for real-world applications, you can implement robust stream processing pipelines and leverage cloud native services (Figure 8-5).

Table 8-6 enumerates some of the failure modes that can occur when integrating with custom APIs. When approaching the integration, it's important to assume that issues might arise in communicating with the endpoint securely, reliably, and accurately.

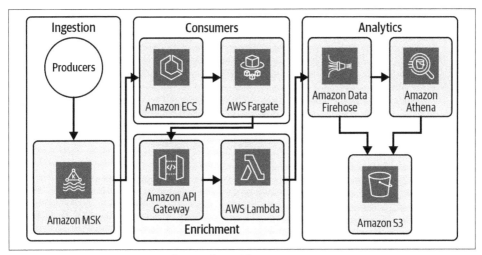

Figure 8-5. Data ingestion pipeline with enrichment

Table 8-6. API integration failure modes

Failure mode	Design pattern	Description
Unauthorized access or security breaches	Authentication and authorization	Implement robust authentication and authorization mechanisms to protect against unauthorized access to your APIs or data sources.
Integration issues or service disruptions	Retries, circuit breakers, fallbacks	Implement retry mechanisms, circuit breakers, and fallback options to gracefully handle service disruptions or integration issues with third-party providers.
Data quality or consistency issues	Data validation, anomaly detection, reconciliation	Implement data validation checks, anomaly detection, and reconciliation processes to ensure the quality and consistency of the enriched data.

Now that you're aware of the potential challenges that might arise, let's explore how you can solve them.

Creating the Connection

You can use Amazon API Gateway to seamlessly integrate with external APIs or microservices for data enrichment in your stream processing pipeline. API Gateway offers a fully managed service that simplifies creating, publishing, and securing APIs.

Using managed API proxies like Amazon API Gateway abstracts away the complexities of invoking external APIs or microservices, making data enrichment within your stream processing pipeline more seamless. API Gateway also offers features like caching, throttling, and authentication, which can boost the security and performance of your data enrichment process.

Here's a Python snippet that shows how a containerized process integrates with API Gateway to enrich incoming trade data:

```python
import os
import asyncio
import requests
from kafka import KafkaConsumer

# API endpoint for data enrichment
API_ENDPOINT = "https://your-api-endpoint.com/enrich"

# Kafka consumer configuration
KAFKA_BOOTSTRAP_SERVERS = os.environ.get("KAFKA_BOOTSTRAP_SERVERS")
KAFKA_CONSUMER_GROUP = os.environ.get("KAFKA_CONSUMER_GROUP")
KAFKA_TOPIC = os.environ.get("KAFKA_TOPIC")

consumer = KafkaConsumer(
    KAFKA_TOPIC,
    bootstrap_servers=KAFKA_BOOTSTRAP_SERVERS,
    group_id=KAFKA_CONSUMER_GROUP,
    enable_auto_commit=False,
    value_deserializer=lambda x: x.decode("utf-8"),
)

async def process_records(records):    ❶
    tasks = []
    for record in records:
        tasks.append(enrich_data(record.value))    ❷

    await asyncio.gather(*tasks)    ❸
```

❶ Asynchronous function to process a batch of records.

❷ Send each record for data enrichment using enrich_data.

❸ Wait for all enrichment tasks to complete using asyncio.gather.

The enrich_data function sends the incoming trade data to the API Gateway endpoint using an HTTP POST request. API Gateway routes the request to an integrated Lambda function or microservice that fetches the required enrichment data and returns the response. The consumer Lambda function then processes or emits the enriched data.

```python
async def enrich_data(data):    ❶
    try:
        response = await asyncio.to_thread(
            requests.post, API_ENDPOINT, json=data)    ❷

        response.raise_for_status()
        print(f"Enriched data: {response.json()}")
    except requests.exceptions.RequestException as e:
```

```
            print(f"Error enriching data: {e}")

async def main():  ❸
    while True:
        batch = consumer.poll(timeout_ms=1000, max_records=10)  ❹
        if batch:
            await process_records(batch.values())  ❺
            consumer.commit()  ❻

if __name__ == "__main__":
    asyncio.run(main())
```

❶ Asynchronous function to enrich data by sending it to the API.

❷ Use `asyncio.to_thread` to run the blocking `requests.post` on a separate thread.

❸ Main loop for consuming and processing records.

❹ Poll for a batch of records from the Kafka consumer.

❺ Process the batch of records asynchronously.

❻ Commit the offsets after processing the batch.

However, integrating with external services or APIs introduces additional failure modes. Unauthorized access, security breaches, or integration issues with third-party services can impact the reliability and integrity of your stream processing pipeline. You should implement proper security measures, such as authentication and authorization mechanisms, and handle potential failures or errors gracefully to maintain the overall resiliency of your architecture.

Designing Consumer State

Designing robust and evolvable stream processing pipelines is important for handling the dynamic nature of data streams and evolving business requirements. Let's explore key considerations and best practices for building resilient stream processing pipelines that can maintain data consistency, fault tolerance, and scalability in your market data analytics application.

When establishing well-defined data schemas to represent the structure of the data flowing through your pipeline, you'll want to specify the fields, data types, and constraints to ensure data consistency and enable compatibility as the data evolves over time.

To manage and share these schemas across your streaming infrastructure, consider leveraging a schema registry like AWS Glue Data Catalog. It acts as a centralized repository for storing and versioning data schemas, allowing consumers and producers to access and validate data against the defined schemas.

Schema evolution capabilities allow you to handle changes to the data structure over time while maintaining backward compatibility. For example, if you add a new property to the stock update message that denotes whether it's from a New York or London market, making this property nullable prevents schema validators from breaking if it can't be provided in every scenario. This is particularly important in real-world scenarios where data formats and requirements may change, ensuring that your stream processing pipeline can adapt to these changes without disrupting existing data flows or downstream consumers.

> AWS Glue Schema Registry is a recommended service for managing and sharing data schemas across your streaming infrastructure when building stream processing pipelines on AWS. It serves as a centralized repository for storing and versioning data schemas, enabling consumers and producers to access and validate data against the defined schemas.

However, there are situations that require breaking changes. For instance, if the market location is part of a database composite key, not having the needed value would prevent inserting the database records and lead to failures.

One common solution is to use message envelopes and declare schema versions. Similar to postal mail, you can use envelopes to encapsulate the message and provide a consistent structure that won't change. The following example implements this pattern for the stock price update:

```
{
  "Version": "2024-06-09",
  "Payload": {
    "symbol": "AMZN",
    "market": "NYSE",
    "price": "185.12",
    "volume": "12345678",
    "timestamp": "1704383560"
  }
}
```

> You can use any incrementing value for the message `Version` property. A common approach is specifying the schema creation or update date (e.g., 2024-06-09). This provides more context than more generic values like v1.

Ultimately, streaming solutions must support business processes by facilitating data movement. By factoring aspects such as schemas into the reliability design, it enables decentralized teams to build and evolve their integrations over time while maintaining quality checks.

By incorporating schema validation and versioning into your streaming pipelines, you can establish quality checks and ensure data integrity throughout the data movement process. This helps catch and handle data inconsistencies early, preventing downstream issues and ensuring the reliability of your streaming solution.

Implementing State Management

Within stream processing pipelines, it's important to consider the trade-offs between traditional SQL databases and NoSQL databases for storing and managing application state. SQL databases provide strong consistency guarantees, enforcing a predefined schema to ensure data integrity and enable complex querying and joins. However, they may struggle with scalability and low-latency access to state in high-throughput streaming scenarios.

NoSQL databases, like Amazon DynamoDB, are designed for scalability and fast key-value lookups, following a schema-on-read approach. This means that the structure of the data is determined during reading rather than enforcing a strict schema during write operations. NoSQL databases are well-suited for handling high-velocity data ingestion and efficient state retrieval.

The schema-on-read approach employed by NoSQL databases allows for flexible data modeling and enables you to store and retrieve state information efficiently. This makes them a good fit for scenarios where data structure may evolve over time and where fast read and write operations are critical.

When working with NoSQL databases in your stream processing pipelines, you can store the application state as key-value pairs or document-oriented structures. This offers flexibility in data modeling while ensuring efficient state storage and retrieval. However, it's important to note that NoSQL databases often sacrifice strong consistency guarantees in favor of scalability and availability, providing eventual consistency instead of immediate consistency. This trade-off is acceptable in many streaming scenarios where the benefits of scalability and fast access to state outweigh the need for immediate consistency.

The choice between SQL and NoSQL databases for managing application state in your stream processing pipelines depends on your specific requirements. If you prioritize strong consistency and complex querying, SQL databases may be a better fit. However, if you need to handle high-velocity data ingestion, scale horizontally, and achieve low-latency access to state, NoSQL databases like Amazon DynamoDB are often the preferred choice.

Handling Concurrency

Maintaining state consistency can be challenging in stream processing pipelines. Conflicts can arise when multiple consumers process events concurrently and update the same state. Implementing mechanisms to handle these conflicts and ensure data integrity is essential.

One approach to handle state consistency is to use optimistic concurrency control techniques, such as versioning and conditional updates. With versioning, each state update is assigned a version number, and the version is checked before applying the update. Suppose the version doesn't match the expected value, indicating that another consumer has modified the state. In that case, the update is rejected or retried.

For example, DynamoDB supports conditional updates using the `ConditionExpres sion` parameter. You can specify a condition that must be met for the update to succeed. If the condition is not satisfied, the update is rejected, and you can handle the conflict accordingly:

```
import uuid

def lambda_handler(event, context):
    payload = json.loads(event["body"])
    stock_symbol = payload["symbol"]

    response = state_table.get_item(Key={"stock_symbol": stock_symbol})
    current_state = response.get(
        "Item", {"total_shares": 0, "etag": str(uuid.uuid4())})

    current_volume = payload["volume"]
    total_shares = current_state["total_shares"] + current_volume
    new_etag = str(uuid.uuid4())

    try:
        response = state_table.update_item(
            Key={"stock_symbol": stock_symbol},
            UpdateExpression=
                "SET total_shares = :val, etag = :new_etag", ❶
            ExpressionAttributeValues={
                ":val": total_shares,
                ":new_etag": new_etag
            },
            ConditionExpression="etag = :etag",
            ExpressionAttributeValues={
                ":etag": current_state["etag"]
            },
            ReturnValues="UPDATED_NEW"
        )
```

```
        updated_state = response["Attributes"]
    except dynamodb.exceptions.ConditionalCheckFailedException:
        print(f"Concurrent update detected for {stock_symbol}")
        return {
            "statusCode": 409,
            "body": json.dumps({
                "message": "Concurrent update detected"
            })
        }

    # Add the total_shares and the new etag to the payload
    payload["total_shares"] = updated_state["total_shares"]
    payload["etag"] = updated_state["etag"]

    # Return the enriched payload
    return {
        "statusCode": 200,
        "body": json.dumps(payload)
    }
```

❶ The etag version is set to :new_etag, which will trigger a ConditionalCheck
FailedException: exception.

By using optimistic concurrency, you gain performance improvements within processes where updates infrequently collide.

While optimistic concurrency control is suitable for scenarios with infrequent conflicts, scenarios involving frequent updates to the same records may benefit from
pessimistic concurrency control. With this approach, exclusive locks are acquired
before modifying the state, ensuring that only one consumer can update a particular
state at a time.

Techniques like semaphores, mutexes, or distributed locking services can be
employed to acquire locks before processing events and updating the state. For example, in a distributed streaming application using Apache Kafka, you could leverage
a distributed lock manager like Apache ZooKeeper or etcd to coordinate access to
shared state across multiple consumers. By acquiring a lock before processing an
event, you ensure that only one consumer can update the state for a particular key at
any given time, eliminating the possibility of conflicting updates.

> In Chapter 9, you'll examine how to implement a distributed lock
> using Redis, while controlling leader selection.

While pessimistic concurrency control provides stronger consistency guarantees,
it can introduce performance overhead and potential bottlenecks, especially in

high-contention scenarios. Therefore, it's crucial to carefully evaluate the trade-offs between consistency and performance based on your specific use case and workload characteristics.

Using Restartability

Kafka's built-in consumer group offset management and state persistence provide a solid foundation for consumer restartability. However, in certain situations, you may need to take additional steps to ensure reliable and consistent data processing. For example, if you introduce a code defect or data corruption, you might need to reprocess events from a specific point in time to restore data integrity.

Let's say you deployed a code defect in your stock price processing pipeline on Tuesday at 10 A.M., causing incorrect calculations or data inconsistencies. After fixing the issue, you would need to update the consumer group offsets to a point before the defect was introduced (e.g., Tuesday at 9:59 A.M.) and reprocess the events from that point onward.

With Amazon MSK, you can use the AWS CLI or the AWS Management Console to modify consumer group offsets. Here's an example AWS CLI command to update the offset for a consumer group named `stock_price_reader` and a topic named `stock_prices`:

```
PARTITION='"TopicPartition":{"Topic":"stock_prices","Partition":0}'
STRATEGY='"ConsumerGroupStrategy":"UseConsumerGroupOffsetConfig"'
OFFSET='{"ConsumerGroupOffset":{"OffsetMetadata":"","Offset":12345}}'
METADATA="\"ConsumerGroupOffsetMetadata\":${OFFSET}"
aws kafka reset-consumer-group-offsets \
    --cluster-arn \
    "arn:aws:kafka:us-east-1:123456789012:cluster/my-cluster/abcd1234" \
    --group-id "stock_price_reader" \
    --execute-service-action "{ ${PARTITION},${STRATEGY},${METADATA} }" \
    --region us-east-1
```

This command resets the offset for the `stock_price_reader` consumer group to offset 12345 for partition 0 of the `stock_prices` topic.

Another approach to support reliable failure recovery is to implement a checkpoint and replay mechanism. Periodically checkpoint the application state and the corresponding consumer group offsets to a durable storage system, such as Amazon DynamoDB or Amazon S3. If a failure occurs or you need to reprocess events, you can restore the application state and consumer group offsets from the last checkpoint and replay the events from that point onward.

The choice between modifying consumer group offsets or implementing a checkpoint and replay mechanism depends on factors such as the complexity of your application state, the frequency of reprocessing requirements, and the level of granularity needed for reprocessing. In some cases, you may need to combine both approaches to achieve the desired level of reliability and recoverability in your stream processing pipeline.

Storing and Querying Processed Market Data

In the previous section, you built reliable Kafka consumers and enriched the market data by integrating with custom APIs. Now, you'll take the next step by collecting and storing this enriched business intelligence for downstream analytics, reporting, and decision-making processes. This is where Amazon Data Firehose comes in handy.

Amazon Data Firehose is a fully managed service that allows you to reliably capture, transform, and deliver streaming data to various destinations, including Amazon S3, Amazon OpenSearch Service, and Amazon Redshift. With Amazon Data Firehose, you can efficiently route batches of data to different storage and analytical services based on your requirements (Figure 8-6).

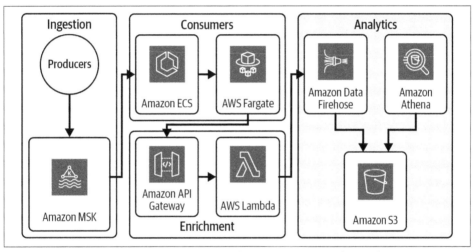

Figure 8-6. Amazon Data Firehose delivers data to Amazon S3 for analytics consumption with Amazon Athena

You can provision the relevant infrastructure using the code snippet provided in this chapter's repository. With this setup, publishers write messages into Firehose, which efficiently batches them into Apache Parquet format. This optimized data storage enables you to perform quick and cost-effective queries using Amazon Athena:

```
def create_data_analytics(self):
    processed_data_bucket = s3.Bucket(...)

    kinesis_firehose = firehose.DeliveryStream(
        self, "ProcessedDataDeliveryStream",
        destinations=[firehose.S3Bucket(processed_data_bucket)],
    )
```

```
athena_database = athena.Database(self, "ProcessedDataDatabase")
athena_table = athena_database.add_table(
    table_name="processed_market_data",
    bucket=processed_data_bucket,
    data_format=athena.DataFormat.PARQUET,
    partition_keys=[
        athena.String.from_json_path("$.date"),
        athena.String.from_json_path("$.stock_symbol"),
    ],
)
```

When choosing storage destinations and implementing monitoring, alerting, and recovery strategies, it's a good idea to consider SLOs for data durability and availability. This will help ensure that your data remains intact and accessible when you need it.

By leveraging Amazon Data Firehose and adopting robust monitoring, validation, and recovery strategies, you can ensure the reliability and durability of your stored market data, enabling downstream analytics and reporting while minimizing the risk of data loss or corruption.

In this example, you'll focus on storing the processed market data in Amazon S3 and querying it using Amazon Athena. Athena is a serverless query service that allows you to run SQL queries directly on data stored in S3, making it easy to gain insights from your market data.

> In Chapter 9, you'll dive into Amazon OpenSearch Service, which enables real-time search and analysis capabilities for your market data. This will give you even more power to unlock valuable insights and make data-driven decisions.

Handling Firehose Failure Modes

Reliability is a key consideration when building streaming data pipelines with Amazon Data Firehose. Firehose captures, transforms, and loads streaming data into various destinations, such as Amazon S3, Amazon Redshift, and Splunk. However, like any distributed system, it can encounter failures and challenges that impact data delivery and processing.

To ensure reliability with Firehose, you need to understand and anticipate potential failure modes. These failure modes can arise from various sources, including network connectivity issues, service outages, producer application failures, data transformation errors, and configuration errors. By proactively identifying and addressing these failure modes, you can build more resilient and fault-tolerant data pipelines (Table 8-7).

Table 8-7. Amazon Data Firehose failure modes and mitigations

Failure mode	Impact	Mitigation strategy
Network connectivity issues	Data delivery disruption, data loss	Implement retry mechanisms, connection monitoring, and failover strategies
Firehose service outage	Data delivery disruption, data loss	Implement retries, fallback mechanisms, and data buffering
Data transformation errors	Incorrect or corrupted data	Implement data validation, error handling, and logging mechanisms
Firehose throttling	Data delivery delays, potential data loss	Implement backpressure mechanisms, rate limiting, and load balancing
Destination service outage (e.g., S3, Redshift)	Data delivery disruption, data loss	Implement retries, fallback mechanisms, and data buffering
Data encryption/decryption failures	Data delivery disruption, data security risks	Implement proper key management, encryption/ decryption error handling
Insufficient Firehose throughput	Data delivery delays, potential data loss	Monitor and scale Firehose resources, implement buffering
Data serialization/ deserialization errors	Data corruption, processing failures	Implement data validation, error handling, and logging mechanisms
Firehose destination configuration errors	Data delivery disruption, data loss	Implement automated testing, configuration management, and validation

To mitigate these failure modes, you can implement various strategies, such as retry mechanisms, fallback mechanisms, data buffering, circuit breakers, health checks, and automatic restarts. It's also important to implement robust data validation, error handling, and logging mechanisms to detect and respond to issues promptly.

Monitoring and scaling Firehose resources are essential for maintaining reliability. By closely monitoring metrics like incoming data volume, throughput, and delivery latency, you can proactively scale Firehose resources to meet changing demands and avoid throttling or performance degradation.

Building reliable streaming data pipelines with Firehose requires a holistic approach. By considering potential failure modes, implementing mitigation strategies, and continuously monitoring and optimizing the system, you can ensure that your data pipelines deliver consistent and reliable performance, minimizing data loss and disruptions. With the right approach, you can build streaming data pipelines that you can count on.

Querying Athena

When working with streaming applications that use Amazon Athena for data analysis, you need to consider reliability and potential failure modes. But first, let's examine how to perform a basic Athena query, then examine the failure modes you'll need to support in a reliable system.

Athena queries data stored in Amazon S3 by employing a distributed query engine that parallelizes the processing of data across multiple nodes in a cluster. When a query is submitted, Athena first reads the metadata of the specified data sources (e.g., tables) from the Athena catalog, which contains information about the location, format, and schema of the data files in S3.

Based on this metadata, Athena constructs an execution plan that involves reading the relevant data files from S3, applying the necessary transformations and filters specified in the query, and aggregating the results. The query engine leverages Apache Spark and Presto to efficiently process large datasets stored in various formats (e.g., CSV, JSON, and Parquet) directly from S3, without the need for intermediate data loading or transformation steps. This serverless architecture allows Athena to scale compute resources up or down dynamically, enabling efficient and cost-effective querying of data in S3 without the need to provision or manage dedicated infrastructure:

```python
import boto3
import pandas as pd

# Create an Athena client
athena_client = boto3.client("athena")

# Define the query
query = """
SELECT date, stock_symbol, AVG(price) as avg_price, SUM(volume) as total_volume
FROM "processed_market_data"
WHERE date >= DATE('2023-04-01') AND date <= DATE('2023-04-30')
GROUP BY date, stock_symbol
ORDER BY date, stock_symbol;
"""

# Start the Athena query
response = athena_client.start_query_execution(
    QueryString=query,
    QueryExecutionContext={
        "Database": "processed_data_database"   ❶
    },
    ResultConfiguration={
        "OutputLocation": "s3://your-output-bucket/athena-results/"   ❷
    }
)

# Get the query execution ID
query_execution_id = response["QueryExecutionId"]

# Wait for the query to complete
while True:
    query_status = athena_client.get_query_execution(
        QueryExecutionId=query_execution_id)
```

```
    state = query_status["QueryExecution"]["Status"]["State"]
    if state == "SUCCEEDED":
        break

# Retrieve the query results
result_data = athena_client.get_query_results(
    QueryExecutionId=query_execution_id)

# Convert the results to a Pandas DataFrame
df = pd.DataFrame([
    row["Data"]
    for row in result_data["ResultSet"]["Rows"][1:]
])

# Print the DataFrame
print(df)
```

❶   Specify the Athena database.

❷   Specify the S3 output location for the query results.

When building a streaming application using Athena to query data in S3, you'll want to consider the potential failure modes that could impact your system's reliability. These failures can affect data ingestion, query execution, data integrity, and overall performance. Table 8-8 lists some common failure modes to keep in mind as you design your application and implement strategies to mitigate their impact.

Table 8-8. Amazon Athena data analysis failure modes

Failure mode	Impact	Mitigation strategy
Kinesis Data Streams service disruption	Data ingestion failure, data loss	Implement retries, dead-letter queues, and alerting mechanisms
Athena query execution failure	Inability to analyze data, data unavailability	Retry failed queries, implement circuit breakers, and monitor Athena service health
Network connectivity issues	Data delivery delays, data loss	Implement resilient network architecture, redundant connections, and monitoring
Data corruption or schema changes	Inaccurate or inconsistent data analysis	Implement data validation, schema evolution strategies, and data quality checks
Insufficient Athena resources (e.g., concurrent queries)	Query throttling, performance degradation	Implement auto-scaling, resource monitoring, and capacity planning

One key aspect to keep in mind is striking the right balance between reliability and cost-effectiveness. Implementing multiple layers of redundancy and failover mechanisms can certainly enhance reliability, but it may also increase operational complexity and costs. To make informed decisions, carefully analyze the criticality of your application, the potential impact of failures, and the associated costs of downtime or data loss. This analysis will help you determine the appropriate level of investment in mitigating specific failure modes while maintaining cost-effectiveness.

Another consideration is the trade-off between real-time data processing and batch processing. While streaming applications often aim to provide near real-time insights, there may be scenarios where batch processing with periodic checkpointing and recovery mechanisms can be a more reliable and cost-effective approach. This is especially true for noncritical workloads or when dealing with large volumes of historical data.

By carefully evaluating these factors and making informed design choices, you can build a streaming application with Athena that delivers reliable results while optimizing for cost and performance.

Optimizing Data Storage and Querying Performance

Optimizing data storage and querying performance becomes crucial as your market data analytics application processes and stores large volumes of data. Table 8-9 shows some best practices and techniques to consider.

Table 8-9. Object storage optimizations for query performance

Optimization technique	Benefits
Data partitioning and bucketing	• Partitions data based on common query patterns (e.g., date, stock symbol) • Uses bucketing to subdivide data within partitions • Improves query performance by reducing scanned data
Data compression	• Compresses data using columnar formats like Apache Parquet or ORC • Reduces storage costs and improves query performance • Uses Kinesis Data Firehose's data transformation capabilities
Indexing and partitioning in Athena	• Defines partitions in Athena based on ordinary query filters • Creates indexes on frequently queried columns, especially low-cardinality columns • Improves query performance by reducing scanned data
Query optimization	• Analyzes and optimizes SQL queries using Athena's EXPLAIN plan or Amazon Athena Query Federation • Uses materialized views or external tables for frequently queried data • Improves query performance and reduces computation costs

Optimization technique	Benefits
Caching and result reuse	• Leverages Athena's query result caching to reuse results from previous queries • Uses Amazon QuickSight's caching capabilities for frequently accessed reports and dashboards • Reduces computation costs and improves performance
Resource management	• Monitors and adjusts Athena's allocated resources (e.g., DPU count, query result cache size) based on workload and performance requirements • Uses AWS Glue Data Catalog's resource policies to control access and limit concurrent queries • Prevents resource contention and optimizes resource utilization

By implementing these optimization techniques, you can improve the performance and cost-efficiency of your data storage and querying processes, ensuring that your market data analytics application can handle large volumes of data while delivering timely insights.

Monitoring and Observability

Implementing effective monitoring and observability practices is essential for maintaining the reliability and performance of your streaming architecture, especially as your consumer groups scale across multiple partitions and topics. As the number of consumer instances and partitions grows, you must proactively track key metrics, logs, and other indicators to identify potential issues that could impact the efficiency of message processing and the overall resiliency of your system.

When monitoring Kafka consumers, several key metrics provide insights into their health and performance. You should closely monitor these metrics described in Table 8-10 to ensure reliable and efficient message processing.

Table 8-10. Common metrics for monitoring event processing

Metric	Description	Potential implications
Consumer lag	Difference between the latest offset in a partition and the offset of the last message processed by a consumer instance	High consumer lag can lead to increased latency and potential data staleness
Processing rate	Number of messages a consumer instance processes per unit of time (e.g., messages per second)	Low processing rate may indicate performance bottlenecks or slowdowns in message processing
Fetch latency	Time taken by a consumer instance to fetch messages from brokers	High fetch latency can impact overall message processing latency and throughput

Monitoring consumer lag and processing rate are two of the most critical aspects of ensuring reliable and efficient message processing. Consumer lag represents the difference between the latest offset in a partition and the offset of the last message processed by a consumer instance. High consumer lag can lead to increased latency and potential data staleness, which can be detrimental in time-sensitive scenarios like financial market data analytics.

It's important to monitor consumer lag at both the individual consumer instance level and the overall consumer group level. By tracking lag for each partition and consumer instance, you can identify if specific instances consistently lag behind others in the same consumer group. This granular visibility can help pinpoint performance bottlenecks or resource constraints affecting individual instances.

Another key metric to monitor is the processing rate, which represents the number of messages a consumer instance processes per unit of time (e.g., messages per second). Monitoring the processing rate helps identify performance bottlenecks or slowdowns in message processing, which could lead to backlogs and delays in processing critical market data.

If you observe that the processing rate of a consumer instance consistently deviates from the average rate of other instances in the same consumer group, it may indicate an issue with that specific instance. Resource constraints, network latency, or application-specific processing logic can adversely impact the processing rate.

```python
def configure_consumer_lag_monitoring(self, kafka_cluster):
    ...
    consumer_lag_metric = cloudwatch.Metric(
        namespace="AWS/Kafka",
        metric_name="ConsumerLag", ❶
        dimensions={
            "Cluster Name": kafka_cluster.cluster_name,
            "Consumer": "stock-trades-consumer-group" ❷
        },
        period=cdk.Duration.minutes(1)
    )

    cloudwatch.Alarm(
        self, "ConsumerLagAlarm",
        alarm_name="ConsumerLagAlarm",
        metric=consumer_lag_metric,
        threshold=100, ❸
        evaluation_periods=1,
        datapoints_to_alarm=1,
        treat_missing_data=cloudwatch.TreatMissingData.MISSING
    )
```

❶ Specify the consumer lag metric name.

❷ Specify the consumer group to monitor.

❸ Set the consumer lag threshold for the alarm.

In addition to consumer lag and processing rate, Kafka exposes a wide range of metrics that provide insights into the performance and health of your consumer instances. Some key consumer metrics to monitor include:

`consumer-fetch-manager-metrics`
> This includes metrics related to the consumer's fetch requests, such as request rate, size, and latency.

`consumer-coordinator-metrics`
> This includes metrics related to the consumer groups coordinator, such as rebalance rate and time.

`consumer-metrics`
> This includes general consumer metrics, such as incoming byte rate, records consumed rate, and fetch latency.

Amazon MSK integrates with Amazon CloudWatch, providing comprehensive monitoring and logging capabilities for your Kafka clusters and consumers.

CloudWatch allows you to collect and track various metrics related to your Kafka cluster, such as broker CPU utilization, disk usage, network throughput, and message throughput. These metrics give you visibility into the performance and resource utilization of your cluster, enabling you to proactively identify and address potential issues before they impact your streaming application.

You can set up CloudWatch alarms based on predefined thresholds for critical metrics, helping you stay ahead of performance degradation or anomalies. For example, you can configure an alarm to notify you when the consumer lag exceeds a certain threshold, indicating that your consumers are falling behind in processing messages.

In addition to metrics, Amazon MSK streams broker logs to CloudWatch logs, providing detailed information about the cluster's operations, including configuration changes, client connections, and error events. These logs simplify troubleshooting and identifying issues within your Kafka cluster.

By leveraging CloudWatch monitoring and logging, you can gain deep visibility into the health and performance of your data ingestion layer, enabling you to troubleshoot issues, optimize resource utilization, and ensure the reliability of your streaming application.

Distributed tracing is a valuable tool for monitoring and troubleshooting streaming applications that span multiple services and components. AWS X-Ray provides end-to-end visibility into your streaming pipelines, helping you identify performance bottlenecks, debug issues, and optimize your application's reliability and performance.

When working with a streaming application that uses services like Amazon MSK, Amazon Kinesis Data Streams, Amazon Data Firehose, Amazon Athena, Amazon ECS, and AWS Lambda, you can leverage X-Ray in several ways:

Instrumenting Kafka producers and consumers
If your streaming application uses Amazon MSK, you can instrument your Kafka producers and consumers with the AWS X-Ray SDK for your programming language. This allows X-Ray to capture and record trace data, such as execution times, annotations, and metadata, for each message or event processed by these components.

Tracing stream processing functions
When your streaming pipeline includes AWS Lambda functions or containerized applications running on Amazon ECS for stream processing, you can integrate the X-Ray SDK into these components. This enables you to trace the execution of your stream processing logic and identify potential bottlenecks or issues.

Monitoring data ingestion and transformation
As you ingest data from Kinesis Data Streams or Kinesis Data Firehose, you can instrument the components or Lambda functions responsible for data ingestion and transformation. This allows you to trace the flow of data through these services and identify any potential issues or performance bottlenecks.

Tracing Athena queries
Although Athena doesn't directly support X-Ray tracing, you can instrument the components or Lambda functions that trigger and execute Athena queries. This provides visibility into the performance of your data analysis queries and helps you identify potential issues or optimizations.

Integrating with monitoring and observability tools
AWS X-Ray integrates seamlessly with other monitoring and observability services like Amazon CloudWatch. This allows you to correlate trace data with metrics and logs for comprehensive analysis and troubleshooting.

Keep in mind that while AWS X-Ray provides valuable distributed tracing capabilities, it's important to use it judiciously to balance visibility and cost. You can configure sampling rules and strategies to control the amount of trace data captured, ensuring that you obtain the necessary insights without incurring excessive costs.

By incorporating AWS X-Ray into your streaming application architecture, you gain deeper visibility into the behavior and performance of your streaming pipelines. This enables more effective debugging, optimization, and ultimately ensures the overall reliability and resilience of your application.

To effectively monitor the health and performance of your Kafka consumers, consider the following consolidated best practices:

Define key metrics
>Identify critical metrics like consumer lag, processing rate, and fetch latency that directly impact reliability and performance.

Implement monitoring and alerting
>Set up a robust monitoring and alerting system to track consumer metrics in real time and configure alerts based on predefined thresholds.

Use appropriate monitoring tools
>Leverage Kafka's built-in metrics and integrate with monitoring tools like Prometheus, Grafana, or cloud native monitoring services.

Monitor at different granularities
>Monitor consumer metrics at the individual consumer instance and overall consumer group levels to identify specific issues.

Correlate metrics with logs
>Combine metric-based monitoring with log analysis to gain comprehensive insights into consumer behavior.

Monitor data quality
>Implement data quality monitoring to detect and address issues such as data corruption, missing or duplicate records, and schema violations.

Monitor end-to-end latency
>Monitor end-to-end latency metrics to measure the overall responsiveness and performance of your stream processing pipelines, from data ingestion to final output or storage.

Regular review and optimization
>Continuously review and optimize consumer configurations based on observed performance characteristics and requirements.

Conduct load testing
>Perform stress testing to assess consumer performance and scalability under different workload scenarios and identify bottlenecks.

By implementing these monitoring and observability best practices, you can proactively identify and address performance issues, ensuring the reliability and efficiency of your Kafka consumers and the overall streaming architecture.

Testing Resiliency

As your market data analytics pipeline becomes more complex and mission critical, it's important to proactively test and validate its resilience against various failure scenarios. AWS Fault Injection Service (AWS FIS) provides a fully managed service that enables you to safely experiment and evaluate your applications' resilience by injecting failures and simulating real-world scenarios.

In the context of your Kafka-based streaming architecture, AWS FIS can help you validate the resilience of your Apache Kafka clusters, producers, consumers, and downstream services like Kinesis Data Firehose, and Amazon S3. By injecting failures such as broker terminations, network latency, data corruption, and service outages, you can observe how your system responds and identify potential weaknesses or areas for improvement.

It's important to implement comprehensive testing and monitoring practices for your stream processing pipelines. This section covers various testing approaches and monitoring strategies to ensure the reliability, performance, and correctness of your stream processing logic. Testing categories are listed in Table 8-11.

Table 8-11. Data pipeline testing

Testing category	Description	Examples	Considerations
Unit tests	Validate individual components and functions of the stream processing logic in isolation.	Test state update functions, business logic, and error-handling scenarios using mocking frameworks.	Ensure test coverage and maintainability of unit tests.
Integration tests	Verify the end-to-end behavior of the stream processing pipeline in a test environment.	Set up a test Kafka cluster, DynamoDB, and test data sources; validate state updates and output events.	Manage test environment setup and teardown, ensure realistic test scenarios.
Fault injection tests	Simulate failures and error scenarios to test the pipeline's resilience and fault tolerance.	Inject Kafka broker failures, network disruptions, DynamoDB errors, and validate recovery mechanisms.	Determine appropriate failure scenarios based on potential real-world failures.
Performance tests	Evaluate the scalability and throughput of the stream processing pipeline under different load scenarios.	Measure processing latency, state update efficiency, and resource utilization under varying loads.	Identify performance bottlenecks and optimize configurations.
Data validation tests	Validate the integrity and consistency of the state data stored in DynamoDB.	Verify that state updates are applied correctly and the stored data matches the expected values based on the processed events.	Implement data reconciliation processes and anomaly detection mechanisms.
Monitoring	Track key metrics and health indicators to proactively identify and address potential issues.	Monitor consumer lag, processing rate, resource utilization, error rates, and data quality metrics.	Set up alerts and notifications and correlate metrics with logs for comprehensive visibility.

By implementing adequate testing and monitoring practices, you can ensure the reliability, performance, and correctness of your stream processing pipelines, enabling efficient and accurate data enrichment for your market data analytics application.

Through effective monitoring, observability, testing, and optimization practices, you can build a resilient and high-performing streaming architecture that can handle the demands of real-time market data analytics while minimizing the risk of data loss, inconsistencies, or performance degradation.

Table 8-12 enumerates some of the built-in chaos experiments for validating your streaming applications.

Table 8-12. Built-in AWS FIS experiments

Chaos experiment	Action
Terminate Amazon MSK broker instances	aws:msk:broker-terminate
Induce network latency between producers/consumers and Amazon MSK	aws:ec2:network-latency-interference
Induce network packet loss between producers/consumers and Amazon MSK	aws:ec2:network-bandwidth-interference
Disable Amazon MSK autoscaling	aws:msk:cluster-scale-in-stop
Corrupt Amazon MSK topic data	aws:kafka:topic-data-corruption
Delete Amazon MSK topic data	aws:kafka:topic-data-deletion
Increase Lambda function timeout exceptions	aws:lambda:function-throttle
Corrupt Amazon S3 bucket data	aws:s3:object-data-corruption
Delete Amazon S3 bucket data	aws:s3:object-data-deletion

The following snippet demonstrates how to deploy one of these chaos experiments into your environment. This example will randomly terminate Kafka brokers, causing Amazon MSK to reprovision them. See Part I of the book for more information about using AWS FIS within your resiliency testing.

```
experiment = fis.CfnExperiment(
    self, "MyFISExperiment",
    experiment_template=fis.CfnExperimentTemplate(
        actions={
            "terminate-msk-broker": fis.CfnExperimentTemplate.ActionProperty(
                description="Terminate an MSK broker",
                provider_configuration=
                    fis.CfnExperimentTemplate.ProviderConfigurationProperty(
                        configuration={
                            "brokerIds": ["<REPLACE_WITH_BROKER_ID>"],
                            "clusterArn": "<REPLACE_WITH_MSK_CLUSTER_ARN>",
                        },
                        service="aws:msk:broker-terminate",
                ),
            )
        },
        experiment_template_name="my-fis-experiment-template",
        stop_conditions={
            "stop-after-time": fis.CfnExperimentTemplate.StopConditionProperty(
                source="none",
                value="PT10M",
```

```
                    )
                },
                targets={
                    "msk-cluster": fis.CfnExperimentTemplate.TargetProperty(
                        filters={
                            "clusterArn": ["<REPLACE_WITH_MSK_CLUSTER_ARN>"],
                        },
                        resource_type="AWS::MSK::Cluster",
                    )
                }
            ),
            role_arn=iam.Role.from_role_arn(self, "FISRole", role),
        )
```

By implementing these testing and monitoring practices, you can ensure the reliability, performance, and correctness of your stream processing pipelines. With a robust testing and validation approach, you can transition to building a resilient and high-performing streaming architecture that can handle the demands of real-time market data analytics.

Cleaning Up

In "Technical Requirements" on page 222, you deployed infrastructure to experiment with this chapter's lessons and explore the various failure modes. When you finish, delete the cloud resources to avoid ongoing costs. The easiest way to clean up is:

1. Navigate a command terminal into the *ch08-real-time_stocks* folder.

2. Run the **cdk destroy** command.

3. Grab another cup of coffee, and return in 30 minutes.

The default configuration uses small instances to minimize any costs. Suppose that you leave these resources deployed for a prolonged time. In that case, you can expect the deployment to cost roughly one dollar daily, prorated to the second. The bulk of these costs come from the kafka.t3.small broker node. Amazon MSK doesn't provide an option for pausing or stopping the cluster, so you must delete and re-create the resource to avoid costs while it's not in use. However, provisioning a new cluster takes around 10 to 15 minutes. Other resources like the AWS Lambda functions for processing the stream qualify for the free tier if your account is eligible for that program. Otherwise, you can expect a few cents consumed monthly by this chapter's serverless resources.

Summary

In this chapter, you explored the principles and best practices for building a resilient and scalable streaming architecture for real-time market data analytics. Supporting fast-paced data streams is key to making informed decisions, seizing opportunities, and mitigating risks. You learned how to design and implement a robust data ingestion layer using Amazon MSK, ensuring reliable and consistent data delivery from multiple sources. By leveraging Apache Kafka's partitioning, replication, and fault tolerance capabilities, you can build a highly available and scalable data ingestion pipeline that can handle high-velocity market data streams.

You also discovered the importance of using AWS Lambda to build fault-tolerant producers and consumers. You learned techniques for ensuring reliable message processing, handling failures, and scaling consumer groups horizontally based on workload demands. Monitoring consumer health and performance is crucial for proactively identifying and addressing performance issues before they impact the overall system reliability.

Additionally, you explored enriching market data through stream processing and API integration. By using services like AWS Lambda and Amazon API Gateway, you can seamlessly integrate external data sources and APIs to enhance trade data with additional context, such as historical trends, company fundamentals, or news sentiment. Maintaining state consistency and fault tolerance during stream processing is an important consideration.

Lastly, you learned about storing processed market data using Amazon Data Firehose and querying it with Amazon Athena. You discovered techniques for optimizing data storage, querying performance, and monitoring costs associated with these operations.

As you progress in your journey of building resilient and scalable solutions on AWS, the next chapter will focus on ingesting news articles and demonstrating real-time search capabilities. You'll explore leveraging AWS services like Amazon Data Firehose, Amazon OpenSearch, and AWS Lambda to build a robust pipeline for ingesting and indexing news articles, enabling real-time search and analysis capabilities.

By applying the principles and best practices covered in this chapter, you'll be well-prepared to tackle the challenges of building a real-time news ingestion and search pipeline, ensuring reliability, scalability, and cost-effectiveness. Get ready to dive into another exciting use case that will further expand your knowledge and skills in building resilient and performant solutions on AWS.

## CHAPTER 9

Building Reliable News Feed Ingestion and Search APIs

In the early 19th century, Nathan Rothschild, a prominent Rothschild banking family member, demonstrated the power of timely information in financial markets. Legend has it that Rothschild received news of the British victory at the Battle of Waterloo in 1815 before official government channels. He used this knowledge to mislead other traders into panic-selling their British government bonds, secretly buying them up at depressed prices. When the official news of victory reached London, bond prices surged, and Rothschild profited immensely.

The story, while disputed, illustrates how access to exclusive information once gave investors a significant advantage before modern communication technologies. Today, businesses across industries consume real-time information to make decisions and stay competitive. You can build reliable systems to ingest, process, and serve news articles and unstructured data, unlocking the power of timely information retrieval and analysis.

In this chapter, you'll explore designing and implementing a resilient news feed ingestion and search architecture on AWS. You'll examine the challenges of fetching articles from unreliable sources and techniques to handle these challenges gracefully. You'll learn about storing and managing article metadata and content using Amazon MemoryDB for Redis and Amazon S3. You'll also discover how to ensure data consistency and real-time synchronization between the primary data store and search index using change data capture (CDC) and the Command Query Responsibility Segregation (CQRS) pattern.

As you progress, you'll learn how to build resilient and decoupled microservices using an API layer with an AWS Application Load Balancer (ALB) and Amazon

Elastic Container Service (ECS) to serve search traffic reliably. You'll explore various resiliency patterns and techniques to handle failures and ensure high availability.

Finally, you'll understand the importance of testing and validating the architecture's resilience through chaos engineering experiments and comprehensive monitoring and observability practices. The chapter also highlights security considerations and best practices to protect against data breaches and unauthorized access.

By the end of this chapter, you'll be able to:

- Design a fault-tolerant data ingestion pipeline using a Scheduler and Worker Node architecture
- Store and manage article metadata and content efficiently using Amazon MemoryDB for Redis and Amazon S3
- Implement a scalable and high-performance search engine with Amazon OpenSearch Service
- Ensure data consistency and real-time synchronization using CDC and event-driven architectures
- Build resilient and decoupled microservices using Amazon ECS and AWS CDK
- Apply chaos engineering principles to test and validate the resilience of your architecture
- Secure your news feed system against data breaches and unauthorized access

Now that you have an overview of what you'll learn in this chapter, let's dive into the technical requirements needed to follow along and build the resilient news feed system.

Technical Requirements

In this section, you'll deploy the news feed ingestion architecture into your AWS account using the AWS Cloud Development Kit (AWS CDK). AWS CDK is a toolset that enables you to rapidly deploy cloud resources in a repeatable manner. Chapter 2 provides detailed instructions for installing, configuring, and troubleshooting the AWS CDK. To deploy this chapter's example:

1. Clone this book's GitHub repository to your local machine.
2. Navigate a command terminal into the *ch09-news_insights* folder.
3. Run the command `cdk deploy`.
4. Take a break, grab a coffee, and check back in about 30 minutes.

Once the deployment is complete, you'll have the following reference architecture available for experimentation. This solution consists of three main components (see Figure 9-1):

Article downloader
> This component orchestrates the download of news articles from a singleton Scheduler across multiple Worker Nodes.

Data replicator
> This component synchronizes two heterogeneous databases (Amazon Open-Search Service and Amazon MemoryDB for Redis) through a CDC process using Redis Streams. It ensures the search index remains up-to-date with the latest article metadata, enabling efficient and accurate search capabilities.

Search API
> This component demonstrates mechanisms for decoupling your clients' search queries from the OpenSearch cluster.

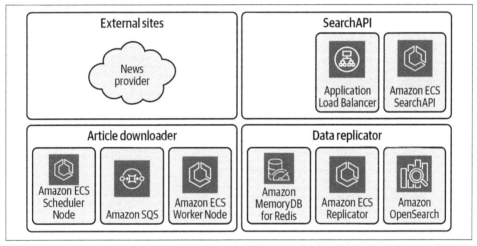

Figure 9-1. High-level architecture diagram of the news feed pipeline, showcasing the flow of data and the interaction between various components

Throughout this chapter, you'll explore the intricacies of each component, discovering best practices for handling failures, ensuring data consistency, and building resilient microservices.

So, how can you create a reliable news feed solution? The following section dives into the challenges of fetching and processing news articles from remote sites, a critical aspect of the process. Let's uncover the strategies and techniques that will help you build a robust and dependable system.

Fetching and Processing News Articles

Developing a dependable news feed solution is particularly valuable for stock trading applications, where users rely on up-to-the-minute financial news to make informed investment decisions. However, fetching and processing news articles from external sources introduces several challenges that can impact the news feed's availability and accuracy.

In today's interconnected world, many applications orchestrate numerous calls to external APIs and systems outside your control. These external dependencies introduce potential failure modes that can disrupt the data ingestion pipeline, leading to inconsistent or outdated information being served to users. One such external dependency is the need to fetch news articles defined in *sitemap.xml* files from third-party news providers.

Sitemaps are simple manifests that provide a structured way for websites to list their available content, such as articles or web pages, along with metadata like the last update timestamp. Search engines and content aggregators crawl these sitemaps to efficiently discover and index the available content:

```xml
<?xml version="1.0" encoding="UTF-8"?>
<urlset xmlns="http://www.sitemaps.org/schemas/sitemap/0.9">
  <url>
    <loc>https://www.example.com/deadbeef</loc>
    <lastmod>2023-05-05</lastmod>
    <changefreq>weekly</changefreq>
    <priority>1.0</priority>
  </url>
  <url>
    <loc>https://www.example.com/about</loc>
    <lastmod>2023-04-20</lastmod>
    <changefreq>monthly</changefreq>
    <priority>0.8</priority>
  </url>
</urlset>
```

However, fetching sitemaps and article content from remote sites can be unreliable due to various potential failure modes:

Remote site outages
Third-party news sites or APIs may experience downtime or outages, preventing the retrieval of *sitemap.xml* files or article content.

Network connectivity issues
Intermittent network disruptions or high latency can impact the ability to fetch sitemaps and article content reliably.

Rate limiting
> News providers may enforce rate limits or throttling mechanisms, restricting the number of requests made within a given period.

Data inconsistencies
> Errors or inconsistencies in the *sitemap.xml* or article content data can lead to incomplete or incorrect information being ingested into the news feed pipeline.

These failure modes can have significant consequences for businesses. Users may make investment decisions based on stale or incomplete financial news, potentially leading to economic losses. Missing or outdated news articles can degrade the user experience and erode trust in the trading application, allowing competitors with more reliable news feeds to gain an advantage.

To mitigate these challenges and ensure a robust news feed solution, you'll explore techniques such as the Producer-Consumer pattern, retry mechanisms, circuit breakers, and event-driven architectures. The following section dives into the Producer-Consumer pattern. This design pattern decouples the production and consumption of tasks, enabling independent scaling and fault isolation. By leveraging this approach, you can build a more resilient and scalable news feed pipeline that can handle the complexities of fetching and processing articles from external sources.

Producer-Consumer Pattern for Article Processing

Fetching and processing news articles from remote sites and handling reliability challenges can be a daunting task, but with a robust and scalable architecture, you can tackle these challenges head-on. The Producer-Consumer pattern, inspired by manufacturing principles, provides a powerful design approach to address these issues.

In this analogy, the Producer takes on the role of the foreman, diligently checking for new orders (*sitemap.xml* files) and assigning tasks to the queue. The Consumers, like skilled assemblers, retrieve these tasks, fetch the necessary parts (article content) from various suppliers (remote sites), assemble the product (store metadata and content), and pass it along for further processing. By separating the task production process from the actual processing, this architecture allows the system to handle disruptions gracefully and ensures continuous operation. The Producer manages the *sitemap.xml* files, identifies pending work, and queues tasks for the Consumers to process. Meanwhile, the Consumers distribute the workload, fetch the article content, and store the metadata and complete content in their respective data stores.

This decoupled approach offers several advantages. It enables independent scaling of the Producer and Consumers based on demand, ensuring efficient resource utilization and fault isolation. If one component encounters issues, it doesn't impact the other, preventing cascading failures. Moreover, the architecture facilitates parallel processing and load distribution, enhancing overall throughput and responsiveness.

Let's dive into an example to see the Producer-Consumer pattern in action (Figure 9-2). Imagine a large news organization that ingests articles from multiple sources, such as RSS feeds, APIs, and web scraping. It has a central Producer service that periodically checks for new articles based on predefined configurations. When new articles are identified, the Producer sends messages to a message queue, like Amazon SQS, triggering the Consumers to process them. The Consumers, running on Amazon ECS, retrieve messages from the queue and begin processing the articles. Each Consumer fetches the full article content from the respective source, extracts relevant metadata, and stores the metadata in Amazon MemoryDB for Redis, and the full article content in Amazon S3. By distributing the workload across multiple Consumers, the news organization efficiently processes a large volume of articles and scales processing capacity based on incoming load.

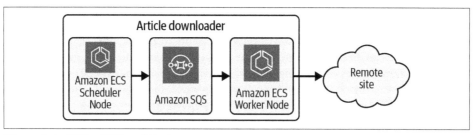

Figure 9-2. ECS + SQS architecture

This example demonstrates how the Producer-Consumer pattern enables efficient ingestion and processing of articles from multiple sources while ensuring scalability, fault tolerance, and decoupling of concerns. The Producer acts as the central orchestrator, identifying new articles and triggering their processing. It reads from a local configuration file, checks for updates, and sends messages to the SQS queue describing articles that need processing. Meanwhile, the Consumers handle the actual fetching, extraction, and storage of article data in a distributed and parallelized manner by pulling messages from that SQS queue:

```
import os
import boto3
import json

sqs = boto3.client("sqs")

def get_sitemap_urls():
    with open("sitemap_config.json", "r") as f:
        config = json.load(f)
    return config["sitemap_urls"]

def process_sitemaps():
```

```
        sitemap_urls = get_sitemap_urls()
        for article_url in get_articles():
            for url in sitemap_urls:
                article_metadata = fetch_and_process_sitemap(url)

                # Publish the article metadata to the SNS topic
                sqs.send_message(
                    QueueUrl=os.environ["NEWS_INGEST_QUEUE_URL"],
                    MessageBody=json.dumps(article_metadata)
                )

def fetch_and_process_sitemap(url):
    response = requests.get(url)
    article_metadata = parse_sitemap(response.text)
    return article_metadata

def parse_sitemap(sitemap_xml):
    # Parse the sitemap XML and extract article metadata
    # Return the article metadata as a dict
    article_metadata = {
        "url": "https://example.com/article/123",
        "title": "Breaking News",
        "author": "John Doe",
        "publication_date": "2023-04-26T10:30:00Z"
    }
    return article_metadata
```

After the Worker Node retrieves the message from an Amazon SQS queue, it downloads the requested URL and stores the content in Amazon S3. Then the article_metadata is persisted into Redis using a hash data type, which behaves like a key-value dictionary with fast access to individual fields. This code example shows how the Worker Nodes consume messages from the SQS queue, fetch the article content from remote sites, and store the metadata in MemoryDB and the full content in S3. Here, the Worker Nodes are fetching article content and storing metadata by consuming messages from the SQS queue, fetching the article content from remote sites, storing the metadata in MemoryDB using Redis hashes, and storing the full content in S3:

```
import os
import boto3
import requests
import json
from redis import Redis

REDIS_ENDPOINT = os.environ["REDIS_ENDPOINT"]
BUCKET_NAME = os.environ['S3_BUCKET_NAME']

def handle_message(message):
    article_metadata = json.loads(message["Body"])
    fetch_and_store_article(article_metadata)
```

```
def fetch_and_store_article(article_metadata):
    response = requests.get(article_metadata["url"])
    article_content = response.text

    store_article_metadata(article_metadata, article_content)
    store_article_content(article_metadata["url"], article_content)

def store_article_metadata(metadata, content):
    redis = Redis(host=REDIS_ENDPOINT, port=6379)
    url = metadata['url'].replace('/', '-')

    redis.hset(
        f"article:{metadata['url']}",
        mapping={
            "title": metadata["title"],
            "author": metadata["author"],
            "publication_date": metadata["publication_date"],
            "s3_uri": f"s3://{BUCKET_NAME}/{url}.html"
        }
    )

def store_article_content(url, content):
    s3 = boto3.client("s3")
    s3.put_object(
        Bucket=os.environ["S3_BUCKET_NAME"],
        Key=f"{url.replace('/', '-')}.html",
        Body=content
    )
```

While this code demonstrates the basic implementation of the Producer-Consumer pattern for article processing, it's beneficial to consider potential failure scenarios and how the system recovers from them. Let's examine some common faults that could occur in this architecture and their corresponding recovery mechanisms (Table 9-1).

Table 9-1. Article downloader failure mode

Potential fault	Description	Recovery mechanism
Producer failure	The Producer service crashes or becomes unresponsive	Amazon ECS automatically restarts the Producer task. The SQS queue retains unprocessed messages, ensuring no work is lost.
Consumer failure	A Consumer instance crashes or becomes unresponsive	Amazon ECS automatically restarts the Consumer task. SQS message visibility timeout ensures the message becomes available for other Consumers to process.
SQS queue failure	The SQS queue becomes temporarily unavailable	AWS manages SQS for high availability. Producer and Consumers implement retry logic with exponential backoff to handle temporary unavailability.
External source unavailability	A news source website or API becomes unreachable	Consumers implement circuit breaker pattern to avoid overwhelming unavailable sources. Failed tasks are sent to a dead-letter queue for later retry.

Potential fault	Description	Recovery mechanism
MemoryDB or S3 outage	Temporary unavailability of storage services	Consumers implement retry logic with exponential backoff. Failed writes are cached locally and retried when the service becomes available.

Amazon ECS's scalability and resiliency allow this architecture to dynamically adjust to changing workloads and recover from failures. The decoupled nature of the Producer and Consumers enables independent scaling and fault isolation.

Leader Election for Scheduler High Availability

Suppose the Scheduler process is a singleton service. Singleton processes may appear in your workloads for various reasons. For example, a central or legacy component might be difficult to partition and horizontally scale, making it a potential single point of failure. If the Scheduler becomes unavailable due to hardware issues, network problems, or other unforeseen circumstances, it could disrupt the entire news feed ingestion pipeline, leading to stale or incomplete data.

To mitigate this risk and ensure high availability for the Scheduler, you can implement a leader election process. Leader election, a distributed computing concept, involves multiple instances of a service coordinating to select a single instance as the leader responsible for performing critical tasks. If the current leader fails, a new leader is elected from the remaining instances, ensuring service continuity.

Achieving fault tolerance and high availability is a crucial consideration for mission-critical applications like the Scheduler. By deploying multiple instances of the Scheduler service across different Availability Zones (AZs), you can ensure that if one instance fails, the others can seamlessly take over, minimizing downtime and ensuring uninterrupted operation.

The key steps involved in implementing the leader election pattern for the Scheduler are as follows:

1. Deploy multiple instances of the Scheduler across different AZs.
2. Implement a leader election mechanism using a distributed lock or consensus algorithm.
3. Instances participate in the leader election process.
4. The elected leader becomes the active Scheduler and processes sitemaps.
5. Standby instances monitor the leader and take over if the leader fails.
6. A new leader is elected from the standby instances if the current leader fails.

To coordinate multiple instances and determine the active Producer processing sitemaps, a leader election mechanism is employed. This typically involves a distributed lock or a consensus algorithm like Raft or Paxos, establishing a single leader among the instances.

When Producer instances start up, they compete for leadership. The instance that successfully acquires the lock becomes the active Producer and begins processing sitemaps. The remaining instances enter standby mode, periodically checking the leader's status and ready to take over if needed.

If the current leader fails or loses the lock due to issues like network partitions or hardware failures, a new leader is elected from the standby instances. This transition occurs seamlessly, ensuring uninterrupted processing of sitemaps and maintaining the Producer service's availability and reliability.

By implementing leader election, the Producer service achieves high availability, fault tolerance, and seamless failover, ensuring continuous sitemap processing even during individual instance failures or other disruptions.

The following code snippet demonstrates how to implement leader election using Redis. You'll notice the main loop attempts to acquire the lock every five seconds. If this instance succeeds, it performs the business logic. Otherwise, the instance knows it's a failover node and waits for its turn:

```python
import redis
import time
import os
import logging

logger = logging.getLogger(__name__)

class LeaderElector:
    def __init__(self, redis_host, redis_port, scheduler_name):
        self.redis = redis.Redis(host=redis_host, port=redis_port)
        self.scheduler_name = scheduler_name
        self.lock_name = f"scheduler_lock_{scheduler_name}"
        self.lock_timeout = 30  # Seconds

    def acquire_lock(self):
        try:
            return self.redis.set(
                self.lock_name,
                self.scheduler_name,
                ex=self.lock_timeout,
                nx=True)

        except redis.exceptions.RedisError as e:
            logger.error(f"Error acquiring scheduler lock: {e}")
            return False
```

```python
        def release_lock(self):
            try:
                self.redis.delete(self.lock_name)
            except redis.exceptions.RedisError as e:
                logger.error(f"Error releasing scheduler lock: {e}")

        def is_leader(self):
            try:
                return self.redis.get(self.lock_name) == self.scheduler_name.encode()
            except redis.exceptions.RedisError as e:
                logger.error(f"Error checking scheduler lock: {e}")
                return False

    def main():
        redis_host = os.getenv("REDIS_HOST", "localhost")
        redis_port = int(os.getenv("REDIS_PORT", 6379))
        scheduler_name = os.getenv("SCHEDULER_NAME", "scheduler-1")

        elector = LeaderElector(redis_host, redis_port, scheduler_name)

        while True:
            if elector.acquire_lock():
                logger.info(f"{scheduler_name} is the leader")

                do_stuff()

                time.sleep(60)
                elector.release_lock()
            else:
                logger.info(f"{scheduler_name} is not the leader")
                time.sleep(5)

    if __name__ == "__main__":
        main()
```

With leader elections, you can ensure that only one instance of the Scheduler actively processes sitemaps at any given time while providing high availability and fault tolerance. If the current leader fails, a new leader is elected from the standby instances, allowing the news feed ingestion process to continue without interruption.

Scheduler Configuration Failure Modes

In this section, you'll explore strategies for handling failure modes related to service configuration metadata.

When working with service configuration metadata, it's important to consider potential failure scenarios and implement appropriate measures to ensure the resilience of your system. Misconfigurations, inconsistencies, or outdated metadata can lead to unexpected behavior and impact the reliability of your services.

In this chapter's example, the *scheduler-config.json* file plays a center role in the news feed ingestion pipeline, representing settings for various aspects of the orchestration, such as lists of `SitemapIndexes` to monitor and process metadata.

A *sitemapIndex.xml* file contains references to multiple *sitemap.xml* files, allowing for more manageable content organization and providing granular information to search engines:

```
<?xml version="1.0" encoding="UTF-8"?>
<sitemapindex xmlns="http://www.sitemaps.org/schemas/sitemap/0.9">
  <sitemap>
    <loc>https://www.example.com/sitemap-main.xml</loc>
    <lastmod>2024-05-05</lastmod>
  </sitemap>
  <sitemap>
    <loc>https://www.example.com/sitemap-blog.xml</loc>
    <lastmod>2024-05-03</lastmod>
  </sitemap>
</sitemapindex>
```

To ensure reliable operation of the news feed ingestion pipeline, you need to maintain the accuracy and consistency of the *scheduler-config.json* file. Outdated or incorrect configurations can lead to missing or inaccurate sitemap processing, resulting in incomplete or stale data.

As different manual and automated processes update the *scheduler-config.json* file, synchronizing it across multiple machines and environments can be challenging. To address this, you should implement a robust configuration management process that ensures consistent maintenance and updates across all environments. Consider the following strategies:

Automated validation
　　Develop automated validation scripts to regularly check the *scheduler-config.json* file for correct hash signatures and verifying the validity of URLs, frequencies, and other metadata. These scripts can be integrated into your CI/CD pipeline or scheduled to run periodically using services like AWS Lambda or Amazon EventBridge. By automating the validation process, you can catch errors or inconsistencies early and prevent them from propagating to the production environment.

Dynamic configuration updates
　　Enable dynamic configuration updates without requiring complete application restarts or redeployments. This can be achieved by leveraging AWS services like AWS Systems Manager Parameter Store or AWS AppConfig. These services allow you to store and manage configuration parameters centrally, and your applications can retrieve the latest configuration values at runtime.

For example, you can store the *scheduler-config.json* file in the Systems Manager Parameter Store or AppConfig and configure your Scheduler and Worker Node applications to periodically check for updates or subscribe to configuration change events. When a change is detected, the applications can reload the updated configuration without requiring a complete restart, minimizing disruptions to the ongoing ingestion process.

The following example demonstrates how to periodically fetch a configuration value from the Parameter store. It uses the `cached_property` decorator to minimize the total requests to AWS Systems Manager:

```python
from functools import cached_property

class MyParameterStoreReader:
    def __init__(self, ssm_client):
        self.ssm_client = ssm_client

    @cached_property(ttl=300)
    def some_configuration_value(self):
        response = self.ssm_client.get_parameter(
            Name='/fetching-news/configuration/my-value',
            WithDecryption=True)

        return response['Parameter']['Value']
)
```

Instead of bundling the *scheduler-config.json* file directly with the application code, store it on a network filesystem accessible by all components of the ingestion pipeline. Table 9-2 compares the network filesystem options provided by AWS.

Table 9-2. AWS filesystem options

Network filesystem	Description	Benefits	Considerations
Amazon Elastic File System (EFS)	A scalable, elastic, and highly available NFS filesystem for Linux-based instances and on-premises servers	Seamless integration with AWS services, automatic scaling, and high availability	Limited to NFS protocol, may have higher latency for some workloads
Amazon FSx for Windows File Server	A fully managed Windows file server with a high performance and highly available file storage solution	Support for SMB protocol, integration with Active Directory, and familiar Windows management tools	Higher cost compared to EFS, limited to Windows environments
Amazon FSx for NetApp ONTAP	A managed filesystem service that provides high performance ONTAP filesystem capabilities	Advanced data management features, storage efficiency, and integration with on-premises NetApp environments	Higher cost compared to EFS, more complex configuration and management

By storing the configuration file on a network filesystem, you can streamline the update process and eliminate the need to redeploy applications or containers whenever the configuration changes. Additionally, this approach simplifies the management of configuration files across different environments, as updates can be made centrally and propagated to all components automatically.

Additional Resiliency Strategies

To further improve the resilience and scalability of the news feed ingestion pipeline, you can apply the Bulkhead pattern and implement a choreographed, event-driven architecture using Amazon EventBridge.

As your large-scale news feed ingestion pipeline grows to support multiple sources and varying workloads, you can ensure resilience and fault isolation by implementing the Bulkhead pattern. This involves isolating the Scheduler and Worker Nodes into separate resource pools and partitioning the Worker Nodes into dedicated bulkheads based on the type of news sources they handle (e.g., financial, technology, or sports news).

Within each bulkhead, you assign dedicated resources like CPU, memory, and network bandwidth to prevent resource contention. This approach ensures that a spike in one bulkhead's workload doesn't impact the others, helping contain the impact of failures and preventing cascading issues across the entire system:

```
cluster = ecs.Cluster(self, "BulkheadCluster")

# Create a task definition for the finance bulkhead
finance_task_def = ecs.Ec2TaskDefinition(self, "FinanceTaskDef")
finance_task_def.add_container("FinanceContainer",
    image=ecs.ContainerImage.from_registry("finance-worker"),
    memory_reservation_mib=4096,
    cpu=2048
)

# Create a service for the finance bulkhead
finance_service = ecs.Ec2Service(self, "FinanceService",
    cluster=cluster,
    task_definition=finance_task_def,
    desired_count=2
)

# Set resource limits for the finance service
deployment_config.deployment_circuit_breaker.rollback_on_failure = True
deployment_config.min_healthy_percent = 50
deployment_config.max_percent = 200
```

By isolating resources that process financial news from those that handle sports news, you can constrain the blast radius of failures and improve overall system resilience.

Amazon EventBridge, a serverless event bus, simplifies the process of connecting applications using data from various sources. Instead of having the Scheduler directly invoke the Worker Nodes, you can implement a choreographed, event-driven architecture using EventBridge to further decouple the components and enhance flexibility.

While earlier examples in this chapter utilized Amazon SQS for message passing between the Scheduler and Worker Nodes, EventBridge offers several advantages that make it well-suited for building reliable and scalable event-driven systems. With EventBridge, you can create rules that match and route events to multiple targets, enabling fan-out scenarios where multiple consumers can process the same event. It also provides event archiving and replay capabilities, allowing you to recover from failures or reprocess events as needed. Additionally, EventBridge supports advanced filtering and transformation of events, giving you fine-grained control over event processing.

In this approach, the Scheduler publishes events to EventBridge whenever new sitemap URLs need to be processed. Each Worker Node bulkhead creates event rules in EventBridge to filter and consume specific events based on the type of news sources it handles. When a new event matches a rule, EventBridge invokes the corresponding Worker Node bulkhead to process the sitemap URL asynchronously:

```
import boto3

eventbridge = boto3.client('events')

# Publish an event to EventBridge
response = eventbridge.put_events(
    Entries=[
        {
            'Source': 'news-scheduler',
            'DetailType': 'sitemap URL',
            'Detail':
                '{"url": "https://example.com/sitemap.xml", "type": "finance"}'
        }
    ]
)
```

EventBridge enables a resilient and flexible event-driven architecture for your news feed ingestion pipeline, offering features like event routing, archiving, replay, and advanced filtering.

To further enhance the resilience of the event-driven architecture, you can combine the Choreography pattern with the Bulkhead pattern. Each Worker Node bulkhead creates event rules in EventBridge to filter and consume events based on the type of sitemap URLs they process (e.g., financial versus sports news). Additionally, you assign dedicated resources to each Worker Node bulkhead, preventing resource contention and ensuring that a spike in resource usage by one bulkhead doesn't impact the others.

Here's a summary of the benefits of combining the Bulkhead and Choreography patterns using Amazon EventBridge:

Flexibility
The loosely coupled architecture allows for easy addition or removal of bulkheads without impacting the entire system. EventBridge enables seamless event filtering and routing to the appropriate bulkheads.

Scalability
Each bulkhead can scale independently based on its specific workload, optimizing resource utilization. EventBridge can handle high volumes of events and automatically scales to accommodate the load.

Resilience
Failures are contained within individual bulkheads, preventing cascading failures across the system. EventBridge provides a highly available and fault-tolerant event bus, ensuring reliable event delivery.

Decoupling
The Scheduler and Worker Nodes are decoupled, allowing for independent development, deployment, and scaling. EventBridge acts as a mediator, enabling communication between components without tight coupling.

You can apply these resiliency design patterns across your applications to effectively isolate failures and increase scalability.

By combining the Bulkhead pattern with a choreographed, event-driven architecture using Amazon EventBridge, you can create a resilient, scalable, and maintainable data ingestion pipeline that adapts to varying workloads and handles failures gracefully, ensuring the continuous and reliable delivery of news feeds to your users.

Syncing Articles to OpenSearch

To enable efficient search functionality for your users, you can leverage Amazon OpenSearch Service alongside storing article metadata in Amazon MemoryDB for Redis and article content in Amazon S3. This combination provides a scalable and durable foundation for your news feed solution. However, it's important to be aware that syncing data between these heterogeneous data stores and the search index introduces potential failure modes. By addressing these failure modes, you can ensure data consistency and reliability across your architecture.

In the news feed architecture, Amazon OpenSearch Service enables efficient search functionality for users. However, syncing data between these heterogeneous data stores and the search index introduces potential failure modes that you need to address to ensure data consistency and reliability.

You'll need to support the following failure modes during this operation:

Network disruptions
Connectivity issues or high latency between the primary data store (MemoryDB) and the search index (OpenSearch) can cause data synchronization delays or failures.

Data corruption
Errors or inconsistencies in the data propagating to the search index can lead to incorrect or incomplete search results.

Resource contention
High workloads or spikes in demand can cause resource contention, leading to performance degradation or failures in the data synchronization process.

Remote site outages or rate limiting
When fetching article content from remote sites, outages or rate limiting can prevent content retrieval, resulting in incomplete search index data.

MemoryDB or S3 outages
Outages or disruptions in the primary data stores (MemoryDB or S3) can impact the ability to retrieve and index article data.

To tackle these challenges, you can leverage CDC in combination with the CQRS pattern. CDC acts as a dedicated messenger, capturing changes made to the primary data store (MemoryDB) and propagating those changes to the search index (OpenSearch) in near real-time. This ensures that the search functionality always reflects the most current information.

To implement CDC replication, you can use a containerized process within Amazon ECS/EKS that subscribes to Redis streams and writes into the OpenSearch indices. The process starts by reading batches of messages from the Redis stream, each containing article metadata such as the S3 location, download URL, and title:

```
redis_endpoint = os.environ["REDIS_ENDPOINT"]
opensearch_endpoint = os.environ["OPENSEARCH_ENDPOINT"]
s3_bucket = os.environ["S3_BUCKET"]

def consume_redis_stream(event, context):
    redis = redis.Redis(host=redis_endpoint, port=6379)
    events = redis.xread({"news-updates": "0-0"}, count=10, block=0)

    for stream, messages in events:
        for message in messages:
            index_article(message, opensearch_endpoint, s3_bucket)
```

It then retrieves the article content from Amazon S3 and persists it into the Open-Search database:

```python
def index_article(message, opensearch_endpoint, s3_bucket):
    article_id = message[0].decode("utf-8")
    article_data = json.loads(message[1][b"data"].decode("utf-8"))

    s3 = boto3.client("s3")
    s3_key = f"articles/{article_id.replace('/', '-')}.html"
    article_content = s3.get_object(
        Bucket=s3_bucket, Key=s3_key)["Body"].read().decode("utf-8")

    credentials = boto3.Session().get_credentials()
    http_auth = AWS4Auth(credentials.access_key,
        credentials.secret_key,
        region,
        service,
        session_token=credentials.token)

    opensearch = OpenSearch(
        hosts=[{"host": opensearch_endpoint, "port": 443}],
        http_auth= http_auth,
            "es"
        ),
        use_ssl=True,
        verify_certs=True,
        connection_class=RequestsHttpConnection
    )
    opensearch.index(
        index="articles",
        id=article_id,
        body={
            "title": article_data["title"],
            "author": article_data["author"],
            "publication_date": article_data["publication_date"],
            "content": article_content
        },
        refresh=True
    )
```

CQRS further enhances the architecture by separating the write (command) and read (query) responsibilities into distinct models and services. The primary data store (MemoryDB) handles write operations for ingesting and storing article metadata and content, while the search index (OpenSearch) is optimized for read operations and provides efficient search capabilities. CDC bridges the two components, ensuring the search index stays in sync with the primary data store.

This loose coupling allows for independent scaling and technology choices for each component based on demand. You can optimize MemoryDB for write-heavy work-loads and OpenSearch for read-heavy search queries, ensuring optimal performance and resiliency.

To further enhance the syncing process, consider using Amazon OpenSearch Ingestion for efficient data ingestion. This service provides a scalable and reliable way to ingest data into OpenSearch, helping to mitigate some of the failure modes mentioned earlier.

Additionally, implement proper index management using tools like Index State Management (ISM) in OpenSearch. This can help in managing index lifecycles, optimizing performance, and ensuring that data retention policies are followed.

When designing your indexing strategy, be aware of OpenSearch naming restrictions for indexes. Proper naming conventions can help avoid conflicts and improve overall system organization.

By employing CDC and CQRS, along with these additional best practices, you can build a resilient and scalable news feed architecture that effectively syncs articles to OpenSearch. This enables you to provide a seamless search experience for users while maintaining data consistency and reliability across the system.

OpenSearch's distributed architecture provides built-in resilience against node failures, but indexing operations can still encounter issues due to network partitions, disk or node failures, or resource constraints. To ensure data integrity and search quality, you need to gracefully handle these failures and ensure successful indexing.

OpenSearch offers several features and configurations to enhance indexing resiliency. You can configure appropriate shard and replica counts for your indices, with a higher number of replicas ensuring data availability even if some nodes fail. Enabling shard allocation filtering prevents shards from being assigned to overloaded or failing nodes, improving indexing resilience.

You can mitigate network partitions and ensure data consistency during indexing by leveraging OpenSearch's quorum-based operations and rack-aware configurations. Configuring OpenSearch's distributed filesystem and data path settings provides resilience against disk failures by distributing data across multiple nodes and disks.

To handle resource exhaustion scenarios, you can utilize OpenSearch's cluster autoscaling feature, which allows you to dynamically add or remove nodes based on resource utilization. Configuring indexing throttling prevents overloading the cluster during high indexing loads. OpenSearch also provides tools like the Force Merge API and shard reallocation capabilities to address shard unavailability issues that may impact indexing (Table 9-3).

Table 9-3. OpenSearch indexing failure modes

Failure mode	Priority	Mitigation
Network partitions	Moderate	Quorum-based operations, rack-aware configurations
Node failures	High	Replica shards, shard allocation filtering
Disk failures	Moderate	Distributed filesystem, data path configuration
Resource exhaustion	High	Cluster auto-scaling, indexing throttling
Shard unavailability	Moderate	Force merge, shard reallocation

Monitoring and alerting are essential for proactively identifying and resolving index-ing failures in OpenSearch. You can leverage OpenSearch's built-in monitoring capa-bilities and integrate with monitoring tools like Prometheus and Grafana to track indexing metrics and set up alerts for anomalies or failures.

Implementing data validation and integrity checks helps identify and handle data corruption or consistency issues during indexing. You can employ techniques like versioning or checksums to detect and resolve data inconsistencies between the primary data store and the search index.

To further enhance indexing resilience, consider implementing a circuit breaker pattern. This can help prevent cascading failures by stopping indexing operations when certain thresholds are reached, such as memory usage or indexing queue size.

Additionally, use the ISM feature in OpenSearch to automate index lifecycle manage-ment. ISM can help you define policies for index rotation, backup, and deletion, which can improve overall system stability and performance.

When designing your indexing strategy, be mindful of the mapping explosion prob-lem. Limit the number of fields per index, and use nested objects or join data types when appropriate to maintain performance and avoid hitting OpenSearch's hard limit on the number of fields.

By leveraging OpenSearch's resiliency features, configurations, and best practices, you can build a robust and highly available search service that can withstand various fail-ure scenarios and ensure reliable indexing operations. Regular testing and simulation of failure scenarios will help validate your resilience strategies and identify areas for improvement.

Serving Search Traffic

You've ingested, processed, and indexed the news articles in OpenSearch. Now, it's time to serve the search traffic and provide a seamless search experience to your users. In this section, you'll learn how to design and implement a scalable and resilient search API using an AWS ALB and Amazon ECS (see Figure 9-3).

Decoupling the search functionality using an API layer offers several benefits but also introduces trade-offs: Benefits include:

- Independent scaling and evolution of the search component
- Enhanced maintainability and flexibility in updating search functionality
- Ability to implement custom access controls and rate limiting

Trade-offs include:

- Increased complexity in system architecture
- Additional infrastructure costs for running the API layer
- Potential for increased latency in search requests

By acting as an intermediary for OpenSearch traffic, the API layer provides more control over search operations, allowing you to:

- Implement custom caching strategies to reduce the load on OpenSearch.
- Apply fine-grained access controls and user-specific query modifications.
- Aggregate results from multiple backend services, not just OpenSearch.

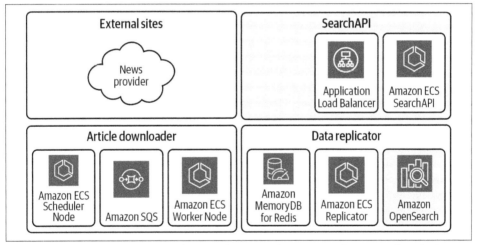

Figure 9-3. Diagram illustrating the Search API architecture with ALB and ECS, showcasing the flow of search traffic from the ALB to the Search API containers running in ECS

Consider the common search failure modes as you design your solution:

ECS task failures
> The ECS tasks hosting the Search API may fail for various reasons, such as resource contention, network issues, or application-level errors impacting the search functionality.

OpenSearch cluster issues
> The OpenSearch cluster may experience node failures, data corruption, or resource exhaustion, leading to degraded search performance or unavailability.

Network disruptions
> Network connectivity issues or high latency between the Search API and the OpenSearch cluster can cause search requests to fail or experience delays.

The following code snippet demonstrates how to define the ALB and the ECS service for the Search API using the AWS CDK, including configuring the task definition, container image, and environment variables:

```
from aws_cdk import (
    aws_ecs as ecs,
    aws_ecs_patterns as ecs_patterns,
    aws_opensearchservice as opensearch,
    aws_ec2 as ec2,
    aws_secretsmanager as secretsmanager,
    aws_ssm as ssm,
    core as cdk
)
from constructs import Construct

class SearchApiStack(cdk.Stack):
    def __init__(self, scope: cdk.Construct, construct_id: str, **kwargs) -> None:
        super().__init__(scope, construct_id, **kwargs)

        # Create a VPC and subnets
        vpc = ec2.Vpc(self, "SearchApiVPC", max_azs=2)

        # Retrieve the OpenSearch domain endpoint
        opensearch_domain = opensearch.Domain.from_domain_attributes(
            self, "OpenSearchDomain",
            domain_endpoint=cdk.Fn.import_value("OpenSearchDomainEndpoint")
        )

        # Retrieve the Secrets Manager secret for the search API
        search_api_secret = secretsmanager.Secret.from_secret_name_v2(
            self, "SearchApiSecret",
            secret_name=ssm.StringParameter.value_for_string_parameter(
                self, "SearchApiSecretName"
            )
        )
```

```
# Create the ECS service for the search API
search_api_task_definition = ecs.FargateTaskDefinition(
    self, "SearchApiTaskDefinition",
    cpu=256,
    memory_limit_mib=512
)

search_api_container = search_api_task_definition.add_container(
    "SearchApiContainer",
    image=ecs.ContainerImage.from_registry("your-search-api-image"),
    environment={
        "OPENSEARCH_ENDPOINT": opensearch_domain.domain_endpoint,
        "SECRET_ARN": search_api_secret.secret_arn
    }
)

search_api_service = ecs_patterns.ApplicationLoadBalancedFargateService(
    self, "SearchApiService",
    cluster=ecs.Cluster(self, "SearchApiCluster", vpc=vpc),
    task_definition=search_api_task_definition,
    public_load_balancer=True,
    service_name="search-api",
    desired_count=2,
    cpu=256,
    memory_limit_mib=512
)

# Export the Application Load Balancer endpoint
cdk.CfnOutput(self, "SearchApiEndpoint",
    value=search_api_service.load_balancer.load_balancer_dns_name)
```

The next snippet demonstrates how to implement the SearchAPI that runs within Amazon ECS and receives web traffic from the ALB. Using frameworks like Flask or FastAPI allows you to rapidly build custom proxies that decouple data consumers from the underlying OpenSearch database.

 This example retrieves the OpenSearch credentials from Amazon Secrets Manager. Secrets Manager provides secure storage and life-cycle management for credentials. Previous examples used AWS IAM authentication because it reduces the operational complexity and increases resiliency. However, your specific deployment (e.g., self-managed Elasticsearch) may only support username and password authentication. Use this pattern for supporting those situations.

```
from flask import Flask, jsonify
from opensearchpy import OpenSearch
from aws_secretsmanager_caching import SecretCache, SecretCacheConfig

app = Flask(__name__)
```

```python
OPENSEARCH_ENDPOINT = app.config["OPENSEARCH_ENDPOINT"]
SECRET_ARN = app.config["SECRET_ARN"]

secrets_cache = SecretCache(
    config=SecretCacheConfig(
        max_cache_size=5,
        secret_refresh_interval=300
    ),
    secret_id=SECRET_ARN
)

# Retrieve and parse the secret
secret = json.loads(secrets_cache.get_secret_string())

# Extract username and password from the secret
username = secret.get('username')
password = secret.get('password')

opensearch_client = OpenSearch(
    hosts=[{"host": OPENSEARCH_ENDPOINT, "port": 443}],
    http_auth=(username, password)
)

@app.route("/search", methods=["GET"])
def search_articles():
    query = request.args.get("q")
    if not query:
        return jsonify({"error": "Missing search query"}), 400

    try:
        response = opensearch_client.search(
            index="articles",
            body={
                "query": {
                    "multi_match": {
                        "query": query,
                        "fields": ["title", "content"]
                    }
                }
            }
        )
        return jsonify(response["hits"]["hits"])
    except Exception as e:
        app.logger.error(f"Error searching articles: {e}")
        return jsonify({"error": "Error executing search query"}), 500

if __name__ == "__main__":
    app.run(host="0.0.0.0", port=8080)
```

When you instantiate a service broker into your architecture, it provides additional control in message routing processes. This capability lets you handle failures transparently for downstream clients and provide a more stable customer experience.

Cleaning Up

In "Technical Requirements" on page 266, you deployed infrastructure to experiment with this chapter's lessons and explore the various failure modes. When you finish, delete the cloud resources to avoid ongoing costs. The easiest way to clean up is:

1. Navigate a command terminal into the *ch09-news_feed* folder.

2. Run the **cdk destroy** command.

3. Grab another cup of coffee and return in 30 minutes.

The default configuration uses small instances to minimize costs. If you leave these resources deployed for a prolonged time, you can expect the deployment to cost roughly one dollar daily, prorated to the second. Most of these costs come from the opensearch.t3.small node. Amazon OpenSearch doesn't provide an option for pausing or stopping the cluster, so you must delete and re-create the resource to avoid costs while it's not in use. However, provisioning a new cluster takes around 10 to 15 minutes. Other resources, like the AWS Lambda functions for processing the stream, qualify for the free tier if your account is eligible for that program. Otherwise, you can expect this chapter's serverless resources to consume a few cents monthly.

Summary

This chapter explored designing and implementing a resilient news feed ingestion and search architecture on AWS. It addressed key challenges like fetching articles from external sources, storing and managing article metadata and content, ensuring data consistency and real-time synchronization, building resilient and decoupled microservices, validating resilience through chaos engineering, and securing the news feed system.

The chapter presented a reference architecture with three main components: the Article Downloader for retrieving news articles from third-party sites, the Data Replicator keeping the primary data store (Amazon MemoryDB for Redis) and search index (Amazon OpenSearch Service) in sync, and the Search API as an entry point for search traffic. By leveraging AWS services and best practices, you can build a scalable, fault-tolerant, and high-performance news feed ingestion and search architecture.

Implementing these architectures and best practices offers several benefits, including improved resilience and fault tolerance, scalability and performance, decoupling and flexibility, data integrity and consistency, enhanced user experience, competitive advantage, and reduced financial losses.

As you embark on building a resilient news feed system, remember that the architecture presented is just the beginning. In the next chapter, you'll explore multiregional disaster recovery strategies for streaming applications, taking your system's resilience to the next level. You'll learn to design and implement a geographically distributed architecture that can withstand impairments and ensure continuous operation of your news feed pipeline.

Are you ready to elevate your news feed architecture? Dive into the next chapter and discover how to build a global and resilient streaming application for this.

## CHAPTER 10

Building Resilient Multi-Region Architectures

As an application architect, you face the challenge of serving users across the globe. In this high-stakes environment, every millisecond of latency and every moment of downtime can impact revenue and user satisfaction. To address these challenges, you can leverage a resilient multi-region architecture on AWS.

A well-designed multi-region application on AWS offers several advantages. It can efficiently manage traffic from diverse geographic locations, maintain consistent data availability, and provide robust fault tolerance against various failure scenarios. While multi-region architectures enhance application resilience and performance, it's important to note that they do not inherently ensure 100% uptime.

This chapter explores the key concepts, strategies, and best practices for building resilient multi-region architectures. You'll gain insights into crucial aspects such as data replication, deployment patterns, and caching strategies. These elements form the foundation of a robust, globally distributed application infrastructure.

Understanding and implementing these multi-region design principles will equip you to create applications that can meet the demands of a global user base. You'll learn how to balance performance, availability, and consistency across different geographic regions, ultimately delivering a more reliable and responsive user experience.

By the end of this chapter, you'll understand how to apply:

- The compelling business drivers behind multi-region architectures
- Fundamental architectural patterns and considerations for designing resilient systems

- Strategies for replicating and synchronizing data across regions using Apache Kafka and Amazon OpenSearch Service
- Best practices for implementing multi-region streaming and search architectures
- Techniques for caching data effectively in a multi-region environment
- Incorporating multi-region secondary databases for improved performance and availability
- Operational best practices for monitoring, testing, and upgrading multi-region architectures

Whether you're an experienced professional or just starting your multi-region journey, this chapter will help you improve your skills and build robust, globally distributed applications on AWS.

The Business Case for Multi-Region Architectures

Multi-region architectures offer compelling advantages for organizations seeking to expand their global reach. Let's explore the key drivers behind this approach.

Latency reduction stands out as a primary benefit. By positioning your application closer to end users, you can minimize response times and enhance the overall user experience. Consider a scenario where a Sydney-based user accesses an application hosted exclusively in North America. The resulting lag could be noticeable and potentially frustrating. Multi-region deployment allows you to mitigate such issues, improving performance for users worldwide.

As businesses expand globally, compliance with data sovereignty laws becomes increasingly important. Multi-region architectures enable strategic data placement to meet regulatory requirements. For example, you might need to ensure that European customer data remains within EU borders. By thoughtfully distributing your infrastructure, you can address these compliance needs while maintaining full functionality.

Resilience improvement is another key consideration. Multi-region setups can help contain the impact of service disruptions by leveraging AWS cloud fault boundaries. Incorporating redundancy and failover mechanisms can bolster your application's ability to withstand, detect, and react to failure scenarios. However, it's worth noting that while multi-region deployments can enhance resilience, they don't guarantee uninterrupted service in all situations.

The concept of multi-region resilience extends beyond mere technological considerations. It encompasses both processes and people. Effective multi-region strategies require well-defined operational procedures and skilled teams capable of managing distributed systems. This includes developing robust monitoring and alerting systems, implementing cross-region deployment pipelines, and fostering a culture of continuous learning and improvement.

While the benefits of multi-region architectures are substantial, they come with trade-offs. These include increased operational complexity, higher infrastructure costs, and greater management overhead. Maintaining data consistency across regions can be challenging and may necessitate advanced replication strategies. Moreover, the expense of running infrastructure in multiple regions can be considerable.

When weighing the option of a multi-region architecture, it's essential to assess the return on investment against these additional costs and complexities. This approach might be suitable for certain workloads within your portfolio, rather than every application in your organization. Factors to consider include the application's importance, performance requirements, regulatory obligations, and budget limitations.

Multi-region architectures can effectively address latency, compliance, and resilience challenges. However, they're not universally applicable. By carefully evaluating your specific needs and balancing the advantages against the costs and complexities, you can determine whether a multi-region approach aligns with your application's requirements. When implemented thoughtfully, these architectures can contribute to building more responsive, compliant, and resilient applications on a global scale.

The decision to adopt a multi-region strategy should be made after thorough consideration. It's a powerful tool, but like any tool, it's most effective when applied to the right job. Some workloads may benefit greatly from this approach, while others might not justify the additional investment. By understanding both the potential gains and the associated challenges, you can make an informed decision that best serves your organization's needs and goals.

Multi-Region Database Architectures

Multi-region database architectures serve applications that need to operate across different geographic locations, maintain high availability during service impairments, or comply with data sovereignty requirements. For the AvailableTrade application, a multi-region setup ensures traders can access real-time data and execute trades swiftly, regardless of their location.

Understanding Consistency Models

Consistency models, which define how data updates propagate across a distributed system, are the foundation of multi-region database design. Your choice of model significantly impacts the AvailableTrade application's behavior and user experience.

Eventual consistency, where updates propagate asynchronously, might be suitable for displaying information that's not time sensitive, like stock news feeds. Monotonic consistency, guaranteeing that reads never go backward in time, could be applied to the display of historical stock prices. Causal consistency ensures that causally related operations are seen in the same order by all nodes, which is valuable for tracking the sequence of trades. Strong consistency, where all reads reflect the latest writes, is essential for real-time stock prices and account balances.

The CAP theorem, which stands for consistency, availability, and partition tolerance, plays a key role in architectural decisions for distributed systems. It states that in the event of a network partition, a distributed system can only guarantee two out of these three properties:

Consistency
　　All nodes see the same data at the same time.

Availability
　　Every request receives a response, without guarantee that it contains the most recent version of the information.

Partition tolerance
　　The system continues to operate despite network partitions.

As a distributed system architect, you must choose between consistency and availability when network partitions occur.

The PACELC theorem extends this concept by considering performance trade-offs in normal operations as well as during partitions. PACELC stands for partition tolerance, availability, consistency, else, latency, and consistency. It states that in case of network partitions (P), one has to choose between availability (A) and consistency ©, but else (E), even when the system is running normally in the absence of partitions, one has to choose between latency (L) and consistency ©. In other words, during normal operations, you choose between latency and consistency, while during partitions, you choose between availability and consistency. This theorem provides a more nuanced view of the trade-offs in distributed system design, acknowledging that even in the absence of partitions, there are still important decisions to be made regarding system behavior and performance.

For AvailableTrade, you might prioritize strong consistency for important operations like trade executions and account balances, accepting higher latency to ensure accuracy. For less time-sensitive features, like user preferences or stock watchlists, you could opt for eventual consistency to reduce latency and improve user experience.

Replication Strategies

Building on the replication concepts, let's explore the active-passive and active-active patterns in the context of AvailableTrade.

In an active-passive setup, AvailableTrade would designate one region as the primary for all write operations, with other regions serving as read-only replicas. This approach simplifies consistency management and maintains a clear write path, which is beneficial for ensuring the accuracy of trade executions. However, it may introduce higher write latency for users distant from the primary region and could lead to potential data loss during failover.

An active-active pattern allows multiple regions to accept writes, providing lower write latency and improved availability. For AvailableTrade, this could mean faster trade executions for users worldwide. However, it introduces complexity in conflict resolution and may lead to data inconsistencies, which could be problematic for maintaining accurate account balances and stock positions.

The choice between these patterns depends on AvailableTrade's specific requirements. If the application prioritizes strong consistency for all operations, an active-passive setup might be more suitable. If the goal is to provide the lowest possible latency for trade executions worldwide and the system can tolerate some level of eventual consistency, an active-active pattern could be more appropriate.

For implementing a multi-region setup using Amazon OpenSearch Service for AvailableTrade's market data analytics, we can extend the OpenSearch setup from Chapter 9. Here's how you might set up OpenSearch domains in multiple regions:

```
from aws_cdk import aws_opensearchservice as opensearch, Stack, App
from constructs import Construct

class OpenSearchStack(Stack):
    def __init__(self, scope: Construct, construct_id: str, **kwargs) -> None:
        super().__init__(scope, construct_id, **kwargs)

        domain = opensearch.Domain(self, "OpenSearchDomain",
            version=opensearch.EngineVersion.OPENSEARCH_2_5,
            # ... other configurations as in Chapter 9
        )

        self.output(f'{construct_id}Endpoint', value=domain.domain_endpoint)

app = App()
OpenSearchStack(app, "PrimaryOpenSearchStack", env={"region": "us-east-1"})
OpenSearchStack(app, "SecondaryOpenSearchStack", env={"region": "us-west-2"})
app.synth()
```

This code creates separate OpenSearch stacks in two different regions, allowing for a multi-region deployment.

To set up cross-cluster replication between these domains, you can use the AWS CLI:

```
aws opensearch create-outbound-connection
--source-domain-info DomainName="primary-domain-name",Region="us-east-1"
```

```
--destination-domain-info DomainName="secondary-domain-name",Region="us-west-2"
--connection-alias "primary-to-secondary-replication"
```

After creating the connection, wait for it to become active, then start the outbound connection:

```
aws opensearch start-outbound-connection
--source-domain-name "primary-domain-name"
--connection-id "connection-id-from-create-command"
```

When using these commands, be aware that:

- The IAM role or user executing this command must have the necessary permissions.

- The connection status progresses through several stages (*validating, approved, provisioning*, and *active*). Wait for the active status before using the connection.

- Cross-region connections may have implications for data transfer costs.

- Consider setting up a bidirectional connection for full replication, if required.

Handling Conflict Resolution

In an active-active setup for AvailableTrade, conflict resolution becomes an important consideration. When the same data, such as a user's account balance, is modified in multiple regions concurrently, you need a strategy to reconcile these changes. Here's how you might implement custom conflict resolution logic using an index template in OpenSearch:

```
import boto3
from requests_aws4auth import AWS4Auth
from opensearchpy import OpenSearch, RequestsHttpConnection

def create_index_template(domain_endpoint, region):
    credentials = boto3.Session().get_credentials()
    awsauth = AWS4Auth(credentials.access_key, credentials.secret_key,
                       region, 'es', session_token=credentials.token)

    client = OpenSearch(
        hosts=[{'host': domain_endpoint, 'port': 443}],
        http_auth=awsauth,
        use_ssl=True,
        verify_certs=True,
        connection_class=RequestsHttpConnection
    )

    template = {
        "index_patterns": ["stock-*"],
        "template": {
            "settings": {
                "index.merge.policy.merge_strategy": "custom",
```

```
        "index.merge.policy.custom_merge_strategy": {
            "type": "script",
            "source": """
            if (ctx._source.last_updated < params.last_updated) {
                ctx._source = params;
            }
            """
        }
    },
    "mappings": {
        "properties": {
            "symbol": { "type": "keyword" },
            "price": { "type": "float" },
            "last_updated": { "type": "date" }
        }
    }
  }
}

response = client.indices.put_index_template(
    name="stock_template", body=template)
print(f"Template creation response: {response}")
```

This script creates an index template that includes a custom merge strategy. The strategy compares the `last_updated` field of conflicting documents and keeps the most recent version. This approach ensures that account balances and trade records remain consistent across regions by always using the latest update.

When implementing a multi-region database architecture for AvailableTrade, you'll face challenges such as data synchronization, conflict detection and resolution, failover and recovery, and monitoring and alerting. To address these, consider using purpose-built databases that natively support multi-region deployments. Implement robust monitoring using Amazon CloudWatch and custom metrics to track replication lag and conflict rates. Develop and test automated procedures for failing over to secondary regions, and conduct regular chaos engineering experiments to verify your system's resilience to various failure modes.

By carefully considering consistency requirements, choosing appropriate replication strategies, and implementing robust conflict resolution and failover mechanisms, you can build a resilient multi-region database architecture for AvailableTrade that provides fast, reliable access to financial data and trading capabilities for users worldwide.

Multi-Region Streaming Architectures

In today's data-driven world, real-time streaming architectures are more critical than ever. And when it comes to building scalable, fault-tolerant streaming systems, Apache Kafka has emerged as a go-to choice for many organizations.

This section discusses implementing a multi-region streaming architecture using Apache Kafka. It builds upon the concepts and best practices covered in "Designing a Reliable Data Ingestion Layer" on page 224, where we explored designing a reliable data ingestion layer.

However, deploying Kafka across multiple regions introduces new challenges and considerations. How do you replicate data between regional Kafka clusters? How do you ensure data consistency in an active-active deployment? And how do you build resilient consumer applications that can handle regional failures?

Let's explore some strategies and best practices for building multi-region streaming architectures with Apache Kafka.

Replicating Kafka Data Across Regions

To achieve multi-region replication in Kafka, you have a few options. One common approach is to use Kafka's built-in MirrorMaker tool, which consumes data from a source cluster and replicates it to a target cluster in a different region:

```
# Example: Configuring MirrorMaker with AWS CDK
mirror_maker_config = {
    "name": "MyMirrorMaker",
    "connector.class": "org.apache.kafka.connect.mirror.MirrorSourceConnector",
    "source.cluster.alias": "source",
    "target.cluster.alias": "target",
    "source.cluster.bootstrap.servers": source_cluster.bootstrap_brokers_tls,
    "target.cluster.bootstrap.servers": target_cluster.bootstrap_brokers_tls,
    "topics": ".*",
}

msk.CfnConnector(
    self, "MirrorMakerConnector",
    connector_name="MyMirrorMaker",
    kafka_cluster=target_cluster,
    connector_configuration=mirror_maker_config,
)
```

You can also explore third-party replication tools like Confluent Replicator or IBM Aspera. These tools offer additional capabilities, such as bidirectional replication and custom filtering of replicated topics, which might suit your specific requirements better.

When implementing cross-region replication, carefully consider factors like replication latency, bandwidth costs, and data consistency guarantees. These aspects will impact the overall performance and reliability of your Kafka setup.

Moreover, design your consumer applications to handle potential data duplication and out-of-order events that can arise from replicating across regions. Implementing idempotency and proper event ordering mechanisms will help ensure data integrity and consistency in your downstream systems. By thoughtfully designing your multi-region Kafka architecture and choosing the right replication approach, you can build a resilient and scalable streaming platform that meets your business needs.

Handling Active-Active Kafka Deployments

In an active-active Kafka deployment, data is produced to and consumed from multiple regional clusters. This introduces additional challenges around data consistency and conflict resolution.

One key consideration is how to handle write conflicts—that is, when the same record is produced to different regions simultaneously. Kafka doesn't have built-in conflict resolution, so you'll need to design your own strategy. This could involve using a "last write wins" approach, leveraging timestamps to determine the latest version, or even building a custom conflict resolution layer.

You'll also need to think carefully about your consumer group design. With consumers spread across regions, you'll need to ensure that each consumer group maintains a consistent view of the data, even in the face of regional failures or network partitions.

Streaming Data to Other Destinations

In addition to replicating data between Kafka clusters, you may also need to stream data to other destinations like data lakes, data warehouses, or analytics platforms. This is where streaming solutions like Kafka Connect come into play.

Kafka Connect is a framework for building connectors that continuously move data between Kafka and external systems. With Kafka Connect, you can easily stream data from Kafka to destinations like Amazon S3, Snowflake, or Elasticsearch:

```
# Example: Kafka Connect configuration for streaming data to Amazon S3
s3_sink_config = {
    "name": "s3-sink-connector",
    "connector.class": "io.confluent.connect.s3.S3SinkConnector",
    "tasks.max": "1",
    "topics": "my-topic",
    "s3.bucket.name": "my-bucket",
    "s3.region": "us-west-2",
    "storage.class": "io.confluent.connect.s3.storage.S3Storage",
    "format.class": "io.confluent.connect.s3.format.json.JsonFormat",
    # ...
}
```

By leveraging Kafka Connect, you can build robust, fault-tolerant data pipelines that keep your downstream systems in sync with your Kafka clusters, even in the face of regional failures or network disruptions.

Multi-Region Search Architectures with OpenSearch

Search is a critical component of many modern applications, enabling users to quickly find and discover relevant content. And when it comes to building scalable, distributed search architectures, OpenSearch has emerged as a popular choice.

This section explores implementing a multi-region search architecture using OpenSearch (previously known as Elasticsearch). It builds upon the concepts and best practices covered in "Syncing Articles to OpenSearch" on page 280, where we discussed deploying OpenSearch in a multi-region architecture (*https://oreil.ly/jWPhR*) and leveraging cross-cluster replication for data synchronization across regions (*https://oreil.ly/Q7upM*).

However, deploying OpenSearch across multiple regions introduces new challenges and considerations. How do you replicate data between regional OpenSearch clusters? How do you ensure data consistency and availability in the face of regional failures? And how do you route search queries to the most appropriate region to minimize latency?

Let's explore some strategies and best practices for building multi-region search architectures with OpenSearch.

Cross-Region Data Replication with OpenSearch

To replicate data between OpenSearch clusters in different regions, you can use OpenSearch's built-in cross-cluster replication (CCR) feature. CCR allows you to create read-only copies of indices in remote clusters, automatically syncing changes from the primary cluster:

```
# Example: Configuring cross-cluster replication with AWS CDK
source_domain = opensearch.Domain(self, "SourceDomain", ...)
target_domain = opensearch.Domain(self, "TargetDomain", ...)

replication_config = {
    "source_cluster": source_domain.domain_endpoint,
    "target_cluster": target_domain.domain_endpoint,
    "indices": ["my-index"],
    # ...
}

opensearch.CfnReplicationGroup(
    self, "ReplicationGroup",
    replication_group_description="My replication group",
    replication_config=replication_config,
)
```

With CCR, you can choose between a unidirectional or bidirectional replication strategy, depending on your use case. Unidirectional replication is simpler to manage but may result in higher read latency for users in nonprimary regions. Bidirectional replication, on the other hand, allows you to accept writes in multiple regions but introduces additional complexity around conflict resolution.

Other Data Replication Options

Beyond CCR, OpenSearch provides the following options for data replication and synchronization:

Index snapshots
> You can use index snapshots to create point-in-time backups of your indices and restore them in another region.

Replication plug-ins
> OpenSearch has various replication plug-ins that enable real-time data synchronization between clusters.

Data pipelining
> You can use data pipelining tools like Logstash to extract data from OpenSearch in one region, transform it, and load it into OpenSearch in another region.

By designing your multi-region OpenSearch architecture with these considerations in mind, you can build a search experience that is fast, reliable, and globally scalable.

Caching in Multi-Region Architectures

Caching is a critical component of any performant and scalable application, and this is especially true in a multi-region architecture. By caching frequently accessed data closer to your users, you can reduce latency, improve throughput, and reduce the load on your backend services.

But caching in a multi-region environment introduces new challenges and considerations. Should you deploy a separate cache cluster in each region, or use a global caching service? How do you ensure cache consistency across regions? And how do you handle cache failures and evictions?

Let's explore some strategies for effective caching in a multi-region context.

One approach is to deploy regional cache clusters—that is, a separate cache cluster in each region where your application is deployed. Each regional cache serves the local application stack, providing low-latency access to frequently accessed data.

The main advantage of regional caches is performance—by keeping cached data close to your application servers, you can minimize latency and improve response times.

Regional caches are also isolated from each other, so a cache failure in one region won't impact the other regions.

However, regional caches also have some drawbacks. First, you'll need to manage and maintain multiple cache clusters, which can increase operational complexity. Second, you'll need to implement a strategy for keeping the caches in sync, whether that's through application-level logic or an external replication mechanism. Finally, regional caches can result in duplication of data across regions, increasing storage costs.

Another approach is to use a global cache with replication. In this model, you deploy a single cache cluster that spans all your regions, with data replicated across regions to ensure consistency.

The main advantage of a global cache is simplicity—you only need to manage a single cache cluster, and you don't need to worry about keeping caches in sync across regions. A global cache can also reduce data duplication and storage costs.

However, a global cache may introduce higher latency for cache access, as requests may need to traverse cross-region network links. It also introduces a single point of failure—if the global cache goes down, it impacts all regions.

A third option is a hybrid approach, where you use regional caches for frequently accessed data that is specific to each region, and a global cache for shared data that needs to be consistent across regions. This gives you the best of both worlds: low-latency access for region-specific data, and global consistency for shared data.

When it comes to implementing caching in a multi-region AWS environment, you have a few options. Amazon ElastiCache supports both Redis and Memcached, and provides features like Multi-AZ replication for high availability within a region, and cross-region replication for Redis clusters.

Here's an example of how you might create an ElastiCache Redis cluster with Multi-AZ and cross-region replication using the AWS CDK:

```
from aws_cdk import (
    aws_elasticache as elasticache,
)

# Create a Redis cluster in the primary region
primary_cluster = elasticache.CfnCacheCluster(
    self, "PrimaryCluster",
    engine="redis",
    cache_node_type="cache.r7g.large",
    num_cache_nodes=1,
    auto_minor_version_upgrade=True,
    multi_az_enabled=True
)
```

```
# Create a Redis replication group in the secondary region
secondary_cluster = elasticache.CfnReplicationGroup(
  self, "SecondaryCluster",
  replication_group_description="Secondary cluster",
  engine="redis",
  cache_node_type="cache.r6g.large",
  num_node_groups=1,
  replicas_per_node_group=1,
  automatic_failover_enabled=True,
  multi_az_enabled=True
)

# Configure cross-region replication
elasticache.CfnGlobalReplicationGroup(
  self, "GlobalReplicationGroup",
  members=[
    elasticache.CfnGlobalReplicationGroup.GlobalReplicationGroupMemberProperty(
      replication_group_id=primary_cluster.ref,
      role="PRIMARY"
    ),
    elasticache.CfnGlobalReplicationGroup.GlobalReplicationGroupMemberProperty(
      replication_group_id=secondary_cluster.ref,
      role="SECONDARY"
    )
  ]
)
```

This code creates a Redis cluster in the primary region with Multi-AZ enabled, a replication group in a secondary region, and configures cross-region replication between them using a global replication group.

Whichever caching strategy you choose, the key is to design your caching layer with the unique challenges of a multi-region architecture in mind. By carefully considering factors like latency, consistency, and fault tolerance, you can build a caching solution that provides a fast, reliable, and scalable foundation for your multi-region application.

Summary

You've made it to the end of our journey through the world of building resilient multi-region architectures on AWS. We've covered a lot of ground, from the fundamental concepts, design patterns, and optimization techniques.

We started by exploring the key business drivers for going multi-region, such as reducing latency for global users, complying with data sovereignty regulations, and enhancing disaster recovery capabilities. We then dove into the architectural considerations, including data replication strategies, deployment patterns, and high-availability techniques.

Throughout the chapter, we looked at specific use cases and technologies, such as multi-region streaming architectures with Apache Kafka, multi-region search with OpenSearch, and multi-region caching with Amazon ElastiCache. We also examined the operational aspects, like monitoring, troubleshooting, chaos engineering, and performance optimization.

By now, you should have a solid understanding of what it takes to design, deploy, and operate applications that span multiple AWS Regions. You've seen how to leverage various AWS services and best practices to build systems that are scalable, resilient, and globally distributed.

But the learning journey doesn't stop here. As you embark on your own multi-region projects, remember to stay curious and keep experimenting. The cloud computing landscape is constantly evolving, with new services, features, and best practices emerging all the time. Stay up-to-date with the latest AWS offerings and industry trends, and don't be afraid to challenge assumptions and try new approaches.

Building resilient multi-region architectures is not just about technology—it's also about fostering a culture of reliability and continuous improvement within your team. Encourage knowledge sharing, embrace blameless postmortems, and always strive to learn from failures. By cultivating a mindset of resilience and collaborating effectively, you can overcome the challenges of operating in a global, distributed environment.

## CHAPTER 11

Putting It All Together

You've made significant progress in understanding how to build reliable software on AWS. Through exploring challenges in frontend onboarding and navigating the complexities of streaming market data, you've gained valuable insights. The knowledge and hands-on experience you've acquired will serve as a solid foundation for designing, implementing, and operating resilient systems.

While there's always more to learn, take a moment to acknowledge the effort you've put in. Let this accomplishment inspire you to continue growing in your journey of creating performant and resilient systems.

Throughout this book, we've explored key aspects of engineering resilient systems on AWS, using a fictitious consumer financial application as our guiding example. From initial design and implementation stages to integrating several resilient design patterns, our aim has been to provide a practical guide to building robust systems capable of withstanding and recovering from various disruptions.

Reviewing Core Concepts

As we near the end of our journey through building highly resilient cloud applications, it's time to review and solidify the core concepts we've covered. Throughout this book, we've explored various frameworks, patterns, and practices that lay the foundation for creating systems that can withstand failures, recover quickly, and provide seamless user experiences. Let's take a step back and reflect on these essential elements that have guided our path to resilience.

Starting with the foundational principles of system resilience, we explored the foundations of resilience and how resilience concepts have changed from traditional resilience approaches to thinking about resilience in the cloud. Each chapter built upon the previous, progressively introducing more sophisticated techniques and patterns, and developing mechanisms for demonstrating resilience through observability and testing.

Reliability Frameworks

Building resilience into your cloud applications is crucial for ensuring high availability, fault tolerance, and exceptional user experiences. By embracing resilience principles and leveraging the right tools and frameworks, you can create robust systems that withstand failures, recover quickly, and maintain continuous operations.

The AWS Well-Architected Framework offers a comprehensive guide for creating and managing robust, protected, high-performing, and economical cloud-based systems. It encompasses six core principles: operational excellence, security, reliability, performance efficiency, cost optimization, and sustainability. By adhering to these pillars, organizations can develop resilient cloud architectures that align with industry best practices.

Complementing the Well-Architected Framework is the Resilience Analysis Framework (RAF), a powerful tool that helps you navigate and mitigate potential failure modes. By analyzing your workload through the lens of SEEMS (single points of failure, excessive load, excessive latency, misconfigurations and bugs, and shared fate), RAF enables you to proactively anticipate and address failure modes, ensuring your systems are better equipped to withstand and recover from failures.

Building resilience is a shared responsibility between you and AWS, as defined by the AWS Shared Responsibility Model. AWS secures and maintains the underlying cloud infrastructure, while you are responsible for securing and maintaining your applications running on that infrastructure. As a customer, it's crucial to understand your responsibilities in the cloud to ensure you're not assuming AWS is handling aspects that fall under your purview.

The Resiliency Lifecycle Framework provides another valuable perspective, guiding you through the continuous process of improving your system's resilience. This framework helps you assess, design, implement, and validate resilience strategies throughout your application's lifecycle.

Embracing the Well-Architected Framework principles, leveraging the AWS Resilience Analysis Framework, understanding your role in the Shared Responsibility Model, and applying the Resiliency Lifecycle Framework allow you to build a robust foundation for resilient cloud applications. These applications can handle failures, recover quickly, and provide seamless experiences, even amid disruptions. Resilient systems foster trust, demonstrate commitment to reliable services, and enhance brand reputation and customer loyalty. Investing in resilience safeguards operations and positions your business for long-term success in the evolving cloud landscape.

Failure Modes with Reliability Patterns

As you've navigated the complexities of cloud computing, you've faced numerous challenges and gained valuable insights into constructing durable systems. Now it's time to take stock of the key concepts and frameworks that have guided your journey. Let's examine how these elements intertwine with the practical examples and AWS services we've explored in each chapter.

Picture your cloud experience as a map to hidden treasure. On this map, each failure mode represents a formidable obstacle, while the corresponding reliability patterns and examples serve as your toolkit for overcoming these challenges (Table 11-1).

Table 11-1. Reliability patterns for common challenges

Resilience challenge	Reliability patterns	Examples
Resource overload	Load shedding, throttling, auto-scaling, connection pooling	High traffic (Chapters 3 and 4), resource exhaustion (Chapters 5 and 9)
Service unavailability	Multi-region deployment, failover mechanisms, HA databases	Single point of failure (Chapter 3), regional service disruptions (Chapters 7 and 10)
Data issues	Data replication, backup and restore, idempotency, CDC	Data corruption (Chapters 1 and 9), state inconsistency (Chapter 8)
Network disruption	Retry mechanisms, circuit breakers, fallbacks, caching	Latency (Chapter 3), network disruption (Chapter 9)
Misconfiguration	Infrastructure as code, configuration management	Misconfiguration (Chapters 1 and 6)
Dependency failures	Asynchronous architecture, message queues, dead-letter queues (DLQ)	Service dependencies (Chapter 8), poison pills (Chapters 4 and 8)

With this map in hand, you're equipped to navigate the treacherous waters of system failures, leveraging the right patterns and AWS services to steer your applications toward resilience. Let's dive deeper into how these learnings manifest in each chapter's adventures.

Connecting the Key Learnings

Throughout this book, we've explored various failure modes, reliability patterns, and AWS services that work together to help you build resilient systems. Let's now examine how these elements interconnect across different aspects of cloud architecture, forming a comprehensive approach to resilience:

Holistic resilience strategy

Our journey has demonstrated that resilience isn't about isolated solutions, but is a comprehensive strategy that spans from client-side experiences to backend services and data management. Each chapter has built upon the last, showing how different components of your system need to work in harmony to achieve true resilience.

Layered defense

We've seen how combining multiple reliability patterns creates a layered defense against failures. For instance, auto-scaling (Chapters 3 and 4) works alongside load shedding and throttling (Chapter 9) to manage resource overload, while circuit breakers and retries (Chapter 3) complement failover mechanisms (Chapters 7 and 10) to handle service unavailability.

Cross-cutting concerns

Certain themes, such as configuration management and monitoring, have emerged as cross-cutting concerns. Infrastructure as code (Chapter 1) and robust monitoring (Chapters 5 and 6) are foundational practices that support resilience across all other areas.

Resilience as a continuum

Our exploration has shown that resilience isn't a binary state but a continuum. From basic practices like proper configuration management to advanced techniques like multi-region deployment, each step improves your system's ability to withstand and recover from failures.

The human element

Throughout our journey, we've emphasized that resilience isn't just about technology. It involves people and processes too. From understanding failure modes to implementing and testing reliability patterns, the human element plays a crucial role in building and maintaining resilient systems.

AWS-specific and general patterns

We've balanced AWS-specific solutions with general reliability patterns, demonstrating how cloud native services can be leveraged alongside universal best practices to create robust architectures.

By understanding these interconnections, you're better equipped to design holistic resilience strategies that leverage the full spectrum of tools and techniques at your disposal. Remember, the goal isn't just to implement individual patterns, but to create a resilient ecosystem where each component supports and enhances the others. As you move forward in your cloud journey, continue to think about how these elements can be integrated in your specific use cases. The resilience map we've created together is not just a collection of individual tools, but a guide to building systems that can withstand the complex and often unpredictable challenges of the cloud environment.

Leading Resiliency Initiatives: Cultivating a Culture of Resilience

You've come a long way in your journey to build resilient systems. Now, it's time to take that knowledge and become a catalyst for change within your organization. As a technical contributor, you're uniquely positioned to drive the adoption of resilience best practices and foster a culture that values reliability above all else.

Nurturing the Seeds of Resilience

Creating a resilient organization isn't just about implementing the right technologies or following a set of best practices. It's about cultivating a mindset that permeates every level of the company. Here's how you can nurture the seeds of resilience:

Spread the gospel of resilience
> Organize engaging workshops and training sessions that highlight the critical importance of resilience. Make these sessions interactive and relatable, using real-world examples that resonate with your colleagues.

Walk the talk
> Your actions speak louder than words. Demonstrate resilience practices in your daily work, showing how prioritizing reliability leads to tangible benefits. When faced with challenges, approach them with a resilience-first mindset, and others will follow suit.

Shine a spotlight on success
> Nothing motivates quite like recognition. Celebrate teams and individuals who go above and beyond in improving system resilience. Whether it's a successful mitigation of a potential failure or the implementation of a clever reliability pattern, make sure these wins are visible and appreciated.

Align goals with resilience
> Work with leadership to integrate resilience-related objectives into performance goals at all levels. This ensures that resilience remains a priority and isn't over-shadowed by short-term gains.

Transitioning from individual contributor to resilience champion requires a shift in perspective. It's no longer just about your technical skills; it's about your ability to influence and inspire others. As you embark on this journey, remember that change takes time. Be patient, persistent, and always ready to lend a helping hand.

Becoming the Go-To Resilience Guru

To truly drive the adoption of reliability best practices, you need to position yourself as a trusted advisor within your organization. Here's how you can become the resilience guru everyone turns to:

Craft your resilience toolkit

Develop a suite of reusable architecture patterns, libraries, and tools that simplify the implementation of reliability best practices. Make these resources easily accessible and well-documented. Your colleagues will thank you for saving them time and effort.

Champion continuous improvement

Foster an environment where learning from failures is celebrated, not feared. Encourage regular retrospectives and post-incident reviews, framing them as opportunities for growth rather than fault-finding missions.

Build your resilience brand

Consistently demonstrate your expertise and commitment to others' success. Be the person who asks the tough questions about reliability in design reviews. Offer constructive feedback that helps teams improve their resilience posture. Over time, you'll build a reputation as the go-to person for all things resilience.

Remember, becoming a resilience enabler is as much about people skills as it is about technical knowledge. Listen actively to your colleagues' concerns and challenges. Empathize with their constraints and help them find practical solutions that work within their unique contexts.

Sharpening Your Resilience Radar

A key aspect of leading resilience initiatives is developing keen insight into your systems' health and performance. Let's explore how you can sharpen your resilience radar:

Master the art of metrics

Regularly review and refine your metrics and dashboards. Ensure they provide meaningful insights into your system's resilience, not just vanity metrics. Conduct quarterly reviews of your SLOs and KPIs, aligning them with evolving business goals and customer expectations.

Elevate your postmortem game

Develop a standardized, blameless postmortem process that focuses on learning and improvement. Encourage open and honest discussions about what went wrong and how to prevent similar incidents in the future. Document and share these learnings widely, turning each incident into a valuable lesson for the entire organization.

Quantify resilience ROI

Measuring the return on investment for resilience efforts can be challenging, but it's crucial for gaining continued support. Track key metrics before and after implementing resilience improvements. Calculate the cost savings from prevented outages or reduced downtime. Don't forget to measure the impact on customer satisfaction and retention rates—these are powerful indicators of the value of your resilience efforts.

As you refine your inspection mechanisms, you'll develop a sixth sense for potential resilience issues. This intuition, combined with data-driven insights, will make you an invaluable asset to your organization's resilience efforts.

Embracing Continuous Resilience

Gone are the days when a one-time implementation of reliability patterns was enough. In today's dynamic cloud environments, we need a more proactive and ongoing approach. Enter the concept of continuous resilience:

Resilience testing

Implement a comprehensive suite of automated tests that simulate various failure scenarios. These tests should verify your system's ability to withstand and recover from different types of failures. Integrate these tests into your CI/CD pipeline, catching potential issues before they impact your customers.

Chaos experiments

Design and run controlled experiments to uncover unknown behaviors and failure modes in your system. Start small, perhaps with simple instance termination tests, and gradually increase the complexity as your team gains confidence. Each experiment is an opportunity to learn something new about your system's behavior under stress.

The shift toward continuous resilience requires a change in mindset. It's about embracing uncertainty and proactively seeking out weaknesses in your systems. As you lead this change, emphasize the learning aspect of these practices. Each test and experiment is an opportunity to improve, not a pass/fail exam.

Making Resilience a Daily Habit

Transforming resilience from a theoretical concept to a living, breathing part of your organization's culture requires consistent effort. Here are some practical ways to weave resilience into the fabric of your daily operations:

Friday resilience hour

Dedicate one hour every Friday for teams to dissect and analyze a specific failure mode or resilience pattern. Rotate the responsibility for leading these sessions among team members, encouraging diverse perspectives and fostering engagement.

Monthly resilience roundup

Organize a monthly review of your resilience metrics, recent incidents, and ongoing improvement initiatives. Use this time to prioritize and plan resilience work for the coming month, ensuring it doesn't get overshadowed by feature development.

Quarterly cross-pollination workshops

Bring together teams from different parts of the organization for resilience-focused workshops. These sessions provide a platform for sharing learnings, discussing common challenges, and collaborating on innovative resilience solutions.

Resilience champions network

Establish a network of resilience champions across different teams. These individuals serve as local advocates for resilience initiatives, helping to spread best practices and maintain focus on reliability concerns.

Resilience improvement backlog

Maintain a dedicated backlog of resilience improvement ideas. Regularly groom and prioritize these items alongside feature work, ensuring that resilience remains a key consideration in your development process.

Implementing these practices creates a sustainable and scalable approach to operationalizing resilience. Over time, you'll find that thinking about resilience becomes second nature for your teams, woven into every decision and design choice they make.

As we wrap up this chapter, remember that building a culture of resilience is a journey, not a destination. It requires ongoing commitment, patience, and continuous effort from everyone involved. But with persistence and the right approach, you can transform your organization into a beacon of reliability, capable of weathering any storm that comes its way.

The tools and techniques we've explored throughout this book have equipped you with the knowledge to build resilient systems. Now, it's up to you to take that knowledge and use it to inspire and lead others. As you embark on this next phase of your journey, remember that every small step toward improved resilience is a victory. Celebrate these wins, learn from the setbacks, and keep pushing forward. The future of your organization's reliability is in your hands—embrace the challenge and lead the way to a more resilient tomorrow.

Looking to the Future

As technology advances at an unprecedented pace, the future of cloud resilience presents both thrilling opportunities and uncharted challenges. While the foundational principles of building robust systems remain steadfast, the terrain in which we apply these principles is perpetually evolving. Let's embark on an exploration of the key trends and developments that will mold the future of resilience in the cloud.

In an era where digital services are integral to daily life and business operations, ensuring the availability and reliability of these services is paramount. The techniques and strategies discussed in this book are not just applicable to financial applications; they are relevant across a wide range of industries and use cases.

Building resilient systems is an ongoing process that requires continuous vigilance, adaptation, and improvement. The landscape of potential threats and disruptions is ever-evolving, and so too must be our resilience strategies. By adopting a proactive mindset of resilience, leveraging the power of cloud services, and fostering a culture of continuous improvement, organizations can better prepare for and mitigate the impact of unforeseen events. This proactive approach empowers you to anticipate potential issues and implement preventive measures, rather than merely reacting to incidents as they occur.

Navigating the Multicloud and Hybrid Cloud Landscape

The adoption of multicloud and hybrid cloud strategies has emerged as a trend in cloud computing. While some organizations perceive these strategies as a means to enhance resilience, it's crucial to understand the realities and complexities involved.

There's a common misconception that if one cloud provider experiences a global outage, services can simply fail over to another provider. However, this oversimplifies the nature of cloud failures and ignores the intricacies of cloud architecture. To gain a deeper understanding of how cloud providers isolate failures and what constitutes a true global failure, readers should refer to the "AWS Fault Isolation Boundaries" paper (*https://oreil.ly/RiQMu*).

Implementing a multicloud or hybrid cloud strategy introduces significant complexity; for example:

- Each cloud provider has its own set of tools, APIs, and management interfaces, creating challenges in maintaining consistency and interoperability.
- Workforce skills need to be diversified to cover multiple platforms effectively.
- Operational complexity increases substantially when managing resources across different environments.

If pursuing a multicloud or hybrid cloud approach, consider these strategies:

- Develop a clear and consistent strategy for data management and synchronization across different platforms.
- Implement standardized APIs and interfaces to abstract away underlying differences between cloud providers.
- Leverage containerization and orchestration technologies like Kubernetes to provide a consistent runtime environment across different clouds.
- Invest in tools and platforms that offer centralized visibility and control over multicloud resources.

Remember, while multicloud and hybrid cloud strategies can offer benefits in certain scenarios, they are not a silver bullet for resilience. Carefully weigh the potential advantages against the added complexity and operational overhead.

Harnessing AI for Resilience

AI and machine learning (ML) are playing an increasingly significant role in managing and optimizing cloud infrastructure. As these technologies mature, they open up new possibilities for building more intelligent and self-aware systems.

One of the key benefits of AI and ML in resilience is their ability to process vast amounts of data from logs, metrics, and traces, uncovering patterns and correlations that might elude human analysts. This capability allows AI-driven systems to take proactive measures, enhancing overall system resilience.

Some examples of how AI and ML can be applied to improve resilience include:

Predictive maintenance
By analyzing historical data on system performance and failure rates, AI models can predict when components are likely to fail and can schedule proactive maintenance to avoid downtime.

Anomaly detection
ML algorithms can be trained to identify unusual patterns or behaviors in system metrics, such as sudden spikes in latency or error rates, and alert operators to potential issues before they escalate.

Log summarization
AI can help digest and summarize large volumes of log data, quickly highlighting relevant information during incident response and postmortems.

Capacity planning

ML models can analyze historical usage patterns and predict future resource needs, helping to optimize infrastructure provisioning and prevent capacity-related issues.

To fully harness the power of AI for resilience, you'll need to invest in building the necessary data infrastructure and ML pipelines to collect, process, and analyze large volumes of telemetry data. This may require collaboration with data scientists and ML engineers to develop and train models that can accurately detect and respond to potential issues.

Embracing Chaos Engineering

Chaos engineering, the practice of intentionally injecting failures and disruptions into systems, has emerged as a crucial discipline for understanding system behavior under various conditions. By proactively exploring how systems respond to different scenarios, teams can uncover previously unknown behaviors and potential weaknesses.

The field of chaos engineering continues to evolve, with advancements in several areas:

- Fault injection frameworks are becoming more sophisticated, capable of simulating a wider range of scenarios across different layers of the stack. These frameworks are increasingly being integrated into CI/CD pipelines for continuous resilience validation.

- Chaos engineering as a service offerings are expanding, providing more comprehensive and customizable experiments for various cloud platforms and architectures.

- Advanced analysis tools are emerging, helping teams derive deeper insights from chaos experiments and correlate results with other observability data.

However, embracing chaos engineering requires more than just tools and techniques. It demands a fundamental shift in mindset and culture. The biggest barrier is often the fear of causing failure or the belief that systems aren't mature enough for such experiments.

It's important to recognize that chaos engineering isn't always about causing failures; it's about learning how your system behaves under various conditions. Sometimes an experiment might validate that your system works as expected, while other times it may uncover unexpected behaviors or vulnerabilities.

Teams can start small with simple experiments, such as injecting latency, simulating packet loss, or inducing CPU stress. These low-risk experiments can provide valuable insights and build confidence in the practice of chaos engineering.

To fully embrace the chaos engineering mindset, organizations must:

- Foster a culture of curiosity and continuous learning, where teams are encouraged to explore and experiment with their systems.
- Provide strong leadership support and allocate resources for resilience testing and improvement.
- Emphasize the learning aspect of chaos engineering, focusing on insights gained rather than pass/fail outcomes.

Leveraging Observability

As cloud environments become increasingly distributed and dynamic, the importance of comprehensive observability grows. Observability goes beyond traditional monitoring, enabling teams to gain deep visibility into the behavior and performance of their systems in real time.

While complex observability setups with high-cardinality data and advanced correlation techniques can provide valuable insights, many teams can achieve significant improvements with well-structured logs, metrics, and traces, combined with thoughtful alarms and dashboards. The key is to start with the basics and gradually enhance your observability practices.

Key trends and developments in observability that will shape the future of resilience include:

- Distributed tracing and context propagation, enabling teams to track requests and transactions across complex microservices architectures and identify performance bottlenecks and failure points.
- Artificial Intelligence for IT Operations (AIOps) platforms that leverage machine learning to automatically detect anomalies, identify potential root causes, and provide intelligent recommendations for remediation.
- Advancements in observability-as-code approaches, making it easier to define and manage observability infrastructure and dashboards as versioned and testable artifacts. Tools like AWS CDK or Terraform are making it infinitely easier to build and maintain repeatable observability setups.

Harnessing the power of observability for proactive management requires a cultural shift toward a more data-driven and collaborative approach to operations. Teams must develop the skills and processes to effectively use observability data to drive decision making and prioritize improvements.

This may involve investing in training to build observability literacy across the organization and fostering a culture of curiosity where teams are encouraged to explore their systems to gain deeper insights and understanding.

As we look to the future of cloud resilience, it's clear that the journey toward more robust and reliable systems is ongoing. By staying informed about emerging trends and technologies, and continuously refining our approaches to resilience, we can build systems that not only withstand the challenges of today but are prepared for the unknowns of tomorrow. Remember, the goal is not perfection, but continuous improvement and learning. Embrace the challenges ahead, for they are opportunities to build ever more resilient and reliable cloud systems.

Summary

Congratulations on completing this comprehensive journey through the intricacies of building resilient distributed systems in the cloud! You've equipped yourself with the knowledge, tools, and mindset necessary to create robust and reliable architectures on AWS.

As you apply these principles in your own endeavors, remember that true resilience extends far beyond technology alone. It encompasses people, processes, and culture, forming a holistic approach to system reliability. We encourage you to:

1. Cultivate a culture of collaboration within your organization, where teams work together seamlessly to address challenges and implement resilient solutions.

2. Embrace continuous learning and experimentation. The cloud landscape is ever-evolving, and staying current with new technologies and best practices is crucial.

3. View failures and setbacks not as defeats, but as valuable learning opportunities. Each challenge you overcome contributes to the overall resilience of your systems and teams.

4. Position yourself as an enabler and trusted advisor within your organization. Share your knowledge, mentor others, and champion resilience principles across all levels.

The future of cloud resilience is both exciting and complex. New technologies, methodologies, and challenges will undoubtedly emerge. However, armed with the foundational knowledge and skills you've acquired, along with the powerful capabilities of AWS, you're well-prepared to navigate this dynamic landscape.

We hope this book has provided you with the insights and confidence needed to build truly resilient systems on AWS. Remember, though, that this is just the beginning of your journey. Continue to explore, experiment, and enhance your skills. The field of resilient system design is vast and full of possibilities, and you are now poised to make significant contributions to its evolution.

As you move forward, your efforts will play a crucial role in ensuring that the digital services we all rely on remain robust, available, and reliable, regardless of the challenges they may face. Your commitment to resilience will not only benefit your organization but will contribute to the overall stability and trustworthiness of our increasingly digital world.

Thank you for joining us on this journey. We're excited to see how you'll apply these principles to create more resilient, scalable, and reliable systems in the cloud. The future of resilient architecture awaits your contributions.

Index

About the Authors

Kevin Schwarz is a technology leader with a proven track record of delivering innovative solutions for complex business needs. He has held key leadership roles at prominent companies, including Amazon Web Services (AWS), Bank of America, and led development at a technology startup. Currently serving as a principal solutions architect at AWS, he designs cloud strategies for top US banks and financial services customers.

Kevin has authored AWS whitepapers, blogs, and workshops. He is an alumnus of the University of Florida, where he earned his MBA, a BS, and a BA.

Jennifer Moran is a Senior Resilience Specialist Solutions Architect for AWS. Her diverse technical background uniquely equips her to address the complexities of building resilient systems. She is a recognized authority and core member of the Technical Field Community for Resilience at AWS, focusing on Business Continuity and Disaster Recovery.

Jennifer is a sought-after speaker known for sharing her expertise on resilience at a wide range of events, including AWS Summits and AWS re:Invent. She has also been a featured speaker at both the Grace Hopper Celebration and the O'Reilly Software Architecture Superstream Series. Jennifer is passionate about educating and enabling others to build resilient workloads on AWS.

In addition to her technical accomplishments, Jennifer continuously advocates for diversity and inclusion in technology. She actively champions women in tech and works tirelessly to create opportunities for and mentor underrepresented individuals.

Dr. Nate Bachmeier (Ph.D. CS; MBA; all AWS certifications) nomadically explores North America one cloud integration at a time. He helps the largest and most complex financial service customers migrate and modernize their workloads into cloud native systems. Nate is a thought leader at AWS Summits, AWS re:Invent, industry conferences, and a content bar raiser for resiliency, machine learning, storage, computing, and AWS best practices. Beyond this, he recently released Computer Vision on AWS and is a core member of the official AWS Disaster Recovery Immersion Day.

Colophon

The animal on the cover of *Resiliency Engineering on AWS* is a wood frog (*Lithobates sylvaticus*). This species can be found in forests throughout North America, including north of the Arctic Circle, where they survive because of a unique adaptation they've developed: freezing themselves over winter. When frozen, their hearts stop, their eyes turn white, and they cease breathing. The wood frog's liver secretes a kind of antifreeze substance that prevents lethal ice from forming within their cells.

Wood frogs have distinctive black marks across their eyes, like masks, and are otherwise varying shades of brown. Females are larger than males. The length of wood frogs ranges from 2 to 2.8 inches. As adults, they primarily eat insects, but the tadpoles eat algae as well.

Many of the animals on O'Reilly covers are endangered; all of them are important to the world.

The cover illustration is by Karen Montgomery, based on an antique line engraving from *Cyclopedia of Natural History*. The cover fonts are Gilroy Semibold and Guardian Sans. The text font is Adobe Minion Pro; the heading font is Adobe Myriad Condensed; and the code font is Dalton Maag's Ubuntu Mono.

Milton Keynes UK
Ingram Content Group UK Ltd.
UKHW012210301024
450441UK00003B/8